Life on a
Mediaeval Barony

By

William Stearns Davis

Life on a
Mediaeval Barony

A Picture of a Typical Feudal Community in the Thirteenth Century

By

William Stearns Davis, Ph.D.

*Professor of History in the
University of Minnesota*

ILLUSTRATED

Harper & Brothers Publishers
New York and London

To Ephraim Emerton
Master Interpreter of Mediæval History
this book is dedicated by
an ever-grateful pupil.

Table of Contents

Table of Contents

Illustrations

Illustrations

Illustrations

Preface

THIS book describes the life of the Feudal Ages in terms of the concrete. The discussions center around a certain seigneury of St. Aliquis. If no such barony is easily identifiable, at least there were several hundred second-grade fiefs scattered over western Christendom which were in essential particulars extremely like it, and its Baron Conon and his associates were typical of many similar individuals, a little worse or a little better, who abounded in the days of Philip Augustus.

No custom is described which does not seem fairly characteristic of the general period. To focus the picture a specific region, northern France, and a specific year, A.D. 1220, have been selected. Not many matters have been mentioned, however, which were not more or less common to contemporaneous England and Germany; nor have many usages been explained which would not frequently have been found as early as A.D. 1100 or as late as 1300.

Northern France was *par excellence* the homeland of Feudalism and hardly less so of Chivalry, while by general consent the years around 1220 mark one of the great turning epochs of the Middle Ages. We are at the time of the development of French kingship under Philip Augustus, of the climax and the beginning of the waning of the crusading spirit, of the highest development of Gothic architecture, of the full blossoming of the popular Romance literature, and of the beginning of the

Preface

entirely dissimilar, but even more important, Friar movement.

To make the life of the Middle Ages live again in its pageantry and its squalor, its superstition and its triumph of Christian art and love, is the object of this study. Many times has the author been reminded of the *intense contrasts* between sublime good and extreme evil everywhere apparent in the Feudal Epoch. With every effort at impartiality, whether praising or condemning, it is dangerously easy to write in superlatives.

Although the preparation of this book was not undertaken without that knowledge and investigation of those mediæval authors, ecclesiastics, and laymen upon which every significant study of this kind must rest, every scholar will recognize the author's debt to many modern specialists. To Th. Wright, Lacroix, Luchaire, Justin H. Smith, Viollet-le-Duc, and Chéruel the acknowledgments are very specific. To Leon Gautier they must be more specific still. It is a great misfortune that his masterpiece, *Le Chivalrie,* is no longer current in a good English translation. The words in quotation, sprinkled through the text, are usually from pertinent mediæval writers, except where they purport to be direct snatches of conversation.

To my colleague in this university, Prof. August C. Krey, who has read and criticized the manuscript with friendly fidelity and professional alertness and acumen, there are due many hearty thanks.

W. S. D.

THE UNIVERSITY OF MINNESOTA.
MINNEAPOLIS, MINN.

Life on a
Mediaeval Barony

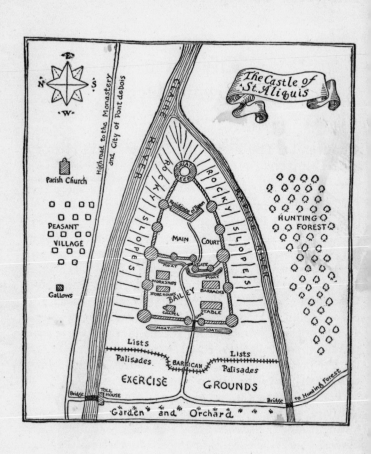

The Castle of St. Aliquis

Life on a Mediaeval Barony

✿

Chapter I: The Fief of St. Aliquis: Its History and Denizens.

IN the duchy of Quelqueparte there lay, in the later days of the great King Philip Augustus, the barony of St. Aliquis. Perhaps you may have trouble in finding any such places upon the maps of Mediæval France. In that case, I must tell you that they did not lie so far from Burgundy, Champagne, and Blois that the duke and his vassal, the baron, could not have many brave feuds with the seigneurs of those principalities, nor so far from Paris that peddlers and pilgrims could not come hence or go thither pretty often, nor the baron of St. Aliquis sometimes journey to the king's court, to do his loyal devoir to his high suzerain, or to divert himself with many lordly pleasures.

About A.D. 1220, when King Philip Augustus was near his end, there was exceptional peace in northern France, and conditions around St. Aliquis were entirely normal. We purpose, therefore (with the help of Our Lady, of holy St. Aliquis himself, and perhaps also of that very discreet *fée* Queen Morgue, "the wife of Julius Cæsar

1

and the mother of King Oberon"), to visit the aforesaid barony as it existed at that time. We shall look around us unseen by the inhabitants, but able to ask many questions and to get pertinent answers. Thereby shall we gather much knowledge, and that, too, not about St. Aliquis only; for this little world by itself is a cross-section, as it were, of a great part of France; nay, of all feudal Europe.

It is fortunate that we are suffered, when we make this return journey to the Middle Ages, to arrive not long after the year 1200. A century or two earlier one might have found conditions decidedly more crude, semi-barbarous, disgusting; one would have indeed been tempted to doubt whether from so lawless and unculti-vated a world any progressive civilization could really develop. On the other hand, had we postponed the excursion until, say, A.D. 1400, we would have found a society already becoming sophisticated and to no slight extent modernized. The true mediæval flavor would have been partially lost. But A.D. 1220 represents the epoch when the spirit of the Middle Ages had reached its full development. The world was still full of ignorance, squalor, and violence, yet there were now plenty of signs of a nobler day. France was still scattered with feudal castles and tales of baronial ruthlessness abounded, but the rise of the royal power and the growth of the chartered communal towns were promising a new political era. The bulk of the people were still illiterate peasants, and many of the nobility even felt very awk-ward when fumbling over books; but the monasteries had never been so full of worthy activities and of very genuine learning. Thousands of scholars were trudging to the University of Paris; and meantime, even in the more starving towns were rising Gothic churches and cathedrals, combining in their soaring fabrics not merely the results of supreme architectural genius, but a wealth of masterpieces of sculpture and of colored glass which were to draw visitors of later days from the very ends of the earth.

The crusading fervor had somewhat waned, but around the castles there were still elderly knights who had once followed Richard the Lion Hearted or Philip Augustus upon the great Third Crusade to Palestine, likewise a good many younger cavaliers who had shared the military glory and moral disgrace of the Fourth Crusade, which had ended not with the recovery of Jerusalem, but the sack and seizure of Christian Constantinople. At Rome the great and magnanimous Pope Innocent III had hardly ceased to reign (1216); while the founders of the remarkable Friar movement—that new style of monasticism which was to carry the message of the Church closer to the people—St. Francis, the apostle of love, and St. Dominic, the apostle of learning, were still alive and active. The world, therefore, was looking forward. The Middle Ages were close to apogee.

We purpose to tell what may be found on the barony of St. Aliquis, first at the castle itself and in the household of Messire the Seigneur, then in the villages of peasants round about; next in the abbey slightly removed; and lastly in the chartered town and cathedral seat of the bishop a few miles further off. But first one must ask about the origin of the principality and how there came to be any such barony at all, for St. Aliquis would have been an exceptional seigneury if it had not had considerable history behind it, and had not represented the growth of several different elements.

3

The castle of St. Aliquis lies at the junction of two rivers. The smaller of these, the Rapide, tumbles down from some hills, cutting a gorge through the dense beech forest until it runs under a precipitous slope, then dashes into the greater, more placid current of the Claire. The Claire is an affluent, perhaps of the Seine, perhaps of the Loire. It is navigable for flat barges a good many miles above its junction with the Rapide, and the tolls upon this commerce swell the baron's revenue.

At the triangle formed by the converging streams rises an abrupt rocky plateau practically inaccessible from the banks of either river and which can be approached only from the third side, where the land slopes gently away from the apex of the triangle. Here rise some jagged crags marking out the place as a natural fortress. Most castles which dot feudal Europe are thus located in the most advantageous spot in their respective regions.

Possibly human habitations have existed upon this promontory ever since God drove Adam and Eve out of Eden. If we consult Brother Boniface, the librarian at the local monastery, the best-read person in the district, the good old man will tell us that long before the Romans came, the ancient Druids ("now in hell") had their pagan altars here, and sacrificed human victims under a great oak. Some chiseled masonry found on the spot also indicates an extensive settlement in Roman days, when Gaul was a province of the Cæsars. Of course, all the pious people know that under the persecuting Emperor Diocletian, the holy Aliquis himself, a centurion in the Legions, was shot to death with burning arrows because he preferred Christ to Jupiter, and that the place of his martyrdom is at the new abbey church about a league from the castle.

Nevertheless, secular history is not precise until after the time of the mighty Charlemagne. Under his feeble successor, Charles the Bald, tradition affirms that the vikings, Scandinavian barbarians, came up the greater river, ascended the Claire in their long dragon ships; then on the site of the present castle they established a stockaded camp, whence they issued to ravage the country. This was about A.D. 870, but after a year they departed, leaving desolation behind them. About A.D. 880 another band of vikings came with similar foul intent, but they met a different reception. The saints had raised up a brave protector for the Christian folk of those lands.

Very uncertain is the ancestry of the redoubtable warrior Heribert, who about A.D. 875 seized the rocky triangle at the mouth of the Rapide, and built the first castle of St. Aliquis. Perhaps he was descended from one of Charlemagne's famous Frankish "counts." He did, indeed, only what was then being done everywhere to check the Scandinavian hordes: he built a castle and organized the levies of the region, hitherto footmen, into an effective cavalry force. This castle was anything save the later majestic fortress. It was merely a great square tower of rough masonry, perched on the crag above the streams. Around it was a palisade of heavy timbers, strengthened on the landward side by a ditch. Inside this compound were huts for refugees, storehouses for fodder, and rude stalls for the cattle. To stop passage up the Claire a heavy chain of iron was stretched across the river and stone piers were sunk at shallow places, thus forcing boats to pass close under the fortress in range of descending missiles. Where the chain was landed there was built another smaller stone tower. All the crossing then had to be by skiffs, although somewhat later an unsteady bridge was thrown over the stream.

The second expedition of vikings found that these precautions had ruined their adventure. They lost many men and a dragon ship when they tried to force the iron chain. Heribert's new cavalry cut off their raiding parties. Finally they departed with thinned numbers and scant spoils. Heribert was hailed as savior of the region, just as other champions, notably the great Count Odo at the siege of Paris, won similar successes elsewhere on a larger scale. The vikings had departed, but Heribert's tower remained. So began the castle of St. Aliquis.

Heribert had taken possession ostensibly as the king's "man," claiming some royal commission, but as the power of Charlemagne's feeble rulers dwindled, Heribert's heirs presently forgot almost all their allegiance to their distant royal "master." This was merely as seemed the case about A.D. 900 all through the region then coming to be called "France." Castles were rising everywhere, sometimes to repel the vikings, sometimes merely to strengthen the power of some local chief. Once erected, the lords of those castles were really little princes, able to defy the very weak central authority. To capture a considerably less formidable fortalice than St. Aliquis implied a tedious siege, such as few kings would undertake save in an emergency.

The result was that ere A.D. 1000 Heribert's great-grandsons had almost ceased to trouble about the king. The person they genuinely feared was the local Duke of Quelqueparte, another feudal seigneur with more followers and more castles than they. Partly from prudence, partly from necessity, they had "done homage" to him, become "his men," and as his vassals rode to

6

hrs wars. The dukes, in turn, full of their own problems, and realizing the strength of St. Aliquis, seldom interfered in the fief, save on very serious occasions. The barons of St. Aliquis therefore acted very nearly like sovereign princes. They, of course, had their own gallows with power of life and death, waged their own personal wars, made treaties of peace, and even coined a little ill-shapen money with their own superscription.[1] "Barons by the Grace of God," they boasted themselves, which meant that they obeyed the duke and *his* suzerain, the king, very little, and, we fear, God not a great deal.

In the recent centuries, however, the barony had changed hands several times. About 1070 the lord had the folly to refuse his ordinary feudal duty to the Duke of Quelqueparte. The latter roused himself, enlisted outside aid, and blockaded and starved out the castle of St. Aliquis. The unfortunate baron—duly adjudged "traitor and felon" by his "peers," his fellow vassals— was beheaded. The duke then bestowed the fief, with the hand of the late owner's niece, upon Sire Rainulf, a younger son of a south-country viscount, who had visited the duke's court, bringing with him an effective battle-ax and fifty sturdy followers. Sire Rainulf, however, died while in the First Crusade. The reigning duke next tried to give the barony to another favorite warrior, but the son of the late baron proved himself of sturdy stuff. He fought off his suzerain and enlisted allies from Burgundy. The duke was forced, therefore, to leave him in peace.

Presently, about 1140, another baron died, survived

[1] Long before the assigned date of this narrative, some king or other potentate had assuredly given the lords of St. Aliquis *immunity—i.e.,* exemption from ordinary jurisdiction, taxation, etc., by outside powers, with corresponding privileges for the local seigneurs themselves.

7

only by a daughter. Her uncles and cousins did their best to expel this poor lady and induced the suzerain duke to close his eyes to their deeds, but, fortunately, the new baroness had been very pious. The influence of the great St. Bernard of Clairvaux was exerted, thereby persuading King Louis VII to warn the duke that if he could not protect his vassals "the king would do justice." So the Lady Bertrada was given in marriage to a respectable Flemish cavalier Gui, who ruled the barony with only the usual wars. He left two sons, Garnier and Henri. Sire Henri, the younger, lived at the inferior castle of Petitmur, went on the Fourth Crusade (1203–04), and perished in the fighting around Constantinople ere the French and Venetians sacked the city. Garnier, the elder, received, of course, the great castle. He was the uncle of the Baron Conon III, the son of Henri, and the present lord of St. Aliquis.

It is well said by the monks that the blessed feel joys in paradise all the keener because a little earlier they have escaped from the pangs and fires of purgatory. Certes, for all laymen and clerics on the St. Aliquis fiefs, there was purgatory enough in Baron Garnier's day to make the present "sage" rule of Baron Conon seem tenfold happy.

The late seigneur ruled about twenty years, filled up with one round of local wars, oppression of the small, and contentions with the great. Baron Garnier was assuredly a mighty warrior. Never was he unhorsed in jousting or in mêlée. His face was one mass of scars and he had lost an ear. Plenty of landless knights and wolfish men at arms rioted around his donjon. His provosts and foresters knew how to squeeze the poor of the seigneury, and by this income and by the ransoms from numerous captives he was able to rebuild the castle of St. Aliquis according to the first military art of the day.

But his sins were more than the hairs of his grizzled head. Having taken dislike to his wife, and the bishop refusing an annulment, he kept the poor Lady Ada mewed up in one chamber for years, and, according to many stories, loaded her with chains and spared not tortures, until in mercy she died. However, he had plenty of less regular consorts. The castle courts had swarmed with loud women, the favorites of himself and his familiars, and with their coarse, unacknowledged brats. No pretty peasant girl's honor was safe in those parts. As for the prisoners—after Messire Conon came into power it was a marvel the quantity of human bones, gnawed by the rats, which they took out of the lower dungeons, as well as how they released four wretches who had been incarcerated in the dark so long that they were blinded. Needless to say, the compartments of the gallows never lacked their swinging skeletons. Women still hush their squalling children with, "Be silent—or Baron Garnier will get you!"

Yet with all these deeds this baron affected great hospitality. He kept a roaring hall, with ready welcome for any cavalier who enjoyed deep drinking and talking of horses, women, falcons, and forays; and a good many seigneurs found his alliance useful. So he continued his evil ways until (praised be Our Lady of Mercies) he came to a fit end. Thrice he had been excommunicated by the bishop. Thrice he had been readmitted to ghostly favor, thanks to large gifts toward the new cathedral at Pontdebois. Then he let his men murder a priest who was traveling with a precious chalice. So he was excommunicated a fourth time. While in this perilous state (though boasting that he would soon make his new terms with the Church) his companion in sin, Suger of the Iron Arm, quarreled with him over their cups and ran him through with a boar spear. The baron lived just long enough to see Suger hewn in pieces by his comrades. Then he died (priestless, of course, and unabsolved) cursing God and crying piteously for help from the devil. Christians cross themselves when they think of his fate hereafter.

Garnier left no legitimate children. He was on very cold terms with his brother's widow, the Lady Odelina, who was rearing her two sons and daughter at Petitmur; but Odelina had faced her brother-in-law down and clung tightly to her own little fief. She had given her children a "courteous" and pious education, and induced a neighboring seigneur to take her eldest son, Conon, to "nourish" as his squire, and rear to be a knight. At length came her reward. The youth was knighted by the Count of Champagne three weeks before his evil uncle perished. Then the suzerain duke was glad to have St. Aliquis pass to so competent a vassal as young Sire Conon.

This is a bare suggestion of the contentions, feuds, and downright wars of which the barony has been the scene, and yet St. Aliquis has probably been freer from such troubles than most of its neighbors.

Although this castle is the center of Baron Conon's power, it is by no means his only strong place. He has three other smaller castles (besides Petitmur, which will go to his brother) that he sometimes inhabits, but which he ordinarily rules through castellans. In the twenty-odd villages upon the fief there are some ten thousand peasants whom he governs through his provosts.[1] Also, there depend on him his own "noble" vassals— about twelve "sires," petty nobles each with his own small castle or tower, hamlet of peasants, and right to

---

[1] On some fiefs, as on the royal domain at this time, there would be a higher seigneurial officer, the *bailli*, set over the provosts.

10

"low justice." These vassals follow the St. Aliquis banner and otherwise contribute to the baron's glory. That seigneur himself is likewise "advocate" (secular guardian) of the neighboring Abbey of St. Aliquis—an honorable post involving delicate dealings with the lord abbot. Also, a few leagues away lies the "good town" of Pontdebois. The baron, as will be explained, has very important relations with that city. In addition he "holds" of the bishop there resident some farms with hunting and fishing rights. For this inferior fief he does homage, of course, not to the Duke of Quelqueparte, but to the Bishop of Pontdebois. Some years previous, when the duke and bishop were at war, the baron was obligated to send twenty knights to fight for the duke, but also six to fight for the bishop. The Scriptures warn us against trying "to serve two masters"; but the baron happily made shift to keep the two contingents of his little array from engaging with one another until his two overlords had made peace!

In addition to all the above, Conon holds still another small castle at quite a distance, for which he does homage to the Duke of Burgundy—a fact promising more complications when Quelqueparte and Burgundy (as is most likely) go to war. Finally, he holds a large farm from his otherwise equal, the Baron of Harcourt. Here he is sure to cut his feudal devoir to a minimum, and leave the Lord of Harcourt to consider whether to pocket his pride, risk a "private war," or attempt a lawsuit before their mutual suzerain, the Duke of Quelqueparte.[1]

---

[1] The Baron of St. Aliquis was fortunate if his feudal relationships, conflicting overlords, etc., were not even more complicated than here indicated. There was nothing "simple" about the composition of a feudal barony!

The Baron Conon would gladly be the direct vassal of the king. The higher your suzerain the higher, on the whole, your own glory in the feudal firmament; but the duke would resent bitterly any attempt to get his vassals away and all the other first-class nobles would support him. Baron Conon must wait, therefore, perhaps until the present elderly duke is dead and the duchy falls under feeble heirs. Then he will find the astute king, if Philip Augustus is still reigning, only too willing and able to meet him halfway. At present, however, Conon is on good terms with the duke, although he is just as jealous himself to prevent his own sires from "holding" directly from the duke as the latter is to check the baron's going over to the king. Everywhere there is this friction over "subinfeudation." "The vassal of my vassal is *not* my vassal": that is the angry comment daily.

All in all, the seigneury of St. Aliquis thus covers three hundred square miles, whereof about one-third is controlled by the baron as his personal domain and the remainder by his vassals. Perhaps there are two hundred similar baronies and countships dotting France, some larger, some smaller, but in their histories, feudal relationships, and general problems much alike. This fief, however, is especially fortunate in that the baron possesses an old charter, wrung from some tottering Carolingian king, giving him the right to collect a sack of grain, a large truss of hay, or a similar quota in kind from every loaded barge traversing down the navigable Claire; also to levy a copper obol for every Christian foot passenger, and three obols for every mounted traveler or Jew (mounted or walking) crossing the very important bridge by the castle. These tolls give messire many fine suits of armor, buy silk gowns for the baroness, and make all the local seigneurs anxious to marry their daughters to the baron's sons as soon as the boys can be knighted.

St. Aliquis, we have said, is happy in its present seigneur. Monks, villeins, and petty nobles agree in praising Baron Conon. When a seigneur is practically a sovereign, everything depends upon his character. If the saints desire to punish certain Christians for their sins, let them merely send them an evil, or only an inefficient, quarrelsome baron! Like the unlamented Garnier, he can soon make their lives into a perfect Gehenna.

Conon III has now ruled for more than ten years. He has kept out of all private wars but one, a feat almost exceptional; but in that one war he struck so hard and so skillfully that his opponent, the Viscount of Foretvert, swore on the relics to a peace which cost him a village of peasants and the transfer of two petty sires to the St. Aliquis fealty. Conon fought also in the great battle of Beauvais so as to win the personal praise of the king himself. He compounded with the abbey over the division of the income of a farm in a manner which left him and the abbot firm friends—a singular piece of diplomacy. Better still, he held to his point about some hunting rights with the Bishop of Pontdebois, and finally won most of his claims without being even temporarily subjected to excommunication. His peasants pay their imposts loyally, for the baron not merely protects them from the raids of brigands and rival feudatories; he also represses worse pillagers still, his own seigneurial officers, who were ravaging harpies in all the little thatched villages through Baron Garnier's day. Therefore, Conon is called "a very gentle seigneur," which means that he is every inch a lord and which term does not prevent him from swinging a heavy sword, and from knocking down a villein with his own fist when there is need of teaching a lesson.

As for Conon's family, his good mother, Lady Odelina, is now resting under the stones of the abbey church; but she lived to see her first-born wedded to Adela, the daughter of a rich Picard sire, a dame of many virtues. The marriage has been blessed with two healthy sons, François and Anseau—the pampered tyrants of all the castle folk. The baron's household also includes his younger brother Aimery, who has just reached the age for knighthood, and his marriageable sister Alienor. So far the family had been marvelously harmonious. There has been none of those passages at arms between elder and younger brothers which often make a castle the antechamber to hell. Adela is "the very *gentle* dame"—beloved of husband and revered by vassals and villeins, but whose "gentleness," like her husband's, by no means keeps her from flogging her maids when their sins deserve it. Alienor is already going to tourneys and has presented at least three young knights with her stockings to tie to their lances; but she knows that it is a brother's duty to find a husband for one's sister, and Conon has promised that whoever he selects will be young, brave, and kindly. Therefore Alienor is not borrowing trouble. As for Aimery, he is proud of being almost as good a hawker and jouster as his brother. He will soon be knighted and rule over Petitmur, but his head is full of a visit to the king's court, of winning vast favor, and finally of being given the only daughter and heiress of a great count—in short, of possessing a fief bigger than St. Aliquis.

There, then, is the little world, ruled by persons perhaps a little more honorable and kindly than the run of North French barons, but by no means of impossible virtue.

It is June, A.D. 1220. The sun is just rising. Let us enter St. Aliquis as the warders unbar the gates; for the castle is the heart of the feudal civilization.

Chapter II: The Castle of St. Aliquis.

HE castle makes the feudal ages possible. It is because western Europe is covered with thousands of strongholds, each of which can stand off a considerable army, that we have the secular institutions of the thirteenth century. To be the owner and lord of at least one castle is the dream of every nobleman, and in fact until he can hoist his own banner from his own donjon he hardly has a defined place in the feudal hierarchy.

As we have seen, the castle of St. Aliquis is now nearly three hundred and fifty years old. Since it has been continuously inhabited by enterprising owners, its structure has been as continuously changing. However, if we had come to the barony only fifty years ago, we would have found a decidedly primitive structure. The general plan of Heribert's original stronghold was then still retained: first, on the landward side of the triangle above the two converging rivers there was a rather deep moat, next a parapet whereof the lower part was made of earth taken from this same moat, and upon the mound rose a strong palisade of tree trunks. Within the palisade were barns, outbuildings, and barracks for such of the baron's men as did not live in the inner stronghold. Then last of all was the donjon, the castle proper—a huge square tower built with little art, but which defied attack by mere solidity. The entrance to this grim tower was by a steep inclined plane leading

16

The Castle of St. Aliquis

TYPICAL CASTLE OF THE MIDDLE AGES
(Without large barbican court)

to a small door in the second story. In case of danger,
if the palisade were forced, the seigneur and his men
retreated into the tower, knocked down the wooden
gangway, and shouted defiance to the enemy. The mass

17

and height of the donjon baffled any ordinary methods of attack save that of blockade and starvation—and there would be six months' supply of wheat, salt beef, and ale in the tower vaults.

Nevertheless, this seemingly impenetrable fortress did not suffice. In the first place, superior methods of siege warfare were developing: the stoutest fortifications could be cracked.[1] In the next place, if the donjon were hard to enter, it was almost equally hard to sally forth from it. No rapid sortie could be made from the door in the second story; the defense must be wholly passive. Finally, this stark masonry tower was a most uncomfortable place, with its cavernous "halls" barely lighted by tiny loopholes, frigid in winter, stifling in summer, unsanitary—in short, almost intolerable for habitation by a large body of men. After the First Crusade (1094–99) numerous cavaliers came home with great tales of the fortresses of the Byzantines and the Saracens. During the twelfth century, consequently, castle architecture underwent a remarkable transformation. Richard the Lion Hearted built Château Gaillard in Normandy. His mighty rival, Philip Augustus, built the famous Louvre to dominate Paris, and erected other new-style castles with cylindrical towers at Montargis, Poissy, Dourges, and elsewhere. Already by 1220 the plans are being drawn for a great castle at Coucy (built between 1223 and 1230) which is to be almost a model for all subsequent fortress builders, until the advent of gunpowder.

Baron Garnier, whatever his crimes, had certainly understood the art of war. He rebuilt St. Aliquis in a thoroughly scientific manner, employing a learned masterbuilder and "sage," an elderly Fleming who had

[1] See chap. xiv.

18

seen the best fortifications of the Infidels and had lived
long in those famous Syrian-Christian fortresses like
Krak des Chevaliers, which by the mere excellence of
construction had enabled small garrisons of western
"Franks" to defy the full power of Saladin. Instead
of a mere ditch, palisade, and then a single vast tower,
St. Aliquis has consequently become a huge complex
of defenses within defenses, each line of resistance a
little harder to penetrate and with every outwork
commanded by an inner fortification. If at last you
come to the central donjon, it still looms up above you—
defiant and formidable, and you can have your fill of
desperate fighting, only perhaps to be bloodily repulsed
in the end. Of course, the donjon can indeed be starved
out, but it is not very often that any enemy of St.
Aliquis will have resources and persistence enough to
keep his troops together until the castle supplies are
exhausted. He must either get possession pretty quickly
or not at all—and Garnier's Fleming certainly took
pains he should not get in quickly!

In examining St. Aliquis or its rivals, one must remember that they are the creations of men who have devoted
most of their thought to the problems of war. Every
possible contingency has been anticipated. The architect and his employer have practically spent their lives
studying "how can a castle be made to hold out as long
as possible?" Being, despite their sins, highly intelligent
men, it is not surprising that they produce remarkable
results.

We are approaching the castle as the morning mists
are lifting from the Claire and the Rapide. Ahead of us,
out of the dispersing fog, is rising what seems a bewilder-
ing mass of towers, walls, battlements gray and brown,
with here and there a bit of green, where a little earth

has been allowed to lodge and a few weeds shoot forth. High above all soars the mass of the great central tower, the donjon, from the summit of which Baron Conon's banner is now idly trailing.

We come down a road that takes us over the toll bridge across the Rapide and find ourselves in a kind of parade ground where there are only a few cattle sheds and possibly a rude cabin or two for such of the baron's herdsmen as must sleep outside overnight. This open ground is the scene for martial exercises, rallyings of the vassals, and even for tournaments. Many people are headed toward the castle, mostly from the village of peasants just westward across the river; but there is also the subprior on a mule, riding over from the abbey, and also a messenger who has spurred down very early from Pontdebois with a communication from the bishop. As we near the castle its tower and inner and outer wards become more distinct. We readily believe that it took Garnier's architect three years to carry through the work; that all the peasants of the barony had been put to grievous *corvées* (forced labor) digging, hewing and dragging stone, or working the great derricks; and that ten expert stonecutters and fully eighty less skilled masons had been hired in from Paris, Rheims, and Orléans, besides a master mason who demanded rewards that seemed outrageous for a mere villein and not for a belted knight.

These speculations end as we come, not to the castle, but to a semicircular palisade inclosing the regular gate on the landward side. This palisade is too high to scramble over; the piles are too sharply pointed and stout enough to stand considerable battering. This outwork is the barbican—the first of the long series of obstacles awaiting the foe. Of course, it could not be

defended in a regular siege, but its purpose is to stop
any surprise attack long enough to enable the garrison
to rally, close the great gate, and man the walls. The
whole crowd of folk now entering make for the heavy
wooden barrier which is just being thrown open by a
rather sleepy porter. Since it is a time of profound
peace, he lets them all stream inside, merely requiring
everyone to leave his weapons in his custody. We pass
unchallenged, thanks to the kind *fée* aforementioned,
who has rendered us as invisible as the owner of Gyges's
ring. If, however, we had been guests of noble rank,
we would have proceeded onward to the inner gate and
rung loudly on a heavy metal gong hanging there.
One of the baron's squires would then have greeted us.
If we had been the baron's equal or superior in the
social scale, Conon himself would next have come down
to lead us in; if somewhat inferior, we would have been
conducted by the squire to the great hall, where we
would have removed hood and gloves before the magnate
presented himself. But we have much to examine ere
we penetrate the seigneurial hall.

Once inside the barbican, one discovers that between
this extreme barrier and the fortress proper there is
another open space with a road, and another place for
equestrian exercises extending from the Claire straight
over to the abrupt slopes of the Rapide. The palisades
run all the way from river to river. This space within
the barbican forms the lists, where two young sergeants
are breaking in a balky stallion. The lists are a great
convenience in peace time, but the real utility is in war,
and they are even more important in the castles that
have land on every side. They supply a good road by
which men can be hurried round the castle circuit in
reasonable safety. On the other hand, if the enemy

suddenly forces the barriers, he finds himself most awkwardly in a limited space between the palisade and the castle moat, with all the arbalists (crossbows) playing on him from the walls above.

Inside the lists and next to the masonry walls runs the moat. It is some twenty feet wide, partly filled now with scum-covered rain water. In the spring the varlets have great joy here hunting frogs, but as the year advances it assuredly breeds mosquitoes. It constitutes, however, another formidable barrier to an enemy, and that is its sole object.

After crossing these lists, the path leads straight to the drawbridge. This has just been lowered by means of heavy counterpoises swung on a kind of trestle overhead, for even in peace times no seigneur will sleep soundly before the drawbridge is up. The portcullis, the frame of iron bars which is lowered whenever the bridge is raised, has also been hoisted in its groove by the gateway. The heavy oaken gates, faced with metal, have not been unbarred, however. A smaller door, just big enough for a horse, has been opened in one of them, admitting to the castle proper. Despite the earlier scrutiny at the barbican, one now catches a watchful eye at the small window in the turret close beside the portcullis. The chief porter has a very responsible position. Many a fortress has been lost because he has been careless or unfaithful. He would, in any case, be chargeable if he admitted unwelcome guests or idle rascals. Porters are often accused of being gruff, insolent, fat, and lazy, but part of their bad name comes because they have to repel bad characters.

And now we are about to enter the outer ward, or bailey, of the castle of St. Aliquis. The walls and towers of these outer defenses are less formidable than those of the inner ward; yet they seem of massive thickness and imposing altitude. There is a solid round tower covering either side of the gate; to about fifteen feet these twain rise above the moat naked and sheer, then are pierced with narrow slits intended, not to let in light, but to permit archers to cover every inch of the way from the barbican to the drawbridge. Even if the foe should cross the moat, shatter the portcullis, and split open the heavy doors, he would be merely at the beginning of terrible hours of ax- and sword-play. He would be in a narrow and low vaulted passage, with many loopholes on either side for archers, and also with slits in the ceiling for pouring down boiling oil, seething pitch, molten lead, and other pleasantries; and if he rushed past all these forms of death into the courts, there, behind him, capable still of very stout defense, would rise the two strong gate towers, rendering every attempt to re-enforce the original attacking party a dice-throwing with death, and making retreat equally dangerous. Few leaders, therefore, will be foolish enough to try to storm St. Aliquis simply by a desperate rush against the gate.

From the two gate towers, right and left, there extends a considerable stretch of sheer wall terminating at either extremity with two more towers which mark the corners on the landward side of the fortress. These four towers, of course, by projecting far beyond this curtain wall, are posted so as to permit a steady fire of missiles on any enemy who may somehow ensconce himself close under the wall. The two sections of curtain wall themselves are some dozen feet thick, with a firm walk along their summit, protected by a stone parapet. To enable the defenders, however, to drop stones and other forms of destruction upon attackers who may be under the very base of the wall and defying the bolts from the towers, a structure of heavy timbers can be built out all along the wall overhanging the moat. These wooden hordings are strong enough to withstand many stones from the casting engines, but they can sometimes be set on fire. In a siege, therefore, they will be covered with raw hides. The same will also be put over the conical wooden roofs which cap the towers. Since this is a time of peace, however, the hordings stand weather-stained and bare. To cover the entire woodwork with hides will be one of the first tasks of the garrison in case of a serious alarm.

As we survey the outer walls of the castle, it is clear that no enemy will try to batter down the towers. Even if he could penetrate their shells, he would merely find himself in a dark, cavernous, vaulted chamber, with the defenders flinging down death from above. He would then have to bore through the inner wall, nearest the court, under every disadvantage. The towers are built so completely of masonry that it is impossible to burn them. Winding stairs, leading up through the stonework, conduct from one stage to another; and these staircases are so narrow and tortuous that a single warrior with an ordinarily lively ax can stop a hundred men ascending.[1] The attack, therefore, must be on the curtain walls. But even here, supposing one has scaled the battlements, more troubles are awaiting. The only way downward from the curtain walls is through the towers at the end of the parapets. To leap into the court inside means broken bones. The gangways along the parapet are intercepted at several points by wooden

[1] Often at dark turns in these towers the floor would be made of wooden scaffolding, easy to destroy; and the attacker would (if not wary) suddenly tumble to the cellar of the tower.

VIEW OF THE COURT AND THE DONJON

bridges. These can be easily knocked away, leaving yawning gaps defying any leaper. If you reach the towers they are all barred, and the arbalists are shooting down on the captured gangways from a dozen loopholes. Finally, be it said, each tower is a little fortress by itself. It has its own cistern, fireplace for cooking, and storeroom. Even if isolated, its garrison can hold out stoutly. So much for the task of attacking merely the outer ward of St. Aliquis.

The problems of the towers and the curtain wall detain one long, for they sum up the fundamental principles of thirteenth-century fortifications. But now before us opens the broad court of the bailey itself, the scene of much of the homely life of the castle; in fact, the place now swarms with people busy with all kinds of activities. The pavement is none too clean. There are large muck piles, and one sees hens and a few pigs and dogs foraging everywhere. A genuine village really exists inside the bailey. To the right of the gate is a rambling, thatched-roof stable where in a long row of stalls the fifty-odd horses of the seigneur are champing their morning fodder. Near the stables stand tall ricks of hay. Behind these are a second line of inelegant wooden structures: they are the barracks for the less favored castle servitors, and for a part of the heavy-handed men at arms whom Baron Conon keeps for instant duty.

On the left side of the gate are several more buildings. To be noted are a commodious carpenter shop where saw and hammer are already plying; a well-appointed smithy where at one ringing forge the baroness's white palfrey is being reshod, and at another the master armorer is putting a new link into a mail shirt. The castle smith's position is no sinecure. He has to keep a great quantity of weapons and armor in constant order; he has to do all the recurring small jobs around the great establishment; and in emergency to manufacture quantities of lance heads and arbalist bolts, as well as perhaps to provide the metal work for siege engines on which may rest the fate of the castle. Conon's first armorer is accordingly one of the most important and best rewarded of all the servitors.

Besides these workshops there is a long storehouse, a repository for not merely the food, but all other kinds of supplies needful in a siege. Near by stands a smaller, shedlike structure, puzzling at first to strangers, but which explains itself by the shrill screams and cries issuing thence. It is the baron's hawk house, the mews, where the chief falconer is now feeding the raw meat to the great hawks and falcons in which his noble masters take delight. Close to these secular buildings, however, there rises somewhat incongruously an elegant Gothic chapel, with soaring pinnacles, a rose window at the end of the small nave, sculptured saints flanking the portal, and within one finds glorious stained glass, more saints' images and carvings, and a rich altar. This is the little castle church to which very many dwellers of St. Aliquis, including messire and madame, had repaired piously at gray dawn, and where now good Father Grégoire has just finished a rather hasty mass.

The bailey, in short, is overrunning with activities. Horses are neighing, cows are being milked, an overladen donkey is braying. Yonder in one corner is a small building with a tall chimney. Here is the seigneur's great oven, whither not merely the castle folk, but a great number of the peasants, resort to bake their bread. In front of the chapel bubbles a little fountain, and chattering women, scantily attired, are filling their water pots. Children in various degrees of nakedness and dirtiness play everywhere. Noises of every kind blend in a hubbub. Lastly we notice, close to the inner drawbridge, another building again with a tall chimney. This is the castle cookhouse, where the dinners are prepared for the great hall within. A glance through the door shows the vast fireplace where one can roast a whole sheep or a small beef entire. The cookhouse is located here because of the danger of fire in the inner castle, and because the position is convenient for the great number of the servitors who must eat in their barracks. When it is mealtime, however, this arrangement compels a prodigious running to and fro all through the dinner hour between kitchen and hall on the part of the twenty-odd sergeants and squires who serve Baron Conon's guests and family. It bothers not the appetites of pious Christians that their food is cooked amid contending odors and that many of the doings near the cookhouse make its condition extraordinarily unsanitary.

We have now crossed the bailey and its teeming life. Before us rises the inner ward of the castle. Here are the gate and the walls of the bailey over again, but far more pretentious and formidable. There is another moat filled with muddy water; another drawbridge larger than the outer one. The two gate towers are higher; their structures are thicker, more solid. The curtain walls are so lofty that arbalistiers thereon can pick off the enemy who may have gained the parapet of the outer defenses. Finally, between the gate towers and the towers at the end of the curtains, both to right and left, there is interposed an extra tower, making the flanking fire much more close and deadly. Consequently, the foe who could force his way into the bailey would thus probably find it merely a bloody cockpit. The retreating garrison would set fire to all the rude wooden buildings, and rake the outer court with their bows and engines. If it would cost dearly to win the bailey, what would it not cost to storm the castle proper?

The gate to the inner ward is flung wide, but the portcullis still slides in its grooves, being dropped every night to make sure that low fellows from the barracks do not prowl around the seigneurial residence in the darkness. Just at present swarms of people are going to and fro between the two great sections of the castle, and jostling ·and laughing in the narrow passages. As we pass through to the inner ward we realize a certain touch of refinement. The pavement is cleaner. Most of the servitors are better dressed and better mannered. Before us opens the great court of the castle, set with stone flags and reasonably well swept. Here the baron and his brother will practice their martial exercises when the weather is bad and they must avoid the tilting grounds. Here the horses will be mounted when Conon, Adela, and all their noble friends assemble to ride out for hunting or hawking. On either side the stately towers set into the walls frown downward, but our gaze is ahead. Straight before one rises first a rather elegant stone building with large pointed windows and a high sloping roof, and then looming before that an enormous round citadel—one that dwarfs all the other towers. It stands at the apex of the triangle; on one side is the castle court, but to right and left the crags at its base are falling precipitously away to the Rapide and the Claire.

The stone building is the *palais,* the actual residence of the baron. The giant tower is the donjon, the great keep of the castle, built on the site of Heribert's old stronghold, but twenty times as formidable. The *palais* is nearest to us, but since the apartments of the seigneur are there, and we wish to examine these later, it is best to pass around one end thereof and visit the donjon first.

Baron Garnier had built his donjon about one hundred and ten feet high and some fifty-five feet in diameter, with walls a dozen feet thick. This size is large, but not extraordinary. At Coucy they are planning a tower two hundred and twenty-five feet high and ninety-five feet in diameter. If Garnier had built a little earlier he would have made it square, like that pitiless tower at Loches, which is only one hundred feet high, but is seventy-six feet on its longest side. To enter the donjon we go over still another drawbridge, although the ditch below is dry, and on penetrating a small door in the masonry we wind up a passageway through the thick wall. Passing from the bright morning light of the court, one seems plunged into pitchy darkness. Strangers stumble up steep stairways, with here and there a twinkle of light from loopholes a couple of feet high, although barely wide enough at their openings to allow the free flight of an arrow. Far below may be caught glimpses of the twinkling, rushing Rapide, and of the bright green country stretching away in the distance.

When St. Aliquis was rebuilt by Baron Garnier's architect, although the donjon was greatly improved, much of the old masonry of the original tower was retained, as well as the general arrangement of the staircases, loopholes, and succession of *halls,* chambers, and lofts. We see what the castle resembled in Heribert's day. By a turn or two in the gaunt entrance we come to the original great hall of the castle. It is

UPPER HALL OF THE DONJON

offensively dark; the windows are mere loopholes at the end of deep, cone-shaped passages let into the walls. Even on this balmy June morning the atmosphere is clammy. As our eyes adjust themselves, however, we see that we are in a huge vaulted chamber with a great fireplace, and with a kind of wooden gallery about eight feet above the floor, around the entire circuit. In this great chamber can be assembled a good fraction of the entire garrison. The seigneur or his spokesmen standing in the center or near the fireplace can give orders which every man present can understand. Directions can thus be given for any move needful for the defense of the castle.

As we shall see, there is now a newer and better hall in the more modern and airy *palais,* but the older hall is still used at great feasts for the overflow of guests. Even now are standing long oaken tables, duly hacked by the trencher knives of many boisterous diners; and on the walls—blackened by the smoke from the great fireplace—are hanging venerable trophies of the chase, antlers, the head of a bear, great boar tusks, as well as an array of all kinds of hunting weapons used by departed generations.

If we were to follow the staircase down from the hall we would come to an even darker vaulted apartment used sometimes as a supplementary dormitory for the humbler guests, but also (to the astonishment of later-day medical usage) with small rooms set off to be used as a kind of sick ward; because every physician, whether schooled at Salerno, Cordova, or Montpellier, will tell you that darkness is the friend of health and that few invalids can hope to get better unless they are kept as shaded and sequestered as possible.

If we wished to pursue still lower, descending a black

staircase with lanterns, the rocks would begin to drip dampness. We could hear the rushing of the Rapide against the base of the castle. The journey would end at a barred iron door. Within would be a fetid, reeking chamber lit only by two or three tiny chinks in the masonry, and with the bare rock for the floor. Here is Baron Conon's prison. He is counted a merciful seigneur, yet he thinks nothing of thrusting genuine offenders therein and keeping them for weeks, if not months, before releasing or hanging. Lucky if Maître Denis, the turnkey, remembers to bring down a coarse loaf each day, and if the rats do not devour the prisoners' toes; but we shall consider all such nice matters later.[1]

It is alleged that from these lower vaults there is an underground passage leading from the castle to a secret sallyport at the foot of the precipice by the Rapide. If a passage exists, however, it is known only to Conon and a very few trusted retainers. But not all such stories are false; many castles have such secret passages; and at Coucy they are quietly planning to introduce a rather elaborate system of the same. Quite possibly St. Aliquis possesses something of this nature.

Far pleasanter is it now to ascend from the main hall through a couple of stages of upper and airier chambers (now used as apartments by part of the castle folk) until by a dizzy ladder we reach the summit of the donjon itself. Here on one edge of the broad platform is a little round turret carrying us still higher. From the turret flutters the orange banner of St. Aliquis, with some kind of a black dragon (in memory, possibly, of the viking raid) broidered upon it, and the arrogant legend of the noble family, "Rather break than bend." To lower this banner were a horrid disgrace. Never is

[1] See ch. x.

it to be struck unless the castle surrenders, when it will be sadly flung into the moat.

Under the flagstaff is a stout projecting beam rigged with a pulley. Here is a gibbet in case the baron wishes to hang offenders as a warning for the countryside. Fortunately, however, Adela has a dislike to seeing the corpses dangling, and has persuaded Conon to order his recent hangings at the ordinary gallows across the Claire by the village. On the flag turret is always a watchman; day or night some peasant must take his turn, and even in peace he has no sinecure. He must blow on his great horn at sunrise, at "cover fire" at night, when the baron's hunt rides out and returns, and again when a strange retinue approaches the gate. The whole wide countryside spreads in a delightful panorama below him at present, but on winter nights, when every blast is howling around the donjon, the task is less grateful. No wonder that peasants impressed for this service complain that "watchmen have the lot of the damned."

So back through the donjon and again to the castle court. The donjon is purely military. In times of peace it is a mere storehouse, prison, and supplementary barrack for the seigneur's people. In war it is the last position where the garrison can stand desperately at bay. A hundred years earlier Adela and her sister-in-law, Alienor, would have lived out most of their days in the cheerless dark chambers directly above the main hall. Now they are more fortunate. They dwell in the elegant Gothic arched *palais*.

The *palais* consists of a long, somewhat narrow building thrusting out into the inner court, and of other structures resting against the western curtain wall on one side, but with their larger inner windows looking also into the court. The rooms are high, with enormous fireplaces where great logs can warm the apartments in winter. The ceilings are ribbed and vaulted like a church, and some of the masonry is beautifully carved. Where the bare walls are exposed they are often covered with a stucco on which are sketched fresco scenes somewhat after the style of stiff Byzantine paintings, or the famous tapestry of Queen Mathilde at Bayeux. All the tints are flat red, yellow, or brown, without perspective or fine lines, and in a kind of demi-silhouette. Little touches of green, violet, and blue relieve the bareness, and despite many awkward outlines and other limitations many of the scenes are spirited as well as highly decorative. Some of the pictures are religious. We notice "Christ on the Cross" between the "Synagogue" and the "New Law," a "Last Judgment," an episode in the life of St. Aliquis himself; also many secular pictures based often on the jongleur's epics. Thus from the "Song of Roland" there is the tearing by wild horses of the traitor Ganelon.

The windows in this *palais* betray the luxury of the owner. They are not closed by wooden shutters, as are most other apertures in the castle. They are of glass, with very small panes set in lead. The panes in the smaller rooms are uncolored, although hardly of transparent whiteness, but in the huge dining hall they are richly colored as in a church, giving a jewel-set galaxy of patron saints (*e. g.*, St. Martin, the warrior saint of France) and of knights and paladins from Charlemagne and King Artus down, gazing benignantly upon the feasters below.

This new hall is, of course, the finest apartment in the castle. Here amid wood- and stone-work deeply carved the baron's household sits down to dinner. It is, however, more than a mere dining room. Great feudal ceremonies, such as the receiving of homage, here take place. Hither also in bad weather or on winter evenings nearly all the castle folk will resort. Messire will sit on the dais upon his canopied chair; everybody else will wedge in as closely as possible, and after infinite chatter, jesting, dice playing, and uproar the ever-popular jongleurs will take station near the fireplace, do their tricks, sing songs, or recite romances. The hall is, in short, the focus of the peaceful life of the castle.

There are other rooms in the *palais,* but, considering the number of people who have to live therein, they seem rather few. There is little real privacy in St. Aliquis. The baron has a special closet indeed, where he can retire and hope that he is not overheard, but the great chamber for himself and the baroness is ordinarily full of servitors. Next to the chamber is a second room where the baron's sons sleep while they are little, and where honored guests can be lodged. Conon's brother and sister have each a large apartment, but there seems a singular lack of anterooms, boudoirs, and other retiring rooms. It is perfectly good manners to ask noble guests to share the same rooms with the family; and a couple of the baroness's maids will sleep on pallets within her chamber, with the baron's favorite squire just outside the door. As for the lesser folk at night, they often stretch unceremoniously on the tables or even on the floor in the main hall. The possession of a strictly private room is indeed a decided luxury; even a great noble is often able to go without it.

The furniture of these apartments seems scanty, but it is at least very solid. In the hall there are lines of tables set upon trestles, faced by long backless seats. Here it is often needful to remove these tables to arrange

INTERIOR OF A THIRTEENTH-CENTURY APARTMENT

From the restoration by Viollet-Le-Duc. At the left the chair where sits the seigneur, the bed separated by a screen from the rest of the hall; at the back, between the two windows, a cupboard; opposite the fireplace, a large table. Tapestries ornament the walls.

for a feudal ceremony or for a dance; but at one end of the apartment is a raised dais, and at right angles to the others runs the ponderous oaken table of the master. Conon faces the hall from a high carved chair under a wooden canopy. The other seats on the dais have the luxury of backs and arms. The fireplace is an enormous construction, thrusting far into the room, where long logs on high andirons can heat the stonework so it will glow furiously for hours. To keep off the heat in winter there are fire screens of osier, but of course in summer these disappear. Every festival day the paved floors of the rooms in the *palais* are strewn, if possible, with new rushes and flowers—roses and lilies, flags and mint, making a soft crackling mass under one's feet. They are fragrant and pleasant while fresh, and even through the winter are allowed to remain to protect against the chill of the floor. By springtime they are dried and are very filthy, for the diners throw their bones and bits of bread and meat into them, and the dogs and cats roaming about cannot devour all of such refuse. Certain seigneurs, indeed are introducing the use of "Saracen carpets," gorgeous rugs either imported from the East or made up in France after imported patterns; but these are an expensive innovation, and Conon as yet keeps to his river rushes.

Of another luxury, however, he is rightly proud. Stowed away in carefully guarded cupboards is a quantity of admirable wall tapestries, some of the precious sendal (taffeta) silk, some of hardly less valuable Sicilian woolen stuff. Their designs are of blazing magnificence. There is one of great elaboration showing "The Seven Virtues and the Seven Vices," another giving a whole sequence of scenes concerning Charlemagne. But such precious ornaments must be kept for great occasions.

The order, "Hang the tapestries," is a sign to the servitors that Conon contemplates a tourney or a great feast or a visit from the duke. For to-day the *palais* contents itself with its simple fresco decoration.

The bedroom furniture is equally simple. The chamber of the baron and his wife is lit by three windows with arched tops pierced into the masonry, overlooking the castle court. There is a little table by the fireplace holding a board of chessmen and there are a few backless stools and long narrow benches. In the window places are comfortably upholstered "She and I" seats facing one another. Opposite the fireplace is a chair of state for the baron, with high carved back and arms, a wooden canopy of equally heavy carving, and a footstool covered with red silk. There are several ponderous wardrobes, and especially a number of very massive iron-bound chests containing valuable garments, jewels, and the like. Bureaus and chests of drawers hardly exist in this age, and ordinary chests take their place. Indeed, no bedroom is fitted properly unless it has a solid chest at the foot of the bed for the prompt reception of any guest's belongings. When a castle is taken the cry, "Break open the chests!" is equivalent to calling to the victors, "Scatter and pillage!"

Near one of the windows in the wall there is also a large crucifix carved of dark wood, and beneath it on a shelf is a small silver box richly chased with figures of saints and angels. This is a reliquary containing a trophy brought from the Holy Land by a crusader—a cluster of hair of St. Philip the Apostle, likewise some ravelings of the robe of St. Anna, mother of the Virgin. Before these sacred objects the baron and baroness kneel on red-silk cushions and say their prayers morning and night.

But the central object of the chamber is the bed. To have a fine bed for the master and mistress is the ambition of every feudal household. It stands under a great canopy, with heavy curtains of blue taffeta. The bed itself, a great mass of feather mattresses and gorgeously embroidered coverlets, projects its intricately carved footboard far into the room. The whole structure is set upon a platform. When the baron and baroness have retired, their attendants will pull the thick curtains and practically inclose them in their own secluded bedroom.

A THIRTEENTH CENTURY BED
Reconstructed by Viollet-Le-Duc, from a manuscript in the Bibliothèque nationale.

The curtains cut off air, but that is no disadvantage, because every physician tells you that night air is most unhealthful.

This nearly completes the furnishings of the chamber, save for various perches, wooden hooks, and racks set here and there for clothes and sometimes for the baroness's hunting hawks, and two bronze lamps swinging on chains, which give a very imperfect illumination. If more brilliance is needed (and if the great fireplace is not throwing out a glare) one can do as they do in the great hall for extra lighting—set resinous torches in metal holders along the walls. However, for ordinary purposes the baron and baroness prefer the less odorous wax candles. In fact, a very tall wax candle stands near to the bed and is allowed to burn all night. This keeps away pixies and the Devil, and makes things generally more cheerful for Christians.

The other apartments of the castle are similarly furnished, although with less magnificence. Of course, in the barracks for the lower servitors and the men at arms each man is lucky if he has a large bag crammed with straw for a bed, a solid blanket, and a three-legged stool whereon to sit by day.

Thus have been inspected exterior, the stone, and the wooden aspects of St. Aliquis. The task is next to see the doings of the people who give to the unyielding fortress its significance and life.

Chapter III: How the Castle Wakes. Baronial Hospitality.

HATEVER the sins of the men of the thirteenth century, they are not late risers. (The lamps and candles are so poor that only rarely, when there is a great festival or imperative work to be performed, do persons remain about many hours after sunset. In winter the castle folks possibly spend nearly half of their entire time in bed; in summer, thanks to the long evenings, they would hardly get sufficient sleep save for a noon siesta.)

Some seigneurs will actually rise considerably before sunup, hear mass, mount their high turret, survey the landscape, then descend to order the washing horn to be blown. We hear, too, of ladies who rise at dusk, have chaplains chant matins while they are throwing on some clothes, then go to the regular chapel mass, next complete their toilet and take a walk in their garden, all before breakfast. There are, indeed, stories of noble folk sleeping even in summer right up to 6 A.M., but these backslidings follow only a deplorable carouse. Conon and Adela are neither indefatigable risers, nor among the slothful. They are seldom found in bed at cock-crow, and the baron is already warning his young sons that "he who sleeps too long in the morning becomes thin and lazy." So at gray dawn William, Conon's first body squire, has yawned on his pallet by the chamber door, tugged on his own clothes, then hastened to the great bed to assist his master to dress. This is one of a good squire's prime duties, but he need not divest his lord of any nightgown. Nightdresses are no more used in the thirteenth century than are table forks. Conon has been sleeping between the sheets, with only the clothing of a new-born babe, although, curiously enough, he wraps around his head a kind of napkin, precursor of the later nightcap.

When the baron has donned a part of his clothes Gervais, the second squire, brings in a metal basin of water and a white towel. The age is one of great contradictions in matters of cleanliness. Baron Conon washes his face and hands carefully and frequently. He also takes complete baths pretty often, using large wooden tubs filled with hot perfumed water. Personally he seems an extraordinarily neat man, and so are all the higher-rank people. But the age has never heard of polluted wells and other breeding spots for malignant fevers. Flies are harmless annoyances. Numerous evil smells can hardly be prevented, any more than cold weather—the saints give us grace to bear them! In short, cleanliness stops with care of the person. Preventive sanitation is as unknown as are the lands which may lie across the storm-tossed Atlantic—"the Sea of Darkness."

There is an old rhyme which is supposed to give the right times for the routine of the day:

"Rise at five, dine at nine,
    Sup at five, to bed at nine,
    Is the way to live to be ninety and nine."

Sometimes dinner came later than nine, but never, if possible, much after ten. People have sometimes become distressed because the meal had to be postponed until noon. This was natural, for everybody is stirring at daybreak and for breakfast probably has had only a few morsels of bread washed down with thin wine—a poor substitute even for the coffee and rolls of the later continental breakfast.

Having dressed and washed, the baron goes down to mass at the chapel. (Attending daily mass is a duty for every really pious seigneur.) One of Garnier's infamies had been his gross irregularity in this matter. If there had been no chapel in the bailey, the service could have been held in a vestibule to the hall of the *palais*. After mass is over, Conon is ready for business or pleasures. It is a time of peace; and, truth to tell, the baron would really be not a little glad of the excitement, bustle, and strenuous preparation which come with the outbreak of war. The list of things he can do to divert himself in times of public quiet seems limited: (He can hunt, fish, fence, joust, play chess, eat and drink, listen to the songs of the jongleurs, hold his court, walk in the meadows, talk with the ladies, warm himself, have himself cupped and bled, and watch the snow fall.) This last amusement is hardly practicable in June. Being bled is not commonly reckoned a regular sport in other ages! Neither can he hold court—receive his vassals and dispense justice— save at intervals. The jongleurs ordinarily reserve themselves for the evenings. (Conon's secret hankering for a war is, therefore, somewhat explicable.)

If this is a fortunate day, however, the horn on the turret will blow, and then the gong at the bailey gate will reverberate. A visitor of noble rank has arrived. Nothing can ordinarily be more welcome in castle communities. Little isolated fractions of humanity as they are, with the remainder of the world seemingly at an extreme distance, the coming of a stranger means a chance to hear news of the king's court, of the doings of the Emperor Frederick II, of the chances of another crusade, of the latest fashions in armor, of the newest methods of training hawks, nay, possibly of rumors of another brave war like that which culminated in the glorious battle of Bouvines. Unknightly, indeed, is the seigneur who does not offer profuse hospitality to a noble visitor; and any priest, monk, or law-abiding merchant will be given a decent, though less ceremonious, welcome. No wonder the inns everywhere are so bad, when the lords of so many castles grow actually angry if a traveler will not tarry perhaps for days.

There are stories of knights who have deliberately caused the roads to be diverted to compel travelers to come close to their castles, where they can be politely waylaid and compelled to linger. Conon is not so absurd, but if to-day a guest of noble rank approaches the castle, all the ordinary routine ceases. At the outer gate the strangers are met by William, the first squire. If he reports that their chief is a baron, the visitors have the gates unbarred before them; they ride straight over both drawbridges to the inner court. Conon himself leads in the horse of his chief guest, and when the visiting nobleman dismounts he usually kisses him upon mouth and chin, although, if the strange knight is an elderly man, or of very exalted rank, he shows his respect by kissing only his shoulders. Adela and her maidens at once conduct the visitors to a chamber, where the best feather beds are piled high in their honor, and next skillfully take off their armor, bathe their feet,[1] and even assist them to don loose clean clothes—a kind of wrapper very pleasant for indoor wear. Meantime their horses are being stabled and given every attention.

[1] Hospitality sometimes went to such a point that we are told the ladies of the castle assisted a visiting knight to take a complete bath—a service quite innocently rendered and accepted. Similar customs, of course, obtained among the Greeks of the *Iliad* and *Odyssey*.

Only after the visitors are dressed, refreshed, bathed, and perhaps fed, will Conon courteously inquire for how long he is to enjoy their company and whether they are making St. Aliquis merely a stopping point or have come to him on business.

Non-noble guests do not receive such ceremony, unless they are high churchmen—bishops, abbots, and their direct subordinates—but even a poor villein, if he appears on a fit errand, is welcome to a solid meal and a bed on the rushes in one of the halls.[1] A jongleur is always received heartily and entertained with the best; the payment will be in songs and tricks after supper. On most feast days, furthermore, the gates of St. Aliquis will open wide. Conon's servitors will say to everyone, "If you are hungry, eat what you please!" There will be simply enormous gorging and guzzling at the baron's expense.

Yet if there are no outside guests the baron is far from being an idle man. Since he has been stirring at 4 A.M. he is able to accomplish a great deal during the morning. All the stables must be inspected; directions are given about a brood mare; the noisy falcon house is surveyed; various stewards, bailiffs, and provosts come in with reports about the peasants, the baron's farms, and especially the contention with a neighboring seigneur's woodcutters about the right to take timber in a disputed forest land—a case calling for major diplomacy to avoid a brisk private war. Then, too, although this is not a court day, the baron as the dispenser of justice has to order two brawling peasants to be clapped in the stocks until sundown, and to direct that an ill-favored lad who had been caught in an honest villein's corn bin shall have his ears cropped off.

[1] See ch. xvii.

The castle is, in fact, an economic unit all by itself. If the baron is idle or preoccupied he leaves its management to deputies; but a good seigneur knows about everything. The estate has its own corn lands and pasture, its stacks of hay, its granaries and storehouses, its mills, cattle byres, slaughter houses, and salting sheds. Practically every scrap of food actually needed in the castle is grown locally. The innumerable women and varlets wear coarse woolen cloth made from wool raised, sheared, carded, spun and woven on the seigneury. The ordinary weapons and tools required in war are made at the smithy in the bailey. The result is that the castle people do very little buying and selling. Conon has a certain income in silver deniers, but, except for the important sums he is laying by for a tournament, his sister's marriage, perhaps a private war, and other like occasions, he spends it almost entirely on the finer articles of clothing, for superior weapons, for cookery spices, and for a few such luxuries as foreign wines. These can be bought from visiting packmen or by a visit to Pontdebois during the fair seasons.[1] St. Aliquis therefore presents what is to us a curious spectacle—a sizable community wherein many of its members seldom handle that thing called "money" from one month to another.[2]

Conon, on many mornings, is thus kept busy adjusting petty matters concerning the estate. The seigneur is the center, the disposing power for the whole seigneury, but he is not the despot. The castle is one huge family, and shares its joys and troubles together. The upper servitors hold their position by a kind of hereditary right.

[1] See ch. xxii.
[2] Even when sums of money are mentioned in connection with peasants' dues, etc., one may guess that often payments in kind are really in question.

Guilbert, who presides over the smithy, is son of the smith before him. In similar case are the chief cook, the master huntsman, and many others. Even the dubious post of baronial executioner is transmitted by a kind of hereditary prerogative. For Conon to dismiss any of these subordinates save for very obvious reasons would be resented by all their fellows and produce a passive rebellion unwelcome to the most arbitrary seigneur. Even tyrannous Baron Garnier had to wait a suitable opportunity ere changing an unwelcome servitor. Every person has his own little sphere of influence and privilege. The successful baron respects all these "rights" and handles each inferior tactfully. The result is that there is a great deal of comradery and plain speaking. The baron and baroness must listen to flat contradictions every day.

"You are absolutely wrong, Messire," says Herbert, the cowherd, to-day, when Conon directs him to wean certain calves. "I shall execute no such order." And the baron (who would have fought a mortal duel with a fellow noble ere accepting such language) wisely acquiesces, with a laugh. Herbert is "his man" and as such has his own sphere of action, and, besides, Herbert and all his fellows will fight for their seigneur to the last drop of their blood, and obey all strictly military orders with touching fidelity.

Indeed, the St. Aliquis people are somewhat like grown-up children. They are often angry, turbulent, obstinate, contentious, even exchanging cuffs and blows. The women are almost as passionate as the men. But tempers cool with equal rapidity. Two varlets who almost drew knives this morning will be communing like twin brothers this afternoon. Furthermore, despite much apparent friction, the three-hundred-odd people who sleep behind the walls of St. Aliquis are fairly well organized. First of all the baron has his three squires, youths of friendly baronial families who are being "nourished" by Conon preparatory to knighthood and whose education will be described later.[1] They are, of course, "noble," and are looking forward to ruling their own castles. Noble, too, is Sire Eustace, the seneschal, the baron's old companion in arms, who carries the great gonfalon of St. Aliquis into battle, and who, in peace times, is chief factotum and superintendent of almost everything about the fief. The marshal who has charge of the stables is also "the son of a good house," and the chamberlain, who has oversight over all that interior economy which does not pertain to food, drink, and mealtimes, is an elderly, childless knight who became lamed in the service of the baron's father, and who really holds an honorable sinecure. There are, besides these, four other petty nobles, whose estates are so small that they find it pleasantest to live at St. Aliquis, ride in the baron's hunts, and command his men at arms.

The remainder of the castle servants are indeed non-noble; but there is nothing dishonorable in personal service, provided you serve a lord higher than yourself. Conon would feel complimented if, on a visit to Paris, he were asked to carry a great pasty and set it before the queen. The importance of a baron is somewhat gauged by the number of his squires and noble servitors. Many a poor sire has to put up with only one squire, and perhaps a seneschal. As for Conon and Adela, they have a cherished ambition that in their sons' day, at least, the St. Aliquis butler, cellarer, dispenser, and even the master falconer should be of gentle blood also; but that

[1] See ch. xi.

would be putting their household practically on an equality with the duke's.

When dinnertime comes there will be a great rush for the hall, but the ceremonies of the table will be told later.[1] Of course, on common days one will not expect a banquet—only one or two plates of meat, some fish, a few vegetables, bread, and common wine, but all in abundance. Hunger seldom troubles St. Aliquis. If the weather is fine, very likely dinner and supper will be served in the garden, outside the barbican, under pleasant shade trees, close to the purling Rapide. There will be long tables covered with linen dyed with Montpellier scarlet. The honored guests will have cushioned benches; the remainder will sit on almost anything.[2] Supper may be either in the hall or in the garden, according to circumstances. It is a long time between dinner and supper, and appetites are again keen. After supper, if by the presence of jongleurs there are excuses for torches and music, the castle folk join in diversions or even in dancing, until a large silver cup is solemnly handed to the baron. He drinks deeply. All his guests are similarly served. Then he rises and the company goes to bed. If there are honored visitors, Conon will escort them to their chambers himself, and take another sup of wine with them ere parting for the night.

The seneschal meantime makes a careful round of the walls, to satisfy himself that the outer drawbridge is raised, the sentries posted, and that everything is safe. Then he will transmit the ponderous keys to be taken to the baron's room till dawn. The seigneur is undressed

[1] See ch. vii.

[2] Mediæval men did not use the floor to the extent of the Chinese and Japanese, but they were certainly often willing to dispense with seats even indoors, and to sit on their haunches upon the pavement or rushes, "Turk fashion."

by his squires and reposes under an avalanche of feather beds thick enough to provide a vapor bath. Soon all the lights are extinguished throughout the whole black mass of the castle, save only the tall taper in the master's apartment. So the castle sleeps through the darkness, unbroken save for the occasional "All is well!" from the yawning sentry on the turret, until the thrushes and blackbirds begin their noise in the garden and in the trees by the rivers. Then again St. Aliquis resumes its daytime business.

Chapter IV: Games and Diversions. Falconry and Hunting. The Baroness' Garden.

IF Baron Conon has been fortunate enough to receive a noble guest, almost the first question is how to divert the stranger. The inevitable program will be to constrain the visitor to tarry at least long enough to cast hawks or to chase down a deer. If that is not possible, at least he will be courteously urged to attempt some game, and it will be most "ungentle" of him to refuse.

Indoor games are in great demand where bad weather often makes open sports impossible and where bookish diversions are limited. The baron frequently plays with his own family when there are no outside guests, and all the household are more or less expert. To understand them is part of a gentle education for both sexes. Indeed, there is no better way for a noble dame and a cavalier to begin a romance than to sit through a long afternoon studying one another's faces no less than the gaming table.

Some of these diversions are decidedly like those of a later age. For example, if all present are reasonably literate they can play "ragman's roll"! Burlesque verses—some suitable for men, some for women, and all often deplorably coarse—are written on slips of parchment wound in a roll. On each slip is a string with some sign showing for which sex it is intended. Everybody has to draw a roll, then open and read it aloud to the mirthful company. The verses are supposed to show the character of the person drawing the same. Also, even grown-up folk are not above "run around" games which are later reserved for children. High barons play blind-man's buff; seigneurs and dames sometimes join in the undignified "hot cockles." A blindfolded player kneels with his face on the knee of another and with his hands held out behind him. Other players in turn strike him on the hand, and he tries to guess who has hit him. If he is correct, the person last striking takes his place. Of course, a large part of the sport is to deliver very shrewd blows. The fact that such a game can be in vogue shows again that even the high and mighty are often like hot-blooded children abounding in animal spirits.

These games Conon will not press upon his guests. He will urge on them backgammon, checkers, chess or, if they seem young and secular, perhaps dice. Backgammon is called "tables." It is a combination of dice playing plus the motion of pieces on a board which goes back to Roman times. The boards and methods of play are so like those of a later age that one need not comment thereon.

Backgammon is a popular diversion, but hardly more so than checkers (Anglice "draughts") known in France as "dames." Here also is a game that hardly changes essentially from age to age. The checkermen at St. Aliquis are square, not round. Otherwise, no explanation is needed.

What men like Conon really enjoy, however, are games of dice. Nevertheless, since the Church has often censured these cubes of ivory, he and his baroness do not dare to use them too often; besides, they realize the havoc often wrought among the young by dice throwing, and wish to keep their own sons from temptation. In parts of France there are laws reading: "Dice shall not be made in this dominion, and those using them shall be looked upon as suspicious characters."[1] All such enactments are usually dead letters, and a high justiciar can ordinarily punish merely the manufacture and use of loaded dice. Although church prelates rail vigorously, their complaints are not merely that games of chance are, *ipso facto,* sinful, but that the blasphemies constantly uttered by losing dice players form a means of populating hell.

Dice playing assuredly is extremely common. It is even impiously called "the game of God," because the regulation of chance belongs to Providence. Did not the Holy Apostles cast lots between Justus and Matthias to select a successor to the wicked Judas; and can good Christians question means acceptable to St. John and St. Peter? So gamesters will quiet their consciences. Vainly does King Philip Augustus command that any person swearing over dice in his royal presence, no matter how high his rank, shall be cast into the river. Dice are everywhere—in the travelers' and pilgrims' wallets and in almost every castle, hut, or town dwelling. Let any three or four men come together for an idle hour and fortunate it is if a set of dice does not appear to while away the time. The thirteenth century is innocent of cards; dice form the substitute.

The swearing is evil, but the gambling is worse. There are at least ten gambling games, some with three dice, some needing six. Adela has been warning François, her eldest son, concerning a recent instance of reckless playing. A young squire, whose father held lands of Conon, set forth to seek his fortune at the king's court.

[1] Such a law was actually enacted for the entire kingdom of France in 1256.

He halted at Pontdebois, where he met an older soldier of fortune at the tavern. The poor young man was induced "to try a few casts." Soon he had lost his travel money; next his horse; next his armor. In desperation he began pledging his ordinary vesture to the tavern keeper (who acted as a kind of pawnbroker). Ill luck still pursued, and he was reduced to his bare shirt[1] before a friend of his father's, chancing about the inn, recovered his necessary clothes between them and sent him home, utterly humiliated. Such calamities are constant. Dice are daily the ruin of countless nobles and villeins—but the accursed gaming continues. It is even rumored that in certain disorderly monasteries these tools of the devil often intrude further to demoralize the brethren.

THE GAME OF CHESS
An ivory plaque of the fourteenth century
(Musée du Louvre).

No such ill odor, however, attends that game in which Conon delights most. To play at chess is part of an aristocratic education. In a jongleur's romance we hear of a young prince who was brought up "first to know his letters," and then "to play at tables [backgammon], and at chess; and soon he learned these games so well that no man in this world could 'mate' him."

---

[1] A mediæval manuscript contains a vivid picture of two gamesters, one of whom had only a shirt left; the other had been reduced to sheer nakedness. Their companions had evidently stripped them almost completely, leaving them to compete for one garment!

François and Anseau, the baron's sons, make no such boasts, but both know the moves, and François takes great pride in having lately forced a visiting knight to a stalemate. Great seigneurs and kings carry chessboards around with them on campaigns and are said to amuse themselves with chess problems immediately before or after desperate battles. Plenty of other anecdotes tell of short-tempered nobles who lost self-control when checkmated, broke the chessboards over their opponents' heads, and ended the contest in a regular brawl.

This royal game has doubtless come from the Orient. Caliphs of the Infidels have long since boasted their skill in taking rooks and pawns, but in western lands about the first record comes from the time of Pope Alexander II (1061-73), to whom complaint was made that a bishop of Florence was "spending his evenings in the vanity of chess playing." The bishop's enemies alleged that this was forbidden by the canons prohibiting dice. But the bishop retorted that "dice and chess were entirely different things: the first sinful; the second a most honorable exercise for Christians." The Pope tactfully refrained from pressing the matter. Nevertheless, austere churchmen regarded the game as worldly, and impetuous religious reformers insisted on confounding it with games of chance. It was only in 1212 that a Council of Paris forbade French clerics to play chess, just as it (for about the thousandth time) forbade dice—despite which fact the Bishop of Pontdebois spent a whole afternoon over the chessboard the last time he visited the castle and could test his skill on the baron.

As for the nobility, no one thinks of refusing to play, although naturally it is the older knights who have the patience for long contests. According to the *Song of*

Roland, after Charlemagne's host had taken Cordova the Emperor and all his knights rested themselves in a shady garden. The more sedate leaders immediately played chess, although the younger champions selected the more exciting backgammon.

The chessmen are often made of whalebone and imported from Scandinavia. They are models of warriors. The kings have their swords drawn; the knights are on horseback; in place of castles we have "warders," a kind of infantrymen; the bishops hold their croziers; and the queens upbear drinking horns like the great ladies in a northern house. Conon, however, has a fine ivory set made in the East; and Oriental models differ from the Norse. The Infidels, of course, have no bishops; instead there is a *phil*—a carved elephant; and since Moslems despise women, instead of a queen there is a *phrez,* or counselor. Chessboards are usually made of inlaid woods, or even metals, and Conon has an elegant one with squares of silver and gilt, the gift of a count whose life he once saved in battle.

Needless to say, chess is a game in which the women can excel. Alienor is well able to defeat her brother, despite his boasting; and among the duties of the ladies of a castle is to teach the young squires who are being "nourished" by its lord how to say "check."

Chess is supposed to be a game of such worth and intricacy as not to need the stimulus of wagering. But, alas! such is the old Adam in mankind that scandalous gambling often goes on around a chessboard. At festivals when nobles assemble, if two distinguished players match their skill, there is soon an excited, if decently silent, crowd around their table. Soon one spectator after another in whispers places wagers to support a contestant; the players themselves begin to bet on their own skill. The final result may leave them almost as poverty-stricken as the dicers in the tavern, as well as compromising salvation by awful oaths.

Young nobles also kill much time with out-of-door games resembling tennis and billiards. The tennis is played without rack- ets, by merely striking the ball with the open hand. The billiards require no tables, but are played on level ground with wooden balls struck with

A GAME OF BALL (STRUTT)

hooked sticks or mallets, somewhat resembling the hockey of another age. Here again reckless youths often wager and lose great sums. Lads and young maidens are fond, too, of guilles—a game resembling ninepins, although the pins are knocked down, not with balls, but with a stick thrown somewhat like a boome- rang. Of course, they also enjoy tossing balls, and young ladies no less than their brothers practice often with the arbalist, shooting arrows with large heads for bringing down birds which take refuge in bushes when pursued by the hawks.

But chess, dice and every other game indoors or out- doors pales before the pleasure of hawking or hunting. There is no peace-time sensation like the joy of feeling a fast horse whisk you over the verdant country, leaping fences, and crashing through thickets with some desper- ate quarry ahead. It is even a kind of substitute for the delights of war. If a visiting knight shows the least willingness, the baron will certainly urge him to tarry for a hunting party. It will then depend on the season, the desire of the guests, and reports from the kennels and mews and the forest whether the chase will be with hawks or with hounds.

Master huntsmen and falconers are always at swords' points. Their noble employers also lose their tempers in the arguments as to venery and falconry, but the truth is that both sports are carried on simultaneously at every castle. If fresh meat is needed, if most of the riders are men, if time is abundant, probably the order is "bring out the dogs." If only the sport is wanted, and the ladies can ride out merely for an afternoon, the call is for the hawks.

LADY WITH A FALCON
ON HER WRIST
From a thirteenth-century
seal (Archives nationales).

Hunting hawks are everywhere. Last Sunday Adela and Alienor rode over to mass at the abbey church. The good brethren chanting the service were nowise disturbed when each of their high-born worshipers kept a great hooded hawk strapped to her wrist during the whole service.[1] It is well to take your hawks everywhere with you, especially when there are crowds of people, to accustom them to bustle and shouting; but we suspect another reason for always taking hawks about is that the carrying of a hunting bird on your wrist is a recognized method of saying, "I am of gentle blood and need not do any disagreeable work with my hands."

[1] We hear scandalous stories of bishops and abbots who did not think it unfit to take their hawks to church. It is alleged that they would strap their precious charges to the altar rail while they were performing the holy offices.

Falcons are counted "noble birds"; they rank higher in the social hierarchy of beasts than even eagles. If one cannot afford large hawks and falcons one can at least keep sparrow hawks; and "sparrow hawk" is the nickname for poor sires who only maintain birds large enough to kill partridges and quails. In short, the possession of a hawk of *some* kind is almost as necessary for a nobleman as wearing a sword, even with knights who can seldom go out hunting. However, it takes a rich noble like Conon to possess a regular falconry with special birds, each trained for attacking a certain kind of game—hares, kites, herons—with the expert attendants to care for them.

Falconry has become a complicated art. Very possibly the good folk in St. Aliquis will have their bodies physicked or bled by physicians much less skillful in treating human ills than Conon's falconers are in treating birds. To climb high trees or crags and steal the young hawk out of the nest is itself no trifling undertaking.[1] Then the prizes must be raised to maturity, taught to obey whistles and calls, and to learn instantly to do the bidding of the master.

THE FALCON HUNT
Thirteenth century; from a German manuscript in the Bibliothèque, de Bruxelles.

In the baron's mews are more

[1] By the thirteenth century a material fraction of the better falcons seem, however, to have been hatched and bred in captivity, thus avoiding this perilous exercise.

than a score of birds; gerfalcons, saker hawks, lanners, merlins, and little sparrow hawks squawk, peck, and squabble along with hugh goshawks. The male birds are generally smaller than the female, and the latter are reserved for striking the swiftest game, such as herons. Some birds will return of their own accord to the hand of the master after taking game, but many, including all sparrow hawks, have to be enticed back by means of a lure of red cloth shaped like a bird. The falconer swings his lure by a string, and whistles, and, since the falcon is accustomed to find a bit of meat attached to the lure, he will fly down promptly and thus be secured

Conon's head falconer is only a villein, but he is such an expert that recently the Count of Champagne offered a hundred Paris livres for him. This important personage is himself the son of a falconer, for the science runs in families. He is a man of shrewd knowledge and a real wizard at breaking in young birds, teaching them to strike dummies and decoys, to remain contented in their cages or hooded on their perches, and yet not lose their hunting spirit. He has precise methods of feeding—so much meat, preferably poultry, and so much of vegetables, preferably fresh fruit. He takes long counsel with Conon how a recalcitrant goshawk can be induced to sit quietly on the baron's fist. He also teaches young François to carry his little sparrow hawk so it will not be incommoded by any horse motion or be beaten upon unpleasantly by the wind, and how to adjust its hood.

There are few more acceptable presents to a nobleman or, better still, to a lady, than a really fine bird. Abbots send five or six superior hawks to the king when craving protection for their monasteries. Foreign ambassadors present His Royal Grace with a pair of birds as the opening wedge to negotiations. The "reception of hawks" is indeed a regular ceremony at the Paris court. Most of Conon's hawks have come from fellow cavaliers who craved his favor. The St. Aliquis gentry pride themselves on understanding all the professional jargon of falconry. Only peasant clowns would confess themselves ignorant thereof; yet even among nobles few speak it really well. The other day a pretentious knight dined at the castle. He put his gerfalcon on the perch provided in the hall for such use by the guests. But, thunder of heaven! how great seemed his foolishness when Conon courteously led the subject around to falconry! "He said: 'The *hand* of the bird'instead of 'the talon'; 'the *talon*' instead of 'the claw'; 'the *claw*' instead of 'the nail.' It was most distressing to find such a man with a claim to courteous treatment!"

NOBLE HOLDING A FALCON
IN EACH HAND
Thirteenth century; restored by Viollet-Le-Duc, from a manuscript in the Bibliothèque de Bruxelles.

Of course, at some excesses in falconry Conon draws the line. He considers impious his neighbor the Viscount of Foretvert, who sprinkles his hawks with holy water prior to every hunt, and says a prayer over them adjuring, "You, O Eagles, by the True God, the Holy Virgin, and the holy prophets, to leave the field clear for our birds and not to molest them in their flight." The church has never authorized this, though the viscount's worldly chaplain certainly condones the practice.

Everything about falcons must be compatible with

their nobility. The glove on which they are carried is embroidered with gold. The hood which keeps them blindfolded is likewise adorned with gold thread, pearls, and bright feathers. Every bird has attached to his legs two little bells engraved with his owner's name. High in the air they can be heard tinkling. If the bird is lost the peasants discovering it can return it to the owner—and woe to the villein who retains a falcon found in the forest! The local law provides that either he must pay a ruinous fine or let the falcon eat six ounces of flesh from his breast. As for stealing a hunting bird outright, there is hardly a speedier road to the gallows; it is what horse stealing some day will become in communities very far from France.

Assuredly it is an exhilarating sight to see the castle folk go hawking on a fine morning. The baron, baroness, and all their older relatives and guests, each with bird on gauntlet, are on tall horses; the squires and younger people have sparrow hawks to send against the smaller prey, but the leaders of the sport will wait until they can strike a swift duck or heron. Dogs will race along to flush the game. Horns are blowing, young voices laughing, all the horses prancing. Conon gives the word. Away they go—racing over fences, field and fallow, thicket and brook, until fate sends to view a heron. Then all the hawks are unhooded together; there are shouts, encouragement, merry wagers, and helloing as the birds soar in the chase. The heron may meet his fate far in the blue above. Then follow more racing and scurrying to recover the hawks. So onward, covering many miles of country, until, with blood tingling, all canter back to St. Aliquis in a determined mood for supper.

Hunting is more serious business than falconry. The

castle folk do not care much for beef and mutton; they prefer venison and boar's meat, and the great woods to the east of the castle supply food no less than diversion.

Hunting is a pursuit quite allowable to pious laymen, and in moderation is even commended by the Church. By hunting one benefits one's soul, for thus we "avoid the sin of indolence, and, according to our faith, he who avoids the seven mortal sins will be saved; therefore, the good sportsmen will

A HUNTER
From a seal of the thirteenth century
(Archives nationales).

be saved." The huntsmen's saints—St. Germain, St. Martin, and above all St. Hubert of Liège, a renowned hunter of the eighth century[1]—are invoked in countless castles oftener, one fears, than such greater saints as St. Peter and St. Paul.

There are many dangerous beasts in the great forests spread over France. Charlemagne (the tale runs) was once nearly hugged to death by a hard-pressed bear. Every nobleman has met with very ugly boars and also powerful stags who fought desperately.

As for the ladies (who, after all, are of one blood with their brothers) the hunt is almost the closest they can

---

[1] The story had it that he was converted to a religious life after meeting in the woods a stag bearing between his horns an image of the Saviour. St. Hubert's feast day was always faithfully celebrated by kings and nobles.

come to martial pleasures. Adela and her sister-in-law can wind horns, follow stags, control dogs almost as well as Conon and Aimery. Of course, they could ride from early girlhood. On occasion of ceremony they ride sidesaddle, but when hunting and hawking they go astride in wholly masculine manner. François has been riding now for years, and even little Anseau, barely seven, can cling to the back of a high steed and keep beside his mother, unless the hunt becomes extremely furious.

The equipments for hunting are simple. The only real luxury is in the hunting horns, the great olifants whose piercing notes can ring a mile through the still forests. These horns are made of ivory, chased with gold, and swung from each important rider's neck by a cord of silk or fine leather. The hunters wear leather gauntlets and use a bow and arrows, a "Danish ax" (a kind of tomahawk), a boar spear (the favorite hunting weapon), and also a large knife for emergencies. As the party mounts in the castle court, around them are leaping and yelping the great pack of dogs—white in teeth, red tongues, straining the leashes and barely controlled by their keepers. Dogs are loved almost as much as falcons, and Conon has a large collection of greyhounds, staghounds, boarhounds, and even of terrible bloodhounds. The kennels are replenished constantly, for stags and old boars can kill many dogs ere they are finally run down and speared. The gift of a litter of fine puppies is, therefore, often as welcome as a cast of hawks.

It is a happy day if a beater comes in with tidings of "a wild boar, the strongest of which anyone has ever heard tell, in the forest of Pevele and Vicogne near the free holdings of St. Bertin." The baron will call out all the castle folk, and, if time admits, will send to some

favorite vassals a few miles away to join the sport. With
ten pairs of hounds and at least fifteen huntsmen and
beaters he will thus organize the pursuit. The hunt
will start at dawn, and it will take much of the forenoon
to reach the forest where the boar has been discovered.
Then (recites a jongleur) will begin "the baying and
the yelping of dogs. They are unleashed. They bound
through the thicket and find the tracks where the boar
has dug and rooted for worms." One of the keepers
then unleashes Blanchart, the baron's best bloodhound.
Conon pats his head and they put him on the track.

The hound soon discovers the boar's lair. "It is a
narrow place between the trunks of two uprooted oaks,
near a spring. When the boar hears the baying of the
hound he stands erect, spreads his enormous feet, and,
disdaining flight, wheels around, until, judging himself
within reaching distance of the good hound, he seizes it
and fells it dead by his side. The baron would not have
given Blanchart for one hundred deniers. Not hearing
his barking he runs up, sword in hand; but he is too
late; the boar is gone."

After that there is nothing for it except to keep up
the chase relentlessly until evening, with the whole
company gradually scattering through the forest until
Conon at last overtakes the chase. But the baron is
now alone save for a few dogs. "The boar has finally
come to bay in front of a thicket. He begins by refreshing
himself in a pool; then, raising his brows, rolling his
eyes, and snorting, he bares his tusks and dashes upon
the dogs, and rips them open or tears them to pieces,
one after another, all except three of the best greyhounds. Then Conon arrives, and first of all he sees
his dogs stretched out dead. 'Oh, son of a sow,' cries
he, 'it is you that have disemboweled my dogs, have

separated me from my friends, and have brought me
I know not where! You shall die!' He leaps from his
steed. At his shout the boar, despite bushes and ditches,
leaps upon him swift as an arrow. Conon lets him come
straight on, and, holding the boar spear straight before
him, strikes at his breast. The point pierces the heart
and goes out at the shoulder blade. Mortally wounded,
the boar swerves to one side, totters, and falls."[1] So the
chase ends and the dogs are avenged. The baron has

THE STAG HUNT
Twelfth century; from a window in the cathedral of Chartres.

to blow his horn many times ere his party finds him.
Luckily the boar has run back somewhat toward St.
Aliquis. They are therefore able to get home in noisy
triumph that night, and all the castle women are under

[1] The quotations are from the story of the boar hunt in the romance *Garin le Lorrain,* with Baron Conon substituted for Duke
Begoy in the original.

the red torches outside the gate to "oh!" and "ah!" at
the boar and to praise the prowess of their seigneur.

Conon is fortunate in being able to return home
without more adventures. His high suzerain, King
Philip Augustus, while a young prince, once followed a
boar until he was lost in the forest, and became justly
anxious; but just as he was commending himself to
God, the Virgin, and "St. Denis, the protector of the
King of France," to his great relief he met "a charcoal
burner, grim to behold, with a face black with charcoal,
carrying a great ax on his shoulder." This honest
peasant guided the prince to safety.

One important part of the St. Aliquis population,
however, regards all hunting parties with far less satisfaction. The chase often goes straight across the
peasants' fields, with twenty horses beating down the
newly seeded ground or even the standing crops. This
is the baron's absolute privilege and any protest is
treasonable. The villeins have not simply to submit
to this, but if deer nibble or boars root upon their fields,
they can merely try to scare the ravagers off. Their
lord and his friends alone may use arrow, blade, or spear
against the game. The St. Aliquis peasants bless the
saints that this time the boar kept conveniently in the
forest and did not sell his life dearly in a half-ripe cornfield.

Hawking and hunting are two great out-of-door sports,
always excepting martial exercises and downright war;
although sometimes Aimery and other young men, for
a tame diversion, take crossbows and try to shoot birds
in the meadows.

If Conon is naturally the master of the hunt, Adela
is as invariably mistress of a very important place—
the garden. Castles are disagreeable residences. Even

with the newer *palais* rising beside the grim donjon, they are usually dampish, illy lighted, and subject to uncanny odors. In northern France there is enough confining weather in any case. Therefore, the more reason there is, the moment the sun shines, for hastening where there are sweet air, bright flowers, and delightful greenness.

The castle garden is outside the barbican, shut off by a dense hedge from the exercise ground. In it are not merely many beds of flowers, but fruit trees and a group of venerable elms much older than the First Crusade. Also, there is a broad, fine stretch of closely cropped grass, shaded by the trees for most of the day. Here all kinds of things can occur. At long tables the whole castle will dine and sup in fine weather. Here Conon will assemble his vassals for ceremonious council. Here will be played innumerable games of chess. And here especially, if a few jongleurs can be found to saw their viols on fête days, all the castle folk, noble and villein, will rapturously join in dances, not in stuffy hall under midnight lamps, but in bright daylight with the merry feet twinkling on God's soft green grass.

Adela has taken great pains with her garden, which fell into a bad condition during Baron Garnier's day. She often councils with Brother Sebastian at the abbey, a real botanist with a true love of plants and flowers. One side of the beds is adorned with roses, lilies, and marigolds. On the other grow useful herbs such as lettuce, cresses, mint, parsley, hyssop, sage, coriander, and fennel. With these, too, are also poppies, daffodils, and acanthus plants, while a vegetable garden supplies the castle with cucumbers, beets, mustard, and wormwood. The fruit trees yield a sizable crop of apples, quinces, peaches, and pears. There is a kind of hothouse in which the baroness has tried to raise figs, but

with no great success; but, of course, there is no difficulty
in maturing grapes and cherries; indeed, cherry festivals
are among the most familiar and delightful holidays in
all this part of France. "Life," say monkish writers,
warning the thoughtless, "though perhaps pleasant, is
transitory, 'even as is a cherry fair.'"

"Crooked" Heman (the hunchbacked gardener) has
considerable skill even without the teachings of Brother
Sebastian. He practices grafting successfully, although
his theories on the subject are absurd. He is trying to
develop a new kind of plum and is tenderly raising some
of the new "Agony" pears—a bitter variety for pickling.
True, he believes that cherries can grow without stones
if you have the right recipe, and that peach trees will
bear pomegranates if only you can sprinkle them with
enough goats' milk. This does not prevent large practical results. His tools are simple—an ax, a spade, a
grafting knife, and a pruning hook; but, thanks to the
unlimited number of peasant clowns which the baroness
can put at his disposal, he keeps the garden and orchard
in admirable order.

Heman's office is the more important because the
garden does not exist solely as a pleasure spot or for its
fruits and vegetables. Flowers are in constant demand,
whenever obtainable, for garlands and chaplets. Even
as with the Greeks, no feast is complete without them.
Wild flowers are in favor, and many a time Adela's
maids are sent out to gather and wreathe woodbine or
hawthorn; but, of course, such a supply is irregular.
On every social occasion from early spring to the edge of
winter the castle garden must, therefore, supply its garlands. It is, accordingly, one of the essential working
units of St. Aliquis, along with the stables, the mews,
and the armory.

Chapter V: The Family of the Baron. Life of the Women.

CONON, we have said, has lived in great harmony with his baroness. Well he might. A short time ago a visiting cavalier, who had learned to string words after the South Country troubadour fashion, saw fit to praise Adela after this manner: "She has fair blond locks and a forehead whiter than the lilies. Her laughing eyes change color with her mood. Her nose is straight and firm. Her fresh face outvies the white and vermilion of the flowers. Her mouth is small and her teeth are white like snow on the wild rose. White are her fair hands, and the fingers are both smooth and slender." Also the baron is very proud of his sister, for whom he is planning a worthy marriage. A Breton jongleur, who found St. Aliquis's hospitality grateful, sang thus of Alienor: "Passing slim is the lady, sweet of bodice and slender of girdle. Her throat is whiter than snow on branch, and her eyes are like flowers set in the healthful pallor of her face. She has a witching mouth, a dainty nose, and an open brow. Her eyebrows are brown, and her golden hair is parted in two soft waves upon her forehead."[1]

Both of these laudators exaggerate. Neither Adela nor Alienor has a monopoly of good looks; yet a life of eager exercise in the open has given them both a com-

[1] These quotations are from Arnaut de Maruelh and Marie de France, respectively.

plexion which many a town-pent rival might envy. Their positions in the castle, as at once the gracious hostesses to equals and the unquestioned mistresses over hundreds of dependents, bestow on them dignity and "noble" assurance. Each lady rejoices in the good fortune of being blond, a first prerequisite to beauty— for in all the romances there is hardly one brunette maiden who comes in for praise. Their hair falls down the length of their arms, to the owners' great satisfaction, and is worn in two long braids, entwined with ribbons, or on gala days with gold thread, resting in front over their shoulders. Adela, at least, has long since become complaisant to all kinds of flatteries, though Alienor is still thrilled when a jongleur or sentimental knight assures her that she has "lips small as an infant's," "cheeks the color of peach bloom," "teeth of perfect regularity," "breath sweet as the censer swung above a church altar," and that "her beauty suddenly illuminates the whole castle." Both of the ladies are tall and slender, again the ideal type of femininity; and they have unconcealed pity for the poor Viscountess of Foretvert, who is short, plump, and afflicted with dark hair.

COIFFURE OF A NOBLEWOMAN Twelfth century (cathedral of Chartres).

Alienor's mother is dead, but her sister-in-law is enough older to take her place somewhat and give much well-meant advice, which the younger damsel must take meekly. Adela often admonishes thus: "My fair sister, be courteous and meek, for nothing else so secures the favor of God and of mortals. Be friendly

71

to small and great. I have seen a great duchess bow ceremoniously to an ironmonger. One of her followers was astonished. 'I prefer' replied she, 'to have been guilty of too great courtesy toward that man, than guilty of the least incivility toward a knight.' Also one must shun foreign fashions at festivals and tourneys, lest one become foolishly conspicuous; and above all beware of lofty headgear, lest you resemble stags who must lower their heads on entering a wood, and in order that you may not by your loud fashions make everyone stare at you as if you were a wild beast."

Recently, too, Adela has been giving sisterly advice on how to walk becomingly: "Look straight before you, with your eyelids low and fixed, gazing forward at the ground six fathoms ahead, not changing your look from one place to another, nor laughing, nor stopping to chatter with anybody upon the highway."

Conon, too, has beset poor Alienor, with all the superiority of an elder brother. He has commended the instructions of a certain *trouvère* (North French minstrel) to a young noblewoman. She must not talk too much; especially she must not boast of the attentions paid by young knights. When going to church she must not "trot or run," but salute "debonairely" all persons she meets. She must not let men caress her with their hands or kiss her upon the mouth. They might misconstrue such familiarities. She must not go around with part of her body uncovered, undress in the presence of men, nor accept presents from any man not a kinsman nor her accepted lover.

The *trouvère* instructor also goes on to warn his fair pupils against scolding in public, against overeating, and against getting drunk, "whence much mischief might arise." Unless she is ugly or deformed, she should not cover her face coquettishly. "A lady who is pale faced or has not a good smell ought to breakfast early in the morning! for good wine gives a very good color, and she who eats and drinks well can heighten her complexion." To avoid bad breath eat aniseed and fennel for breakfast. Keep your hands clean and cut your nails so as not to retain dirt. When you are sharing the same dish at table with some one else (as is the custom) do not pick out all the best bits for yourself; and beware of swallowing too large or too hot a morsel of food. Also, wipe your mouth frequently, but on your napkin, and particularly not upon the tablecloth. Also, do not spill from your mouth or grease your hands too much. Young ladies also should keep from telling lies.—Alienor wishes the impertinent *trouvère* in purgatory.

But following Conon and Adela, Father Grégoire, the chaplain, and then even holy Brother Matthew, the prior of the abbey, takes her in hand. She must avoid sin by never letting her mantle trail disgracefully, lest she seem like a fox whose glory is in his tail. Her maids must avoid repeating gossip. She must never travel without proper retinue, lest she be caught in compromising situations. She must attend mass regularly and not be satisfied "merely with hearing low mass and hurrying two or three times through the Lord's Prayer and then going off to indulge herself with sweetmeats." Alienor should also avoid all games of chance, including backgammon (advice, indeed, at which Conon laughs) and not to waste too much time even at chess, nor to take indecent pleasure in the low songs and antics of the jongleurs. No wonder the poor girl vows she will peversely do these very things at first opportunity![1]

---

[1] All the above advice to noblewomen is from contemporary etiquette books or clerical writers. The trouvère quoted is Robert of Blois, a writer of the thirteenth century.

Alienor tells herself, however, that she is fortunate she is not troubled by worse things than hortatory friends. Champions of "equality of sexes" from a later age can become horrified over the legal status of women in the feudal centuries. Females can never bear arms; they must remain perpetually as minors before the law. Even a great heiress will be under severe pressure to take a husband who will perform the military duties of her fief as soon as possible. If a baron dies, leaving only a young daughter, the suzerain can complain that he has been injured in one of his most important rights— his claim to armed service from the fief holder. Where now is the vassal to follow his banner? Perhaps a decent suzerain will wait until the heiress is twelve. Then he will "give" her to some battleworthy follower. She will not have any real choice, even if the bridegroom is old, ugly, and brutal.

On the other hand, many a fatherless girl becomes terribly anxious to be married. Only married women have a fixed status in feudal society. Only a husband can keep an heiress's lands from shameless plunder. There is the familiar story of a young noblewoman who went straight before the king and said: "My father has been dead two months. I demand of you a husband." She never dreamed of suggesting any particular husband. *That* was the suzerain's business; but to leave her in unprotected celibacy was an outrage which no lord had a right to inflict upon an orphan.

Legally and morally, husbands have the right to treat their wives harshly if the latter provoke them. Every girl around St. Aliquis knows the story of the silly wife who often contradicted her husband in public, and how, after he had vainly remonstrated, "one day raised his fist, knocked her down, and kicked her in the face while

74

she was prostrate, and so broke her nose." The story conveys the plain lesson that she was directly to blame, "for it is only right that words of authority should belong to her lord, and the wife's duty requires that she should listen in peace and obedience." It is, indeed, repeated as something rather exceptional that Adela has recently boasted to certain relatives: "My husband since our marriage has never once laid hands on me." Not that all castellans are brutal—but after all, men will be men, lose their tempers, and treat their wives accordingly. Everybody knows the scene from an epic poem where a certain king is angered at a tactless remark by his queen, and therefore "shows his anger in his face, and strikes her in the nose so hard that he draws four drops of blood, at which the lady meekly says 'Many thanks. When it pleases you, you may do it again!'" Such submissiveness is the best way to disarm a husband's anger.

Conon has been mildly ridiculed among his fellow knights because he takes counsel with his wife. Minstrels like to make fun of such cavaliers and to commend the baron who told his officious spouse: "Woman, go within and eat and drink with your maids. Busy yourself dyeing silks. Such is *your* business. *Mine* it is to strike with the sword of steel!"[1] Of course, many knights do worse things than to tell their wives not to meddle, and, if not obeyed, occasionally knock them down. It has been told how Baron Garnier imprisoned his unhappy consort. This was harsh, but not exceptional. Philip Augustus, the reigning king, kept his unlucky bride, Ingebord of Denmark, long years in captivity, notwith-

---

[1] Students of the *Odyssey* will recall a similar command which Telemachus addressed to his mother, Penelope. Homeric society and feudal society had many viewpoints in common.

standing the menaces of the Church; holding her tight in the gloomy Tower of Éstampes, where she complained she had not enough either to eat or to wear. Many nobles sometimes imitate their lord. Thus over in Burgundy, Gautier of Salins recently threw his wife into prison, whence, however, she contrived to escape to her parents. In any case, when, for the sake of her fiefs, a girl of twelve to eighteen is wedded to a husband of forty or fifty, all kinds of unhappy things can happen. The devil can fill the poor damsel's mind with love for a handsome squire. Her lord may neglect her scandalously until suddenly he finds himself required to avenge "his honor" by some deed of startling cruelty. Such things make the kind saints weep. Not without reason does Conon make discreet inquiries concerning a certain widower knight who has sought Alienor's hand: "Does he horsewhip his servants save for good cause? Did he leave his last wife to mope about the hall while he spent his months riotously at the king's court?

Nevertheless the chatelaines and baronesses of these parts are not always meek doves at the mercy of their husbands. Are they not sprung themselves from a domineering stock? Are they not reared around a castle, which is a great barrack, and where the talk is ever of feuds and forays, horses, lances, and armor? Many a noble lady can answer her husband's fist with a rousing box on the ear, and, if he is not a courageous man, make him quail and surrender before her passions. Her habits are likely to seem very masculine. If she can quarrel like a virago, she can also prove a she-wolf in times of danger. A knight will ride away to the wars, leaving his castle under the command of his wife and feel certain that it will be defended to the inner donjon. The rough men at arms will obey her orders as implicitly as her husband's. In short, the feudal noblewoman is, as might be expected, a compound of mortal weaknesses and excellencies, but all of these qualities are somewhat naïve and elemental.

In any case the castle women cannot complain of being shut up in a harem. They have perfect freedom to meet strange men. If we accept the epic poems, when noble maidens believe a visiting knight to be very handsome they do not hesitate to tell him so to his face. In many love stories the first advances come from the lady, and not infrequently these advances are rather coldly received by the knight. Your average mail-clad cavalier is a man of strong passions, but he is often more interested in war and the chase than in fair maidens. He is seldom a philanderer.

If we visited the castles around St. Aliquis and listened to typical jongleurs' tales, we should gather abundant material for monkish preachments. Noble ladies are said to make few difficulties about inviting male visitors to their chambers to sit on their beds while they are still within the same—or entering the room of a male guest and sitting on *his* bed while conversing very familiarly. Women often meet strangers in scandalously insufficient garments. Ladies also talk with the uttermost freedom to men, quite as openly as young men will talk on ticklish matters among themselves. Many a story, jesting question, or "gab" which is utterly coarse, not to say worse, will be exchanged in mixed company. Young women are seldom well chaperoned. In place of the duenna there is the "waiting woman," herself apt to have her own lover and ready to help her mistress push matters with hers. If there is a sensual intrigue, all criticism ceases if there is, at the end, a formal marriage; but many romances (according to the current stories)

77

in no wise end in marriages. A wedding is by no means the standard climax even to a happy love affair.

The monks, of course, are scandalized at less harmful things than these. They assert that the fair sex, besides being sinful coquettes, are spendthrifts, ruining their husbands by their own extravagance. Women as a sex are inordinately fond of false hair, rouging, and other forms of giving a lie to the faces which God has vouchsafed. As for controlling them, Brother Guyot, of Provins, wrote in despair thus: "The wisest are astray when they wish to judge or correct a woman. She has never found her master, and who can flatter himself that he knows her? When her eyes weep her heart laughs. There are men who teach astronomy, necromancy, geometry, law, medicine, and music; but I have never known a person who was not a fool to take *woman* for a subject of study."

All the above seems true. Yet when due allowances are made, the number of noblewomen who lead happy, honorable lives is great; and if many barons are unkind to their wives, many others reckon them as their greatest treasures. If reasonable care has been taken not to force the mating of obviously uncongenial couples, a decent respect is likely to result, even after a marriage arranged wholly by outsiders. If, in many of the epics, sundry fair ladies seem unprudish, very many others are superlatively faithful, devoted to their husbands, foes to all evil thoughts and seducers, and know how to draw the line very sharply between those familiar attentions which courtesy demands and those where real sinfulness begins. Even a baron who will curse his wife roundly and switch her shoulders treats her also as his *jurê*, the holder of his pledge, to whom he can trust his honor and leave the command of his castle when he rides to war.

"A great deal depends upon the woman herself," Adela assures Alienor. Husbands and wives are shut up together in a castle often for weary months, and a clever wife can easily make herself indispensable to her husband, and then rule the whole barony. In short, in treatment of women, as in all things else, the Feudal Age is a jumble of contradictions. You can find the worst and the best. "A good woman suffices to illuminate a kingdom," a poet declares; while even a crusty monk writes that "we ought to love, serve, and honor woman, for out of her we all come." And what, in one sense, is the intense worship of the Virgin but a sign that woman is extraordinarily venerated and very powerful? "God, thou son of St. Mary"—is that not a standing invocation among the knights?

As for the pursuits of the women, there is little about the castle to which they cannot devote themselves. Sometimes they have even to replace the men on armed expeditions. Adela is grateful that she has not had to imitate the great Countess Blanche of Champagne, who (while guardian of her young son) has recently, in 1218, conducted an invading army into Lorraine and burned Nancy, and then again, near Château-Villein, has led her knights in person and won a real pitched battle. Adela, however, understands all the technic of defending the castle in a siege, she can help her husband about the entire peace-time economy of the seigneury, check up the provosts's accounts, sift out the complaints of the peasants, arrange the alms to the poor, and, best of all, knows how to manage the local bishop and abbot, with a mingling of piety, harmless coquetry, and firmness—a great asset for the weal of the barony.

Her greatest task, however, is to direct the perpetual weaving, knitting, embroidering, and sewing of the castle women. Even if some of the finer cloth is imported, nearly all the garments must be made up in St. Aliquis; and the ladies must set their maids as good an example with their needles as the baron must furnish to his men with his sword. The chambers of the *palais*, and even the garden in summer, seem given over to incessant cutting and sewing; and many a time can you watch the fair Alienor, like the girl in the romance, "seated in her brother's chambers, working a stole and 'amise' in silk and gold, right skillfully; and she made it with care, and many a little cross and many a little star she sets therein, singing all the while the 'Song of the Cloth'"— a gentle, lilting air suitable for the movements of her white hands and her needle.

It was when so engaged that her brother, coming in early from the hounds, vowed he would not spare the dowry to get her a gallant husband; and that night he cast five deniers to the jongleur who praised her to her face before the applauding hall:

> She is the rose, the lily, too,
> The sweetest violet, and through
> Her noble beauty, stately mien,
> I think her now the finest queen
> Which mortal eyes have ever seen.
> Simple, yet coy, her eyes flash joy:
> God give her life without annoy
> And every bliss whereof I ween!

Of course, the prime centers of Adela's life are the rearing of her children and the management of her servants. When little François and Anseau were being born, the castle bell, and that, too, of the village church, were all the time rung furiously to induce the saints to ease their mother's labor. Sensible Father Grégoire had to interpose his ghostly authority to check the midwife from at once plunging the feet of the newly born into icy water to toughen them to the cold, or rubbing their cheeks with a gold piece to make them rich. Of course, Conon was delighted each time they told him, "A sturdy son!" On François' advent he called all his vassals to a feast. "Be joyous!" he proclaimed. "There is born the seigneur from whom you will hold your lands. He will give you rich furs, white and gray, beautiful arms, and horses of price. Yes, in twenty years my son will be dubbed a knight!"

The young St. Aliquis barons were rocked in beautifully carved cradles. They were bathed before a great fire and wrapped, not merely in the usual long baby clothes, but in little robes of silk and furs, even of precious ermine, to proclaim their noble rank. They were, of course, baptized at first opportunity, because unbaptized children had very dubious chances in the next world. Adela had been unable to go to the ceremony for either, but there had been a great gathering of relatives and vassals; for a christening is the formal acknowledgment of the child's legitimacy and settles many claims to inheritance. A child must have three godparents, two of its own sex and one of the other. At the font, one of these holds the babe round the body, and each of the others grasps a leg. Then the priest dips the child completely in the water. "Bare as a babe at baptism," runs the saying. Of course, the higher the rank of the godparents, the luckier the infant. François is proud already because the Duke of Quelque-

CRADLE
Thirteenth-century manuscript in the Cambridge Library (Green).

parte calls him "godson," and Anseau because he is styled the same by the high Countess of Blois.

Up to seven the young boys were left to the care of their mother. Adela nursed her own sons, although wet nurses were the rule in many noble families; but at least three maids were constantly in attendance on each young sprig of St. Aliquis. Neither François nor Anseau is spared the wholesome diet of many blows. Monkish preachers are always warning against sparing the rod and spoiling the child, and every father and mother heeds this particular admonition. Truth to tell, conditions round a castle often tend to make boys little demons of rascality. All the hall has laughed at the epic "Daurel and Beton," in which a child at four was clever enough to steal his guardian's gloves, and at five to play chess and dice and to ride a tall horse. But François and Anseau are growing up reasonably honest, thanks to frequent dermal pain. They have enjoyed a great variety of toys, most of them of types as old as the Pyramids and which will be a delight in succeeding centuries. There are dolls with hempen wigs, carved wooden soldiers with helms and hauberks, windmills, all kinds of animals made of baked clay, wooden horses, and, of course, an armory of wooden weapons. The scores of children swarming the bailey are at their disposal as playfellows, with the sons of the higher officers preferred. There are innumerable games of the tag variety, but already François is learning to marshal his playmates in military companies. What greater delight than to defend some tower against their father's old foe, Foretvert? It will be lucky if they do not filch real arbalists and shoot deadly bolts at one another.

François is now being taken in hand by his father and taught many things needful for a baron's son to know before he is sent away to be "nourished" by some friendly seigneur. He has no sisters, but his aunt Alienor is just emerging from the usual education of a girl of family. If there had been a local nunnery she might have been sent to the convent school. As it was, Conon took in the daughter of a petty noble, a kind of sister under minor vows, who was half teacher, half attendant.

This good soul has given Alienor rather more of book-ish learning than François will probably obtain. The young lady has learned to read and write Romain (North French) and at least to read Latin. The result is that she devours every romance manuscript which she can borrow or can persuade her brother to buy. She has been taught arithmetic fairly well; she has learned the names of the chief stars and constellations and the legend about the "Way of St. Jacques" (the Milky Way). She has picked up a knowledge of healing herbs and is not afraid of the sight of blood, nor does she flinch when binding up a wound. Warfare and tourneys require that young girls should become expert nurses and even make shift to set shattered bones. Of course, she can ride, and at hawking or hunting upon her dear roan Marchegai can keep up with the best; and, like every fortunate maiden in France, her lips are perpetually light with songs—pious or secular, from quaint little chants in honor of the Virgin to the merry

> Easter time in April
> Sings each small bird gentle,
> *"Zo fricandés, zo, zo!—*
> *Zo fricandés, zo!"*

Assuredly, Father Grégoire and the monks have not neglected her religious education. She has learned many prayers, besides the Credo, Ave, and Paternoster, which every Christian child must memorize as soon as possible. Her brother one Easter gave her a finely illustrated psalter, and she has most of the chants by heart. By constant attendance at mass she knows practically the entire service and understands its symbolism. She has plenty of quaint little superstitions, but no degrading ones. At bedtime she repeats a prayer which is popular with all the girls of France: "I implore thee again, Virgin Mary, mayest thou, with all the saints and the elect of God, keep close to me and council me, and further all my prayers and desires: and be with me in all my sorrows and necessities, in all that I am called upon to do, to say, or to think; on all days, at all hours, through all the moments of my life."

Her dolls, of course, have been much finer, and have been retained much longer, than those of François. In her chamber her pet falcon is seldom lacking from his perch—a fact which does not add to cleanliness. She has also a caged magpie which she is laboriously teaching to talk. At the last fair she longed vainly for a rare Eastern parrot, but has consoled herself with a very small lap dog presented by a friendly vassal. Cats abound in the bailey, but they are not pets for noblewomen. There is something plebeian about them. Ill-famed old crones always possess black cats, which possibly partake of the devil. The Church, however, does not support this last belief, because in most nunneries the sisters are forbidden to keep any animals except cats, which evidently belong less to this world than dogs, the companions of secular warriors.

There is one thing which Alienor really loves even better than riding and hawking—*a long, hard dance*. The mania young people have for dancing is sinful. The Church vainly tries to restrain it. Preferably,

Alienor would dance with a handsome knight or squire, yet if these lack, the most indifferent music and company will suffice. The truth is that her robust, vigorous body demands a violent outlet. It is vain for the graver Adela to tell her of the count who allowed so much dancing in his castle that finally at a *bal* on Christmas Day so many joined the revel and all danced so violently that the floor of his great hall suddenly collapsed. The whole company were flung to the cellar, and the foolish count's own daughter was the first body to be taken out.

At the time of the great Church festivals, of course, comes the delight of the mystery plays, and Alienor herself has participated therein, once as an angel and once also as Queen Esther at the Easter play arranged at Pontdebois by the cathedral clergy. She has hopes now that next Easter she can be Herodias's daughter—which is surely the best part open to women, except that of the Holy Virgin herself.

While Adela is, on her part, graciously assisting her family, she is also more explicitly directing her servants. She need not reckon the lack of domestic help among her troubles; hundreds of young men and women from the peasants are only too glad to enter service in return for a straw pallet, a suit of clothes yearly, and a seat in the great hall after the regular diners have risen. Money wages need hardly be considered, although everybody expects a few obols at Christmas and Easter. The importance of a baron is partly indicated by the number of his dependents wearing his insignia, "eating his bread," and attending him and his lady everywhere. Conon is hardly less vain than his peers. The result is that St. Aliquis has twice as many servitors as are really required. The courtyards swarm with busy idlers, although there is a certain organization and hierarchy of service, and all but the least responsible lads and damsels enjoy the honor of having at least *one* inferior whom they can afflict with cuffings and snappish orders.

Adela commands some twenty young women. One or two of these are *pucelles,* daughters of petty nobles and entitled to a certain consideration, even as are the baron's squires. They dress their mistress and Alienor, accompany them, and discreetly share their pleasures. The others, strong-limbed Aiglentine, Jeanette, Martine, and their sisters, by their loose, sleeveless aprons betray peasant origin. They have been carefully selected by the baroness from thrice as many candidates. She has taken pains to learn whether they come of honest parents, are greedy or inclined to drink, are respectful, and whether they are accustomed merely to answer on receiving an order, "It shall be done pretty soon."[1]

These maids are trained to clean the apartments; next to wipe down all the stools and benches; next to feed the "chamber animals"—dogs and cage birds. After that the mistress must assign to them their task of weaving, cutting, sewing, etc. They are fed plentifully, "but only on one meat, and have only one kind of drink, nourishing but not heady, whether wine or otherwise." They must also eat promptly, "not reposing on their meal, or halting or leaning on their elbows," and "they must rise as soon as they begin to talk and lounge about." After supper they must go immediately to bed, unless with the remainder of the castle they sit up for a jongleur.

So passes the routine of many days until at last the prospect dawns of an event which will tax the full

[1] The directions about engaging servants given in mediæval handbooks on domestic economy contain much practical common sense for any age.

administrative capacities of the baroness, and which sets Adela and Aimery each in a different kind of a flutter.   Conon is about to give his sister in marriage and immediately after that to knight his brother.   There will be a festival which will carry the name of St. Aliquis all over northern France.

Chapter VI: The Matter of Clothes. A Feudal Wedding.

INASMUCH as from time immemorial a wedding has seemed primarily a matter of clothes, what better place than this wherein to consider the costumes of the good folk of St. Aliquis? Assuredly, the Scripture warns us, "Take no thought saying . . . 'Wherewithal shall we be clothed?'" but that admonition (so Adela tells the abbot) was doubtless intended only for the Holy Apostles, not for a Christian woman who must make a fair showing for her husband in the face of Heaven knows how many critical baronesses and countesses.

Already Western folk have made that great change in their general style of costume which is to last for many generations later. The Greeks and Romans *wrapped on* their garments; all of them were forms of slightly elaborated shawls, fastened with fibulæ or buckles, but devoid of buttons. Even as late as Frankish times the garments of Charlemagne's contemporaries seemed fairly loose, after the antique model. But with the Feudal Age has come elaborately made clothing which must be *put on* and securely fastened. We have reached the epoch of the shirt, the stocking, and even of objects later to be styled "trousers." Perhaps the life constantly spent in the saddle requires this; also, the demand for garments easily worn under the hauberks, the great

coats of mail.[1] The great transition has been made.
The men of St. Aliquis wear garments strange enough
to another epoch, but without those sartorial differ-
ences which will separate the twentieth century from
the age of Nero.

Another thing to observe is that nearly all garments
are still made of wool, save, indeed, the leathern leggings
and gauntlets of the hunters, and crude garments of skins
for the peasants. Cotton and silk, if not quite unknown,
have been rare, with linen not very common. The
woolen fabrics have usually been coarse, home spun
literally, made up in the castles or farmhouses. Such
garments are warm and durable, but they are prone
to collect dirt, hard to wash, and very irritating to the
skin. Probably it is the general use of woolen clothing,
along with the fact that much of the population possesses
no other raiment than what it is wearing incessantly
every day, which accounts for the number of skin
diseases, from leprosy downward, which are direfully
prevalent. Matters are improving, however. More flax
is being spun up into fine linen. People of quality
change their clothes pretty often. Cotton and silk are
coming from the Levant at prices that permit the ordinarily rich to command them. Wash day is even developing into a fixed institution around most castles.
All this makes for health and comfort. Still, the great
majority of all garments are woolen; and, Holy saints!
how the fleas jump out of a villein's doublets whenever
you beat their wearer!

Conon normally dons the following peace-time garments. First, his squire helps him into underdrawers

[1] Of course, the northern climate and the fact that the Germanic
tribes wore many garments of skins and leather were contributing
factors.

of fine white linen; next come long hose which can be of various fabrics or colors. Upon a gala day he will proclaim himself to be a rich baron by wearing silk hose; otherwise they are of fine wool. Good taste forbids stockings of brilliant color, they should be black, brown, or, at most, black with red stripes. After that comes the chemise, a shirt of white linen, but *sans* cuffs or collar.

The baron is now ready for his regular outer garments. He will put on his pelisson. This is a long fur-edged

garment, very warm and pleasant in winter when the castle is a barnlike place. In summer it is often hot, and as substitute one wears the *cotte* without fur and made of very thin stuff. Over the pelisson is thrown the bliaut, a tunic, fairly loose, which is pulled on over the head like a shirt. The best bliauts are of silk, but for common use one wears fustian or, perhaps, even cotton. Finally, if the baron is going abroad, he will swing his mantle over his shoulders. It is a semicircular cape, with a fur lining even in summer, and very likely ornamented by many silk tassels.

A KING IN THE TWELFTH CENTURY WEARING PELLISON
Restored by Viollet-Le-Duc, from a manuscript of the Bibliothèque nationale.

The shoemakers are already masters of their art. Anybody can buy well-cobbled leather shoes or high boots, but if a nobleman wishes to dress in state he will wear cloth shoes, and display his wealth by having them plated with gold and embroidered with jewels; for good taste here permits elaborate ornaments.

Conon's most variable garment is his headdress.
In the house, or on state occasions, he wears a chaplet
of flowers, or even a thin gold wreath of floreated design;
outdoors he is likely to appear as do
meaner men, in a cloth bonnet—a kind
of Phrygian cap of bright color. If,
however, the weather is bad, he will
probably pull on a *chaperon*. This
is a combination cap and cape which
is drawn on over the head, and which
sticks up or is pulled back in a kind
of peak, at the same time covering
cheeks and shoulders, while the face
shows through a long slit cut in the
upper part.

WREATH MADE OF
METAL FLOWERS
SEWED ON BRAID
Thirteenth century
(church of St. Thibaut;
Côte-d'Or).

These are the orthodox male garments, while the female dress is much
the same, albeit with certain simplifications here and
elaborations elsewere. Adela's maids ordinarily put
upon her a long linen chemise, preferably white, which
descends to her knees. Over that comes the pelisson,
again with the fur edging. It can be made of some very
fine wool or silk, and falls over the chemise clear to her
feet. Above this again is the bliaut, sometimes worn
rather loosely, but more often close fitting and showing
off the figure. The baroness's maids lace it tightly and
take pains adjusting the long trailing sleeves. It is held
in place by a girdle of woven cords, preferably of silk.
The bliaut, of course, can be of very fine material, and
oramented with gold embroideries and pearl beadwork.
Finally there is the mantle, a loose trailing cloak, often
cut as a long semicircular cape and made, on gala occasions, of the richest stuffs available.

Plenty of elegant fabrics can be had by the wealthy.

You can bring back from the Champagne fairs figured silk, woven with silver and gold thread; also very heavy silks woven with large threads of white, green or red. This is the fair *samite* whereof the poets delight to sing. But perhaps more useful is the thin, airy, shimmery sendal silks, useful both for delightful summer garments and for making those brilliant banners which noble ladies give to the knights of their choice. Naturally, too, there are plenty of Oriental silks, with strange Egyptian and Persian figures. For humbler wear (if homespun is not desired) you can buy all kinds of of honest woolens; Flemish and Picard, Champagne products, or those from Languedoc. They come in serges and rough goods, as excellent as anyone could ask. Linen is available bleached to a dazzling whiteness for those who have the price; but cotton cloth is still costly, although the mercers often spread out to the ladies "silk at a marvelously low price" which is really naught but cotton, woven up, perhaps, in Sicily.

However, the finest samite and sendal cannot take the place of suitable furs. *Wearing furs is practically a sign of nobility,* like wearing a sword or carrying a hawk. Many a petty noble will cling to his frayed tippet of black lambskin, even in the hottest weather, merely to proclaim that he is not a villein. Fox- and wolf-skins and civet are, of course, common, but your high noble seeks something better. He will line his pelisson and other garments with red or white marten, black sable, with the gray of the beautiful northern squirrel, and especially (if his purse can compass it) with ermine, the precious fur of the white weasel. The choicest furs probably come from those dim countries called "Russia." You cannot make a noble friend a much more acceptable present than a fine ermine skin; and many a baron has pledged lands to the Jews merely to satisfy his wife's taste for miniver, a superior form of marten. In fact, there is more extravagance over furs than over jewelry, or even over falcons!

Fashions in dress do not change around St. Aliquis so rapidly as in other ages, yet there are constant innovations. For example, the surcoat is coming in. Originally it was a longish woman's garment, but recently a fine knight riding down from Rheims wore one cleverly adapted to masculine necessities. It was a close, sleeveless jacket cut short at the hips and made with big armholes for easy movement. Conon must have one very soon. Inevitably too, at the king's court all kinds of new fashions, luxuries and ornamentations are to be observed. Women cover themselves with gold embroidery, wear gold buttons, and gold girdles set alternately with agates and sapphires. They protect their hands with chamois-skin gloves, and swing a silken alms purse from silver chains at their belts. Fine cavaliers load themselves with a dozen buckles set with sardonyx, and pieces of enamel, and even wear small emeralds in the embroidery on their mantles. Pointed shoes are coming much into style, with the use of colored thongs to bind them to the feet.

FELT SHOE
Thirteenth century
(various monuments).

Yet the St. Aliquis simplicity is hardly undermined. Except on fête days the seigneur is not much better clad than the upper servitors, and Adela never ceases to warn her sister-in-law against extravagance of dress. "Consider always your husband's rank and fortune, but never disgrace them by seeming to devote too much study to your costume or by constantly plunging into new fashions. Before leaving your room be sure your appearance is neat, and see especially to it that the collar of your gown is well adjusted and is not put on crooked."[1]

WINTER COSTUME IN THE
TWELFTH CENTURY
From a manuscript in the Bibliothèque
nationale (Viollet-Le-Duc).

The dress of the humbler folk is of the above nature, of course simplified, and of more sober hue. Blue is the color of the baronial house and nearly all its lord's followers wear bliauts of that color. This is their livery, because twice per year there is a distribution (a *livraison*) of garments to all whom Conon undertakes to clothe and feed.

Noble folk thus display their rank by wearing furs. They also show it by their headdresses. When the baron wishes to put on dignity he assumes a velvet bonnet in place of the ordinary cloth one. On formal occasions, however, this bonnet will be embroidered with gold thread and become his "cap of presence." Sometimes these caps are elaborated and made with a flattened square top. These are the *mortiers,* and in generations later great lawyers and doctors will wear the mortarboard as a professional badge long after the high barons have absolutely discarded the fashion.

As for the head covering of women, the thirteenth century is as yet rather innocent of those towering constructions of peaks and veils common in the suceeding

[1] From a mediæval *Treatise of Instructions to a Young Lady.*

age. Even noblewomen are usually content (as we have seen) with the long braids of their hair intertwined often with ribbons. If the sun is hot or the weather bad they will wear thin veils or solid woolen hoods, according to the seasons; and on gala days they will don either floral chaplets or genuine crowns of gold and pearls, according to the wealth of their fathers or husbands.

Conon's appearance differs from that of his grandsire's in one important particular. Until rather recently gentlemen had their hair cut short in front, although rather long behind, and wore beards, often divided into a great many little tufts which they might even wind with gold thread. By 1200, however, noblemen were usually smooth shaven, although the hair was allowed to grow to some length and sometimes was arranged in little curls.

HEADDRESS OF A MAN
Popular in the thirteenth century (tomb of Saint-Denis).

Thus ended a long struggle, for the Church has for generations disapproved of lengthy beards; many a bishop has warned that "they are the sign of the children of Belial," and the great Pope Gregory VII uttered a regular anathema against them. The reign of the barber is renewed, and the St. Aliquis tonsor twice or thrice per week scrapes over the chins of all the knightly males in the castle. For the servitors and villeins, however, there is no such luxury. All the humbler folk wear beards of great bushiness, as well as unsanitariness; and their hair is cut so seldom that often it can be almost braided like the women's.

Every person of consequence wears a ring. Its signet device is often equivalent to a personal signature. All a man's friends know his ring and will give credence to messengers who produce the same. Women give rings to their lovers, as well, of course, as receiving rings in return. It is believed that many rings have charmed virtues. Conon's signet has been in the family at least since the First Crusade. It has a green Egyptian turquoise cut with a serpent, and is called "The Luck of St. Aliquis." The servitors profess confidence that so long as the baron keeps this ring the castle cannot be taken; and François has already had his head filled with such stories as that of the father who on his deathbed

gave his son a ring, "the virtue of which was that whosoever should wear it should have the love of all men"; or the tale of Princess Rigmel, who gave to her lover a ring so potent that "whoever bore it upon him could not perish; he need not fear to die in fire or water, nor on the battlefield nor in the mêlées of the tournament."

Such are the ordinary articles of costume and adornment. One need not dwell on the buckles and brooches, the golden pins and the jewel-set necklets which Adela treasures in her coffers. They come from Oriental, Byzantine, or Venetian workshops. Some are very beautiful, but fine jewelry, generally speaking, has changed comparatively little from age to age.

COSTUME OF A NOBLEWOMAN

Thirteenth century; restored by Viollet-Le-Duc, from various monuments.

The baroness is not above certain frivolities of toilet herself, but Alienor's approaching marriage has given her fair opportunity to admonish the younger lady on the sins of false adornments. Indeed, these iniquities are thundered against nearly every Sunday at the churches, because the shrewd preachers know that all the men in the congregation will grin approval the fiercer the invectives become. Women are regularly accused "of turning their bodies out of their natural form" by means of laces and stays, of dyeing their hair, of painting their faces. It is affirmed that David was first impelled to desire Bathsheba because she combed her long hair at a window too openly, and all her sore troubles came justly upon her "for the overgreat attention which she sinfully gave to the ornamenting of her head.'

Then, in another sermon, there is approvingly repeated the sarcastic story by the monk Guyot of Provins, that the saints have brought suit at the Assize of God against the race of women because the latter have used so much color for their faces there is none left wherewith to paint the holy images in the churches! The noble ladies are told that when they smear on vermilion, saffron, or quicksilver, or apply poultices of mashed beans and mare's milk to improve their complexions, they are adding centuries to their durance in purgatory, if not taking chances of eternal damnation.

Lastly, there is the iniquity of false hair—as if the good God did not know the proper amount of herbage to grow from each female head! Once there was a holy man who could heal the sick. A young noblewoman suffered from grievous headaches. The miracle worker took one glance at her

COIFFURE OF A WOMAN
Thirteenth century
(cathedral of Rheims).

towering headpiece. "First," said he, "remove that scaffolding which surmounts your head. Then will I pray for you with great confidence." The sacrifice was too great, and she refused; yet erelong her anguish became unendurable and the holy man was recalled. He compelled her to cast away all her false hair and colored bands and swear never to resume them. Immediately then he began to pray—and, behold! her headache departed.

These sermons and Adela's sisterly warnings produce as much result as such admonitions can. Alienor will go through life, now dreading for her comeliness and now for her soul, but never quite imperiling either. Yet she is surely less frivolous than the family rivals, the Foretvert dames—who (tasteless creatures!) could adorn a whole cathedral of saints' images with their paint pots.

There are sometimes seen around St. Aliquis certain obnoxious people who are compelled to wear conspicuous garments in order that others may be warned and thus avoid physical or moral contamination. If you meet a man with a gray coat and a scarlet hat, pass at a distance—he is a leper. If he has a big circle of saffron cloth sewed on his breast, look to your money—he is a Jew. If he has a cross sewed on each side of his breast, say a prayer—he is a released heretic. Finally, if you go to Pontdebois and come upon sundry unveiled females in scarlet dresses, accost them not if you are a decent man—they are women of the town.

At last we have seen the general nature of the garments which are to make gay Alienor's wedding. It is time for the wedding itself.

Marriage, in noble families often does not mean the union of two souls, but of two fiefs. The average baron marries to extend his seigneury and to rear up sons to defend it. A wife represents an estate and a castle. Not many young men marry before they have been knighted. After that they are glad to enter into holy wedlock, for the normal way an aspiring young cavalier whose father is living can gain independence is through his wife's dowry, unless his father allows him a share of the barony.

Since young men are not often knighted until late in their teens or even beyond twenty, weddings on their side seldom take place early. Girls, however, become marriageable sooner. South Country troubadours assert that love can begin to claim a girl when she is thirteen; she is then eligible for marriage. If she has not "given her heart" by the time she is twenty-one there is no hope for her, save in a nunnery; and old maids find no recognized place in society whether in castle, city, or peasant hut.[1]

A ROYAL MARRIAGE IN THE THIRTEENTH CENTURY

From a manuscript preserved in the British Museum (Green).

Of course, couples can marry younger than that. Not many years earlier Count Baldwin VI of Hainault was wedded to Countess Marie of Champagne. The bride was only twelve, the bridegroom only fourteen. Boys and girls are thus sometimes merely "so many pieces on a chessboard," to suit the ambitions of guardians.

If a noblewoman's husband dies she need not expect to be a widow very long, for a man is required to manage her fief. It was one of the greatest proofs of Conon's mother's strong character and ability that when his

---

[1] Troubadour and romance love stories were thus likely to revolve around very young and flighty people. If they survived this critical period of youth they were likely to be staid and sober enough the rest of their lives.

father died she prevented Baron Garnier from forcing her into nuptials with one of his boon companions—a roistering daredevil who, as guardian of her children, would have ruined them, body and soul. Also, if an heiress's husband does not prove suitable to the prevailing powers, strange things can happen. In 1190, when the crown of Jersualem became vacant, Isabella (the new queen) was forcibly separated from her husband, the Seigneur Onfroy, by the barons of the Crusaders' realm, and was given to a more powerful noble, Conrad of Montferrat. Twice the poor queen's husbands died, and twice her barons forced new spouses upon her. The wishes of Isabella herself, who sincerely cared for Onfroy, were in nowise consulted.

In all the romances you can find stories of marriages consummated with amazing haste. There is, *e.g.*, the tale of the old Baron Aimeri, who wished to find his son an heiress. The lad, unaware of what was to happen, was summoned into the presence of a duke, his father's friend. "Young sir," said the duke, "you are of high lineage. I am going to give you my pretty daughter." The boy stood silent while the pucelle was brought in. "Belle," said her father, "I have given you a husband." "Blessed be God!" she replied promptly. The next to come in was a bishop. The ceremony was immediately over; the young people were mated for life, seemingly before either could get his or her breath. Here, at least, the lad was as much the helpless tool of his elders as was the maid.

A story in the "Lorraine" romance makes the proceedings hardly less precipitate. The Count of Flanders is resolved to give his bereaved sister to his valiant friend, Fromont. She had never seen this hero, but has heard much about him. Suddenly her brother takes her by the hand, saying, "My beautiful and dear sister, let us converse a little apart." Then he announces "to-morrow, you shall have a husband." The lady protests that she has been a widow only a month and has an infant son. "You will do this, however, my sister," insists the count. "He whom I give you is far richer than your first husband." Then he says much in praise of Fromont, whereupon the lady responds, "Sire brother, I will do according to your desires." Thereupon, runs the story, "They did not wait a day, they did not wait an hour. On the spot they proceeded to the church. Clerics and priests were notified. There they were blessed and married."

This is a strange state of things, but, fortunately, the Church comes partly to the rescue. It demands first that the maiden shall be at least fifteen years old (a point sometimes waived), that she shall not be too closely related to the man, and that she shall give her "free consent" (another matter not always investi-gated). The question of the "forbidden degrees" is, however, a bar to many projected alliances. The Church endeavored formerly to forbid the marriage of cousins up to the seventh degree, but that rule had proved unworkable, since god-parents were reckoned the same as relatives. The Lateran Council of 1215 has therefore ordained invalid marriages between cousins through the *fourth* degree; and the saints know that this rule makes complications enough, considering how the great families are interrelated! Of course, the regulations are wise, otherwise heiresses would always be given in an outrageous manner to near kinsmen. On the other hand, the forbidden degrees are sometimes a little trenched upon to give the contracting parties an excuse for repudiating each other in case they get tired of their bargain—although here again is a practice which the Church treats with just anger.[1]

The Church does not formally permit divorce, but it cannot thwart many of the currents of the age. Nobles frequently repudiate their wives for trivial reasons— mere ill health, for instance; and often the women take the initiative. There are worldly bishops who will give their help toward an annulment on grounds of "lack of inward consent." Again, if a very desirable marriage with a cousin comes in question, often a "dispensation" can be obtained from the same complaisant authorities. It is easy to become cynical if you study how easily the "holy bonds of matrimony" can be put on and off by the powerful, although sometimes a great pope like Innocent III will teach even a mighty king a lesson, as Philip Augustus learned when he tried to repudiate poor Ingeborg of Denmark.

If a maiden has a father, a competent brother, or an uncle she is lucky. Otherwise, the bestowal of her hand belongs to her suzerain. This right to bestow heiresses or the widows of vassals on faithful retainers is one of the most precious privileges of a great seigneur. Many a knight is kept loyal by the hope that presently his lord will say: "One of my barons is dead without sons. I will give you his fiefs and his daughter"; or, "Take the widow of the late Sire X. . . . You may have the land along with the lady." Under feudal usage it is well-nigh impossible to deprive an heiress of her estates directly, but her marriage practically gives her husband

---

[1] How serious the problem of the "forbidden degrees" could be is shown by the case of the pious Louis VII of France, who put away his wife, the great heiress Eleanor of Aquitaine, because he was the fifth in descent from Hugh Capet, who had married a sister of the great-great-grandfather of Eleanor. Of course, the marriage had actually proved uncongenial before this point was raised.

the ownership of the property. No wonder the Duke of Quelqueparte is anxious to see whether the sickly Count of Greve is about to die and leave only a daughter, so that he can secure the desirable allegiance of the Baron of St. Saturnin, who has been a widower now these six months, yet has remained still "uncomforted" just in hope of this particular happening.

What wonder if under these conditions strange romances occur; if the lady gives "her love and kiss" to some young knight, not her husband; if South Country troubadours assert that "married couples cannot truly love;" and if barons sometimes bring irregular consorts straight into their castles, while perhaps winking at their wives' uncanny doings? All this is true. Yet, as stated before, not everything is bad. Girls are taught not to expect too much of their spouses. They usually accept the situation as they accept stormy or sunny weather. Besides, if some fathers or guardians are scandalously careless in disposing of their charges, many fathers and brothers are full of honest affection and accept the duty of marrying off their daughters or sisters as a solemn responsibility; and if they are wise custodians the results are usually happy. There is no need of pitying Alienor too much because she has not the right to elope.

Conon has negotiated a most satisfactory marriage. He will give his sister to Sire Olivier, the eldest son of the Count of Perseigne. The Perseignes are a great Burgundian family with many castles, and counts think themselves a little higher in the social scale than do barons, but St. Aliquis is also a powerful fief, and its alliance will be useful to Perseigne when he has his expected war with the Vidame of Dijon. Conon will give the young couple his outlying Burgundian castle (not of great value to himself) and the alliance will enable him to talk roundly to his uncivil neighbors. A most excellent match; another sign that St. Aliquis has an extremely sage seigneur!

Alienor is now nearly seventeen and has been thinking about a wedding since before she was fifteen. Her nurses have long since reviewed all the eligible cavaliers for her. Her great dread has been lest she have to wed some old and very stupid man—as befell her cousin Mabila, who had been sent away tearful and pouting to Picardy, the bride of a three-times widower. Who can measure her relief when Conon declared he would not give her to old St. Saturnin? It was all very well for the jongleurs to sing, "An old man who loves a young maiden is not merely old, but a fool!" The thing has happened so often!

Her ideal is to have a "damoiseau (squire or young knight) just with his first beard"—one who is brave, valiant, and is, of course, courteous and handsome. She had once hoped that Conon would give a great tourney and award her to the conqueror; but this desire faded when she learned that the victor in the last tourney was ugly and brutal. She has been on very brotherly terms with William, Conon's first squire, but William is still too young, and it is not always honorable for a squire to push intrigues in the house of his lord. Thus she is in a very open state of mind when her brother says to her one day: "Fair sister, I have arranged your marriage with Olivier of Perseigne. He is a gallant cavalier. Any maiden might rejoice to have him. Consider well what I say because (here he adds a phrase which he hopes will not be taken too literally) I would not have you wed him against your wish."

If Alienor has anything against Olivier, if her antipathy were violent and based on reason, Conon, as a genuinely affectionate brother, might give it weight; but in fact, though she has met Olivier only a few times at a tourney, at the Christmas fête at the Duke of Quelqueparte's court, and once when he stopped at the castle, she has not the least objection. He has certainly large blue eyes, blond hair, a large nose, and a merry laugh. He is reported to be kind to his servants, generous to a fault, and not overgiven to drinking or brawling. At the tourney he broke three lances fairly against a more experienced knight. His family is excellent and her brother's desires are obvious. She will not have to live too far from St. Aliquis. What more could be said? After a few hours of decent reflection she informs Adela that she will comply with Conon's wishes. After that the castle takes on a joyous activity.

Before the wedding had come the betrothal. It was a solemn ceremony, blessed by the Church. Sire Olivier visited the castle with a great following of relatives and met the shy and blushing Alienor. In the chapel, after suitable prayers by Father Grégoire, the pair had awkwardly enough exchanged their promises! "I will take you for my wife." "And I for my husband." After this there would have been great scandal had either side turned back. The Church affirms energetically, however, that betrothal is *not* marriage. Otherwise the affianced pair might have considered themselves somewhat wedded on trial, only to repudiate their obligations later. Also, not merely the young couple, but their parents or guardians, had to be present and add their consent; and, of course, all the pledges were sworn to over the holiest relics available.

Olivier, during all this happy time, has lodged at the castle of a friendly vassal of St. Aliquis, and he rides over frequently to visit his betrothed. He is excellently bred and knows everything expected of a prospective bride-groom of good family. The alliance has been largely negotiated by his parents, but he has been consulted, understands that Alienor is witty and beautiful, and he is wholly aware of the worldly advantages of being Conon's brother-in-law. At meals he and his beloved are allowed to sit together and above all to eat out of the same por-ringer, when he delicately leaves to his intended all the best morsels. He consults a competent jongleur, and with his aid produces suitable verses praising his finacée's beauty. He gives her a gold ring with both his own name and hers engraved thereon. In return, besides a sleeve and a stocking to hang on his lances (gifts which she has already sent in mere friendship to other cavaliers), she bestows a lock of her hair set around a gold ring; like-wise a larger lock which he may twine around his helmet. The happy pair are permitted to take long walks to-gether, and to promenade up and down the garden, with Olivier holding his lady in the politest manner by one finger—the accepted method of showing intimacy.[1]

We have said that Conon is resolved to knight his brother at the same time he gives his sister in marriage. This involves holding a tourney and many other pro-ceedings really unnecessary for a wedding; but, of course, it will attract a much greater number of guests and advertise the prosperity of the baron of St. Aliquis to all northwestern France. The knighting and tourney will come after the bridal, however, and it is easier to explain the two things separately. We omit the gathering of the wedding guests—the coming of distant counts, barons, and sires; the erection around St. Aliquis of a real village

---

[1] Friends would seldom walk arm in arm. Two persons of the same sex or of different sexes would walk familiarly hand in hand, or, if especially friendly, one leading the other by a single finger.

of brilliant tents and pavilions; the ceremonious greetings; the frenzied efforts of the castle folk to make all
ready; the inevitable despair, not once, but many times,
of Adela, who directs everything. At last it is the morning of *the* day, in midsummer. No rain and, blessed be
St. Martin, not too much heat. Alienor is surrounded by
a dozen women, old and young, arraying her for her
wedding.

There is no regular bridal costume. Alienor does not
dress much differently from what she does on Easter or
at some other major festival. Her two great braids of
hair are weighted down over her breasts with an extra
intertwining with gold thread. Her chemise is of very
fine saffron-tinted linen. Her pelisson is completely
fringed with magnificent ermine, the gift of the Countess
of Perseigne, and the garment itself is made of two cloths
sewed together, the inner of fine wool, the outer of
beautiful bendal of reddish violet. The whole is laced
tightly until Alienor can hardly breathe. Above this
garment floats the elegant bliaut, of green silk with long
sleeves, many folds, and a long train. There is more silk
embroidery and elaborate flouncing. Fairest of all is the
girdle, made of many pieces of gold and each set with a
good-luck stone—agate to guard against fever, sardonyx
to protect against malaria, and many similar. In the
clasp are great sapphires which Baron Garnier originally
"acquired" from a town merchant shortly before he
hanged him. Finally, there is the mantle—again of silk
intricately embroidered and dyed with a royal purple.

Alienor's pointed shoes are of vermilion leather from
Cordova, with still more of gold-thread embroidery.
While one female minister is clasping these, her chief
pucelle is putting on a small saffron-colored veil, circular, and held down by a golden circlet—a genuine

crown; beautifully engraved and set with emeralds. Inevitably the whole process of dressing is prolonged. Alienor is too excited to feel hot or pinched, but her attendants find her very exacting. They bless the Virgin, however, that she is not as some noble brides, who fly into a passion if every hair in their eyebrows is not separately adjusted.

Meantime, in a secluded part of the castle, the groom has been wrestling with a similar problem, assisted by his two squires, although requiring less of time and agony. His legs are covered with fine brown silk stockings from Bruges; but it is effeminate to wear a silk shirt—one of fine white linen will answer. His pelisson is like his bride's, although less tightly laced—of cloth and silk, trimmed with rich fur; and the outer color is pale red, inevitably with much gold embroidery around the neck and sleeves. His bliaut does not come below his knees, but it is of blue sendal silk; his mantle is also edged with fur and of the same color as his pelisson. Simple as it is, it must hang exactly right. Everybody will ask, "Did the groom wear his mantle like a great baron?" The squires take a long time adjusting it. Olivier's shoes are of very fine leather. On his crisply curled hair they set a golden chaplet set with flashing gems— very much like that worn by his bride.

Hardly are the happy twain ready before the wedding procession forms in the bailey. So large a company could never crowd into the castle chapel. It will go across the bridge over the Claire to the parish church by the village—a Gothic structure sufficiently pretentious to suit the occasion. The Perseignes reckon a bishop among their cousins, and he is on hand to officiate.

So the procession forms. Ahead go a whole platoon of jongleurs puffing their cheeks for their flutes, twanging their harps, or rasping their viols. The Feudal Age delights in music, and does not mind if sometimes melody is exchanged merely for a joyous noise. Alienor comes next. She is on a black mule with extra long ears and a finely curried shining coat. His harness is of gold and his trappings of scarlet samite. She has been swung into the saddle by her eldest brother ("Alas! that her father, who should do this, is dead!" murmur all the women), and he as her guardian leads the mule. Olivier rides a tall white palfrey with a saddle of blue leather. His mother, Adela, and all the St. Aliquis and Perseignes female relatives follow on other mules, led by gayly dressed squires. Then come all the noble guests, the Duke of Quelqueparte at their head. No wonder there is no work being done in all the villages for miles around, and that all the villeins are lining the road, doffing caps, and cheering as the dazzling cortége sweeps past.

The details at the church we pass over. Among other features to be noted is the fact that the bride is swung down from her mule upon a great truss of straw, that the bishop meets them at the sacred portal, and that outside the actual building Olivier and Alienor exchange those vows which form the essential part of the marriage ceremony. After that Conon's chief provost recites in loud voice all the estates, horses, fine garments, and servitors which the bride brings as her dowry. This customary publication may avert bitter disputes later. Next the happy pair scatter newly coined silver deniers among the swarm of ill-favored mendicants permitted to elbow and scramble among the more pretentious guests.

Finally, the church is thrown open. The great nave opens mysterious and dark, but galaxies of candles are burning and the lofty stained-glass windows gleam like jewels. Olivier and Alienor occupy seats of honor in the choir, while the bishop says the very solemn mass of the Trinity and pronounces a special blessing over them. "Let this woman," intones the prelate, "be amiable as Rachel, wise as Rebecca, faithful as Sarah. Let her be sober through truth, venerable through modesty, and wise through the teaching of Heaven."

So at last the mass ends. The "Agnus Dei" is chanted. The bridegroom advances to the altar and receives from the bishop the kiss of peace. Then he turns, and right at the foot of the great crucifix embraces his wife and transmits the kiss to her. This act completes the ceremony. Away the whole company go from the church. They have been condemned to silence for nearly two hours, and are glad now to chatter like magpies. When back at St. Aliquis they find the great hall has been swept, garnished, and decorated as never before. The walls of the hall are hung with the pictured tapestries or beautiful pieces of red and green silk. Your feet crush fresh roses and lilies scattered on the floor. Alienor almost bursts with delight at the number of high-born cavaliers and dames who press up to kiss and congratulate. All the remainder of her life she will match weddings with her friends: "I had so many counts and barons at my marriage." "But I had so many!"

All these guests, however, expect to receive presents— bliauts, mantles, goblets, and other things, each suitable to the recipient. It is well that Conon has saved many livres in his strong box. The presenting of the gifts by the host is quite a ceremony; each article has to be accompanied by a well-turned speech. By the time this reception to the bride and groom is over the trumpets sound furiously. They tell that the feast is ready in the fragrant garden under the trees. There is a fine tent of blue silk for the bridal party and the more exalted guests. All the others must sit on long tables open to the glad sunshine.

What Messire Conon's guests have to eat and drink is so serious a topic that we must tell thereof separately. We speak here merely concerning the festivities of the wedding. Olivier and Alienor are served by two barons as squires of state. The groom drinks from a great goblet, then sends it to his wife, who ceremoniously finishes the draught. In the bridal tent there is a reasonable amount of decorum, but elsewhere (Blessed martyrs!) what noise and tumult! All the ville ns appear to be there, and burghers have even wandered up from Pontdebois. It will never do to have men say, "The bride was charming, but her brother stinted his hospitality." Enough food and drink is gorged and guzzled to stave off a famine next winter. The jongleurs keep quiet during the first part of the feast; later they earn their dinner by singing of the loves of Jourdain and Orabel or of Berte, who was the faithful wife of Girard of Roussillon through all of her lord's adversity. At many of the tables the jesting and horseplay become unspeakably ribald. After the wine circulates two petty nobles quarrel; one strikes the other with a drinking cup, but the sergeants pull them apart before they can whip out swords.

After three hours of this some guests are sleeping stertorously under the trees; but those nobles who have kept their wits go to another large tent, and, despite their heavy meal, dance with vigor. The bride and groom are expected to dance together, and everybody is prepared to admire the beauty of one and the grace and strength of the other. As evening advances a priest appears. He solemnly blesses the nuptial couch strewn with roses, while the new couple piously kneel. The couch is then "censed" like an altar, and the women guests join in the bizarre usages of "putting the bride to bed."

The morning after the marriage the newly wedded pair attend mass in the castle chapel. Here they are expected to make privately all kinds of vows of good conduct, and Alienor especially promises always to obey her husband, and call him dutifully "mon sire" and "mon baron."

The festivities will last two weeks longer, and conclude with the dubbing of knights and the tournament, whereof more presently. After that Olivier and his wife will depart for their Burgundian castle without anything like a honeymoon to strange parts. . . .

So they celebrate the wedding at St. Aliquis. Very far is it from being a love match of a later day; yet there is a decent hope of happiness for the two most deeply interested. A new spirit in the relations of men and women has been creeping into the world since Greek and Roman days, and if this spirit too often manifests itself in illicit romances it is something if romantic love can exist at all, and if, also, in many an instance (as the jongleurs already like to tell us), their story can run that "thus the twain were wedded, and forevermore lived together happily."

It was as early as about 1160 that the South Country troubador, Bernart de Ventadoun, sang about the great motive which was coming to add beauty to the world:

> "For indeed I know
> Of no more subtle passion under heaven
> Than is the maiden passion for a maid;
> Not only to keep down the base within a man,
> But teach high thought and amiable words,
> And courtliness and the desire of fame
> And love of truth, and all that makes a man!"

Chapter VII: Cookery and Mealtimes.

OW it is as certain as that God reigns in heaven, that if one desires a wedding and a tournament, although the first thought must be of raiment, the second must be of food and drink. When Conon bids Adela make ready for the festivities, straightway that prudent dame sends for the butler and the cellarer and takes account of everything stowed away in the great vaults under the castle. Then she orders the chief huntsman muster all his beaters and course the forests, not for sport, but for victuals. At the same time nets are set out in the Claire; purveyors with their carts are ordered up from Pontdebois, and a messenger is even sent to Troyes to bring back a tun of rare Grecian wine. All available maids from the village are requisitioned to make great pasties, and a master cook is imported from Paris to prepare special cakes and pastries. In short, it is no light thing even for the huge St. Aliquis household to prepare to feed several thousands without aid of those miracles which caused five loaves and two fishes to suffice in the days of our Blessed Lord.

For the baron's feast the great fireplace in the bailey cookhouse is insufficient. They build fires in the open out in the tilt yard or garden and all day perspiring varlets stand feeding on great logs over which roast long spits of chickens and geese, or boil caldrons of meat. In the cookhouse, where the finer dishes must be prepared, the master cook has a true arsenal of utensils—

pots, trivets, mortar and pestle, a table for mincing
herbs, pothooks, caldrons, frying pans and gridirons,
saucepans, platters, a pepper mill, dressing board, scum-
mer, ladle, and many things else. There is no lack of
help in the kitchen. Half a dozen loutish boys gladly
work there all day long (receiving, incidentally, many

COOKS

From a manuscript in the Bodleian Library at Oxford (Wright).

of the cook's hard knocks) in return for being allowed
to lick the pans and gnaw the scraps, so cheap is human
labor.

On ordinary days we would marvel at the quantity
of boiled meat served at St. Aliquis. About the only
way to preserve meat is to salt it (the vats of the castle
are full of salted meat kept against winter or a siege),
and this flesh must ordinarily be boiled. The result is
that a great copper meat pot seems always in action,
with a boy pumping the bellows to make the caldron
bubble. But fowls and fresh meat are often boiled as
well. Butcher's meat, however, is less welcome at feasts
than is game. An ideal dish is a stag, roasted whole in
the great fireplace, crisped and larded, then cut up into
quarters and served on very large plates. Upon such

114

dishes is poured a hot, steaming pepper sauce. Therefore a stag will be served at the wedding banquet besides many other kinds of choice game.

Since there are no iceboxes, unsalted meat must be eaten soon after being killed, although your feudal epicure is not squeamish. Beef and mutton are often killed, cut up, and cooked almost on the spot. There is a story of a butcher who, coming late to a town, got a lodging at the priest's house, and to pay for his quarters killed the sheep which they ate for supper. But pork is probably the commonest meat.

PORK BUTCHERS (BOURGES)

Conon has great droves of hogs fattening out in his oak forests, which supply abundant crops of acorns. Pigs seem to penetrate almost everywhere save into messire's and madame's chamber. They are the general scavengers and apparently replace plumbing and sewerage systems. They infest castle courts and the streets of towns. In 1131 the Crown Prince of France was killed in Paris by a pig which ran between the legs of his horse as he rode from the Hotel de Ville to the Church of St. Gervais. People will tell you that pork promotes leprosy, but, nevertheless, they devour it. Pork, too, is the main substance of those great sausages and black puddings in which everybody delights, especially on Easter, when you break your Lenten fast with as much heavy food as possible. Veal, too, is desirable, as is the flesh of kids; but lamb is by no means so much in favor.

Almost all kinds of birds are counted edible. Herons, cranes, storks, cormorants, and such fowl as can be taken by hawks are in preference, but crows are considered very fair eating. The flock of stately swans by the mouth of the Rapide has just been depleted, for these elegant birds are kept for the kitchen rather than for ornament. As for small fowl—thrushes, starlings, blackbirds, quail, partridges, and cuckoos—the varlets can bring in as many as possible with their crossbows and snares. Young rabbits, likewise, are welcome, but older rabbits are too tough save for the diet of the least-considered villeins. Everybody knows the saying, "An old hare and an old goose are food for the devil!"

There is plenty of poultry around St. Aliquis. Most Christians hold that birds are of aquatic origin, hence, like fish, can be eaten on fast days, although the Church opposes this opinion, and is slowly overcoming it. Chickens have been fattened for the feast by shutting them up in dark coops and gorging them. Droves of geese have been coming in from the fields, great honking armies, crowding the narrow way, hissing and biting, but all propelled steadily ahead by the cracking whips of the small goosegirls. Ducks are more commonly preferred in their wild stage; but out in the exercise ground several peacocks have been preening themselves, and at least two of these are now sacrificed to make a gala dish to serve the highest seigneurs, for peacocks are counted especial "food for the brave." Indeed, there is the old proverb that "thieves have as much taste for falsehood as a hungry man for a cooked peacock."[1]

Fish is hardly in great request. One is likely to have too much of it on the numerous fast days. Still, out of

[1] Peacocks, as especially desirable poultry, practically took the place of the turkey of later days.

the Claire they draw excellent barbel and eels; there
are carp in a near-by pond, and splendid trout in the
brooks that feed the Rapide. The lads bring in many.
If you go to Paris you can eat salt herring taken in the
North Sea. All through the spring, furthermore, the
St. Aliquis folk have had their fill of frogs' legs from the
castle moat and the numerous bogs, and Conon has a
"snail bed" to provide snails for garnishings and salads
during Lent and on Fridays.

One cannot stay at the castle long and not discover
the vast importance of soup. One partakes thereof at
least twice per day: "dried peas and bacon water," water-
cress soup, cabbage soup, cheese soup, and "poor man's
soup" (made up of odds and ends collected on short
warning), and fish soups for Lent. All the better soups
are spiced with marjoram, sage, and sweet basil, if not
with the favorite condiment, pepper. But what are
soups compared with meat pies? Whenever the castle
cook is in doubt how to please their lordships he decides
upon a noble pasty. Much thought has been con-
centrated upon this subject. There are little poems to
be memorized by illiterate cooks explaining this triumph
of their mystery—*e.g.*, that they should use "three
young partridges large and fat, not forgetting six quail
put on their side"; add to these thrushes, some bacon,
some sour grapes, and a little salt. Then if all is made
aright, the crust nicely rolled of pure flour, and the
"oven of proper heat with the bottom quite free from
ashes," when all is baked enough "you will have a dish
to feast on"! Other pasties can be made of chickens,
venison, salmon, eels, pigeons, geese, and other kinds
of meat. Probably, in fact, more energy goes into making
the pasties than into any other one form of culinary effort.

The St. Aliquis folk are not at all vegetarians, but

they cannot eat meat forever, and the poorer peasants seldom touch flesh save on important feast days. The cooks have at their disposal onions and garlic, cabbages and beets, carrots and artichokes, lentils and both long and broad beans, peas, turnips, lettuce, parsley, water cress—in short, nearly all the vegetables of a different age save the all-important potato. Turnips are in favor, and figure in far more dietaries than they will do later. Cabbages, too, are in request: there are Roman white cabbages, huge Easter cabbages, and especially the Senlis cabbages, renowned for their excellent odor. Cucumbers are supposed to cause fever, but Herman raises some in the garden for the salads.

As always, bread is the staff of life. Naturally, the villeins have to use flour that is very coarse and made of barley, rye, or oats—producing black bread, before which noble folk shudder. It is one of the signs of messire's prosperity that all his household are ordinarily fed on white bread. In the castle ovens they make a great variety of loaves—huge "pope's" or "knight's" loaves, smaller "squire's" loaves, and little "varlet's" loaves, or rolls. There is a soft bread made of milk and butter, a dog bread, and two-color bread of alternate layers of wheat and rye. Then there are the table loaves, sizable pieces of bread to be spread around the tables, from which courteous cavaliers will cut all the crust with their knives and pass the remainder to the ladies, their companions, to soak up in their soup. The servants have less select common bread, although it is still wheaten. Finally, there are twice-baked breads, or crackers. These are often used in monasteries, also in the provisioning of castles against a siege.

Fancy jellies, pastries, and sweet dishes are coming into vogue, although they have not reached the perfection to be attained by later French cookery; but for the St. Aliquis feast they are able to prepare great molded structures of lions and suns, made of white chicken and pink jelly. The quantity of spices used is simply enormous. To enjoy food thus charged, especially with pepper, is an acquired taste, which developed following the First Crusade. The cooks, too, use a liberal supply of mustard, and a favorite sauce is made from strong garlic. Fresh and pickled olives are sent up from Provence, likewise a good deal of olive oil; but the oil used in common cooking is often extracted from walnuts or even from poppies. Another favorite flavoring is with rosewater. All through June you can see great basins of water filled with rose petals steeping in the sun. The liquor thus obtained will add zest to sauces for the next twelve months. There is also a certain whitish substance known as "sugar." It comes from the Levant, in small irregular lumps. Its flavoring qualities are delightful, but it is too expensive to use in cookery. A small quantity is passed about among Conon's higher guests, to be eaten as a confection. The ordinary sweetening is still that of the Greeks and Romans, honey, supplied from the well-kept hives of the bees belonging to the monastery.

Cheeses hardly figure in feasts, but for everyday diet they are important. On feast days they often replace meat. Their varieties are legion—white, green, large, small, etc. Some places produce famous cheeses exported all over France, and in Paris one can hear the street venders shrilly chanting:

> "Buy my cheese from Champagne,
> Or my cheese from Brie!"

As for eggs and butter, they are gifts of the kindly saints, to carry men through Lent and fast days.

Theologians have said that hens were aquatic creatures, like other birds; that hence good Christians could eat their eggs freely. But butter (by some unaccountable notion) if eaten during times of abstinence, must be freshly churned. It must not be salted, nor used for cooking purposes.

Passing next to beverages, be it said that the St. Aliquis denizens are fairly abstemious folk. All of them sometimes get tipsy, even Adela and Alienor, but only seldom. Conon's servants help him to bed once or twice per year. Down in the villages there are disgraceful guzzlings among the peasants, especially on saints' days. But the beverages are not very alcoholic—one must absorb a great deal to be really upset. The region grows its own wine for ordinary consumption, and a little thereof is shipped to Paris and even to Flanders and England, along with the more famous vintages of Gascony, Saintonge, Macon, Rheims, the Marne, and the Orleanais. The most desirable French wine is that of St. Pourcain, in Auvergne, and the baron has a carefully cherished tun of the same in his cellars. Poems, indeed, exist in praise of this St. Pourcain wine, "which you drink for the good of your health." On occasions of great state, however, imported wines will be produced, mainly because they are unusual and expensive. The St. Aliquis feasters are consequently offered heady Cyprian and Lesbian from the Levant, also Aquilian from Spain, and not a little Rhenish from the German lands, less distant.

In the autumn when the apples and pears are falling, the peasants will make cider and perry, and get outrageously drunk when these beverages grow hard; but outside of Normandy such drink seldom appeals to castle folk. There are also in common use many substitute wines, really infusions of wormwood, hyssop, and rosemary, and taken mostly to clear the system; although "nectar" made of spices, Asiatic aromatics, and honey is really in request.

The great competitor of wine is beer. In northern France we are in the dividing zone between the land of the winepress and the land of the brewhouse. Everybody drinks beer and makes beer. The castle has a great brewhouse; likewise the monastery. Beer is made of barley, and only late in the Middle Ages will hops be added to add to the zest. Really fine beer is *god-ale* (from the German "good" and "ale") or "double beer." Common beer is "small beer." Since the Crusaders have returned from the East, spiced beer has been growing in favor—charged with juniper, resin, gentian, cinnamon, and the like, until the original taste has been wholly destroyed.

The St. Aliquis folk do not, however disdain buttermilk. This they like to ferment, boil up with onions and garlic, then cool in a closed vessel. The product is *serat*, the enjoyment of which is surely difficult for a stranger.

Another form of beverage is not quite unknown. Some physicians prescribe water of gold and allege it "prolongs health, dissipates superfluous matters, revives the spirits, and promotes youth." Also it "greatly assists the cure of colic, dropsy, paralysis, and ague." Of a surety, it aids the patient temporarily to forget his troubles. Yet this is hardly more than a costly medicine. Many years later it will become more common; but its name will be changed to "brandy."

The usages even of a great dinner depend largely on the customs of everyday life. One cannot understand the splendors of the marriage feast of Sire Olivier and Alienor without knowing what goes on regularly in the hall of St. Aliquis.

When the day is started we have seen how everybody arises to a very light breakfast of bread and wine, although sometimes, as in the epic of Doon of Mayence, when the work promises to be arduous, the baron's squire may bring him a favorite pasty because "eating early in the morning brings health and gives one greater courage and spirit." Dinner also, we have discovered, can begin as early as nine in the morning, and a good part of the day's business comes after this heavy meal. Sometimes when dinner is late you do not serve your guests any regular supper, but when they go to bed have the attendants bring cakes and fruits and wine. If you entertain guests, however, always it is proper to try to make them eat and drink as much as possible. There is a story of an overhospitable Count of Guines who not merely constrained any knight passing through his dominions to a feast, but kept quantities of white wine always on hand, so that if his visitors asked to have their red wine diluted with water, they might be hoodwinked by seeing a white liquid mixed in their goblets. In this way he once rendered the whole suite of a bishop gloriously intoxicated!

The ingenious Bartolomes of Granvilla has laid down the following requisites for an ideal banquet: (1) a suitable hour, not too early nor too late; (2) a pleasant place; (3) a gracious and liberal host; (4) plenty to eat, so one may choose one's dishes; (5) the same as to things to drink; (6) willing servants; (7) agreeable company; (8) pleasant music; (9) plenty of light; (10) good cooking; (11) a seasonable conclusion; (12) quiet and repose afterward. A marriage feast and a tourney can hardly provide this twelfth desideratum, but they ought, with proper management, to supply everything else.

The tables for the notables are laid and served by two classes of attendants; first by Conon's three squires, aided on this grand occasion by several young nobles

SERVANTS BRINGING THE FOOD TO THE TABLE
From a manuscript of the thirteenth century in the library of Munich (Schultz).

who have actually received knighthood; second, by the older professional servitors of villein stock. The first class of attendants are resplendent in bliauts of colored silk with fur trimmings. Most of the dishes will be passed to them by the soberly clad villeins, then to be presented on bended knee by noble hands to noble guests. The whole process is under Sire Eustace, the old seneschal, who orders about his platoons of attendants with as much precision as he might command the men at arms for defense of the castle.

It is part of a squire's education to learn to wait on table. One may have to do this for some superior all one's life, unless one be king or emperor! Conon's squires have been taught to stand at perfect ease; not to roll their eyes or stare blankly; not to laugh save when guests are laughing; to keep their finger nails clean and hands well washed. If they sit at table them-

123

selves they are models of propriety. They do not gobble
down their food, but put a little from every plate into
the basket of collected leavings for the poor; they do
not chatter, nor fill their mouths too full, nor chew on
both sides of the mouth at once, nor laugh or talk with
a mouthful, nor make a noise by overeating, nor handle
cats or dogs during mealtime, nor wipe their knives on
the tablecloth, nor pick their teeth publicly, nor wipe
their noses with their fingers, nor (last but not least)
spit across the table or beyond it.[1]

The tables are nearly always long and narrow. In the
great hall they are fixed and of heavy oak planks, but
there are plenty of light tables of boards to be set on
horses, if the seneschal suddenly says, "The weather is
fine; Messire will dine in the garden." The favored
guests are provided with cushions, and, of course, in
the hall the baron and his immediate friends and family
sit on the long master-seat on the dais, facing the company, and with the baron's own chair under a canopy.
This canopy is the sign of high seigneurial privilege. One
will be set for Conon even when he sits in the garden;
and he will never surrender his place save when he
entertains a superior, like his suzerain the duke, or
when, as at present, all other claims fade before those
of a bridal couple.

Indoors or outdoors, it is no mean art to lay the tables.
Enormous tablecloths have to be spread out smoothly,
and set with napkins neatly doubled; also at each place
a suitable drinking vessel, and a knife and spoon. These
articles, gold or silver, are carefully handed out by the
seneschal. They represent a good fraction of the portable
wealth of the castle and must be laboriously counted

[1] The existence of many of these prohibitions in the etiquette
manuals shows that they were not unneeded.

before and after use. The knives are sharp steel for
serious business. The drinking cups are often of bizarre
forms—lions, birds, and dragons, while for the humbler
folk there are huge cups of wood and also large "jacks"
of leather. At every place, too, there must be a good-
sized cake of fine white flour, and between every two
places there is a large porringer (pewter or silver) to be
shared by each pair of guests.

Feast day or fast day, it is the loud blast on trumpets
which sends the mighty and the humble bustling toward
the garden or the hall. Of course, at a wedding feast
there is some little formality, but ordinarily in the St.
Aliquis household the good-natured jostling and scam-
pering is prodigious. Men and women live close to
nature and are always conscious of rousing appetites.
On ordinary days when you entered the baron's hall,
you would take your turn at the lavatory close to the
entrance. Here would be several little washstands with
pitchers and basins, and everybody would fall in line
in order of precedence: first, any visiting clergy; then
visiting knights; then the seigneur's family, etc. The
hand washing presents a great chance for flirtation among
the young: Olivier and Alienor had great delight "passing the towel" to each other during their betrothal.
But now at a great festival, when you enter the special
banqueting tent you are met by two handsome varlets.
The first holds a water jug and a small basin. Water is
dexterously poured over your fingers, and as promptly
wiped off by the second varlet, and each guest patiently
waits until the persons ahead have enjoyed this courtesy.
So they enter the tent, and the magnates make for
the seats of honor.

The placing of the company has been a matter of
serious deliberation between Messire Conon and the

sage Sire Eustace. Of course, to-day the bride and groom take the canopy. At Olivier's right must be the officiating bishop. At the bishop's right must be the suzerain Duke of Quelqueparte, and at Olivier's left must be the bride and the Count and Countess of Perseigne. All that is standardized. But how locate the dozen other counts and barons who, with their dames, have honored the bridal? Will the old rival Foretvert stomach it now if he is seated farther from the canopy than the Count of Maric, who is richer and of a more ancient house? Bloody feuds have started from failure to seat guests properly. It is a matter for supreme diplomacy. So far as possible, a lady is placed beside each cavalier. The two will use the same dish and the

YOUNG GIRLS OF THE NOBILITY SERVING AT THE TABLE
From a thirteenth-century manuscript of the library of Munich (Schultz).

same goblet during the entire feast—obviously another case where one is compelled to test one's brains while selecting partners.

So the feast begins after grace by the bishop. An endless procession commences between the cookhouse and the banqueting place—boys running with great dishes which they commit to the more official servitors to pass to the guests. It is a solemn moment, followed by cheering, when into the bridal tent, with clash of cymbals and bray of trumpet, Sire Eustace in a bright scarlet bliaut enters, waving his white wand and followed by all the squires and upper servants, each carrying shoulder high a huge dish of some viand. A great haunch of the stag is set on the table. The baron's carver cuts ample slices, while two jongleurs blow at their flutes. He holds the meat "by two fingers and a thumb" (no fork), plying a great knife as a surgeon might his scalpel. Equal skill is demanded of the cup-bearers when they fill the flagons, not spilling a drop. Even the bride and groom are now hungry and ready for the venison.

The banqueters have little need of plates. They take the loaves lying ready, hack them into thick slices, place the pieces of meat upon the same, then cut up the meat while it is resting on the bread. These "trenchers" (*tranchoirs*) will not ordinarily be eaten at the feast; they go into the great alms basket for the poor, along with the meat scraps. However, the higher guests to-day enjoy a luxury. Silver plates are placed under their bread trenchers. For most guests, however, the bare tablecloth is bottom enough for these substitutes for the porcelain of another day. Whatever does not go into the alms basket will be devoured by the baron's dogs, who attend every meal by prescriptive right. Indeed, early in the feast the Duke of Quelqueparte benevolently tosses a slice of venison to a fine boarhound.

Time fails to repeat all the good things which Conon and Adela set before their guests. The idea is to tempt the appetite to utter satiety by forcing first one dish upon the feasters, and then another. There is not really a good sequence of courses. Most of the dishes are heavy; and inasmuch as vegetables are in great demand on common occasions, the average banquet seems one succession of varieties of meat. The noble folk in the bridal pavilion have at least a chance to eat their fill of these comestibles:

First course: Slices of stag, boar's head larded with herb sauce, beef, mutton, legs of pork, swan, roasted rabbit, pastry tarts.

Second course: Pottage of "drope and rose" mallard, pheasant and roast capon, pasties of small birds.

Third course: Rabbits in gravy heavily spiced with onion and saffron; roasted teal, woodcock and snipe; patties filled with yolk of eggs, cheese, and cinnamon, and pork pies.

No salads, no ices, no confectionery; nevertheless, some of the dishes are superb—notably the swan, which is brought once more on with music, prinked out as if he were alive and swimming, his beak gilt, his body silvered, resting on a mass of green pastry to represent a grass field, and with little banners around the dish, which is placed on a carpet of silk when they lay it on the table. The cooks might also serve a peacock with outspread plumage. Instead, toward the close of the repast, two squires tug in an enormous pasty. Amid an expectant hush Conon rises and slashes the pasty open with a dagger. Instantly out flutter a score of little birds which begin to dash about the tent; but immediately the baron's falconers stand grinning at the entrance. They unhood a second score of hawks which in a twinkling pounce after the wretched birds and kill them, to the shouts and delight of the feasters, right above the tables. Inevitably there is confusion, rustling by the ladies and merry scrambling, before the squawking hawks can be caught, hooded, and taken away. In fact, from the beginning the feast is extremely noisy. Everybody talks at once. The

A FEAST OF CEREMONY IN THE TWELFTH CENTURY

It was the custom during the repast to bring in enormous pâtés which held little live birds; these flew about the hall when the crust of the pâté was broken; immediately the servants loosened falcons which gave chase. This part of the feast is represented here.

appearance of the stag has started innumerable hunting stories. The duke has to tell his loyal lieges how he slew a bear. Two of the baron's dogs get to fighting and almost upset the chair of a countess. Everything is very merry.

If an elaborate dinner had been required on a so-called fast day, the cooks could still have met the occasion and yet have kept within the commands of the Church; although not merely would there have been much fish, but also more vegetables. The guests could have been served with roast apples garnished with sorrel and rosemary; then might have come a rich soup made of trout, herring, eels salted twenty-four hours, and salt whiting soaked twelve hours, almonds, ginger, saffron, and cinnamon powder. If possible to bring them up from the ocean, there would have been soles, congers, turbots, and salmon—and in any case these can be had salted—the rivers in turn supply pike (preferably with roe), carp, and bream. For side dishes there can be lampreys, porpoise, mackerel, and shad served with juice of crab apples, rice, and fried almonds. Finally might come stewed or ripe fruits—figs, dates, grapes, and filberts; the whole washed down with spiced wine (hippocras). To the minds of men of a later age this fast-day dinner might seem only a little less gorging than the orthodox feast upon meats.

But elaborate as is this wedding banquet, at last everybody has had his fill. The concluding baked pears, the peeled walnuts, dates, and figs have been passed. The noble dames have chewed their unfamiliar sugar plums. A last cup of spiced wine is handed around, but nobody has drunk too much to become worse than merrily talkative. Before rising the guests have all very properly "thought of the poor," called in the servitors and piled all the loose food upon great platters to be kept for the needy. To-day, in fact, all the indigent in the region are eating voraciously at the outer tables, but on the morrow of a festival day you will see a great collection of halt, sickly, and shiftless hanging around the barbican in just expectation that Conon and Adela will order a distribution.[1]

At last the bishop returns thanks; basins, pitchers, and towels are again carried around. Then the guests rise, some to mingle with the less exalted visitors outside, some to repose under the shade trees, some to listen to the jongleurs who are now tuning their instruments, and many (especially the younger) to get ready for the thing we have seen they liked almost the best—extremely vigorous dancing.

Outside of the state pavilion the service has naturally been less ceremonious and the fare less sumptuous, but all of the countryside has been welcome to wander into the castle gardens and to partake. Greasy, unkempt villeins have been elbowing up to the long tables, snatching joints of meat, bawling to the servitors to refill their leather flagons, and throwing bits of cheese and bread around in an outrageously wasteful manner. Thousands of persons, apparently many of whom will be happy if they can have black bread all through the winter, are trying to-day to avenge past hunger by devouring and drinking just as much as possible. Sire Eustace is continually calling; "Another tun of wine! Another vat of beer! Another quarter of beer!" These viands for the multitude are not select, but there are bread, flesh, and drink without stinting. Fortunate it is that Conon has not *two* marriageable sisters, or there would be naught left to eat on the seigneury!

[1] See p. 275.

Wholesale Hospitality

As the shadows lengthen everybody seems satisfied. The villeins and petty nobles lay down their flagons. Groups of friends, if sufficiently sober, begin to sing songs in a round, each member improvising a doggerel verse, and the group thundering out the chorus. But many of the guests do not retain wits enough for recreations. While their noble hosts are dancing, the others throw themselves on the grass in companies to watch or listen to the jongleurs: then as the wedding dances finish, Olivier and Alienor come out of the great tent to take their seats on flower-wreathed chairs before the principal minstrels, and by their presence give some decorum to what threatens to become a disgracefully confused and coarse form of reveling.

For a great feast the jongleurs seem, in fact, almost as indispensable as the cooks. We have now to ask the nature of North French minstrelsy.[1]

---

[1] What actually was involved in the way of mere victuals for a public feast in the Middle Ages is shown by the following record of the hospitality dispensed by an archbishop of York, England, in 1466. There is no reason for believing such lavish "feeding of the multitude" was not fairly common also in France a little earlier. This festival required, by formal record, "300 quarters of wheat, 300 tuns of ale, 100 tuns of wine, 104 oxen, 100 sheep, 304 calves, 304 swine, 400 swans, 2,000 geese, 1,000 capons, 2,000 pigs, 100 dozen quails, 4,000 mallards and teal, 204 cranes, 204 kids, 2,000 ordinary chickens, 4,000 pigeons, and over 500 stags, bucks, and roes." In addition there were made up "4,000 cold venison pasties, 3,000 dishes of jelly, 4,000 baked tarts, 1,500 hot venison pasties, 2,000 hot custards" and proportionate quantities of spices, sweetened delicacies, and wafer cakes.

Evidently the archbishop was deliberately planning to feast the entire population of a considerable area of England. Conon's hospitality herein depicted was, of course, nothing like this.

Chapter VIII: The Jongleurs and Secular Literature and Poetry.

THE St. Aliquis folk delight in music. It is very desirable for a cavalier to have a rich voice and know how to twang a harp. Aimery, soon to be Sire Aimery, can sing and play as well as many minstrels. Adela spent many hours at her viol and at a little portable organ before family cares took up her time. Five or six of the servitors hold their places mainly because they can play so excellently at those impromptu dances which Conon gives on every possible occasion.[1] You cannot linger long around the castle without hearing the lutes, the flutes, and the castanets, and in confining weather in winter the music keeps up almost the whole day long.

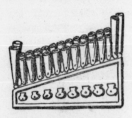

SMALL PORTABLE ORGAN
OF THE THIRTEENTH
CENTURY
From a manuscript in the
Bibliothèque nationale.

However, variety is the spice of life. It is a red-letter day when a new jongleur or, better still, a troupe of jongleurs arrive. They will teach new music, new songs, new tricks to the regular denizens, and break up that desperate monotony which sometimes causes the barons to fret with a pent-up

---

[1] If St. Aliquis had been a slightly larger fief, its lord would probably have allowed himself the luxury of a professional minstrel in residence—half musician and half jester.

132

energy and to precipitate new wars merely to get relief. As for a great fête like the present, obviously a large corps of entertainers must be mobilized. The mere news through the region that messire proposed a marriage feast and a tourney has been enough to start many such itinerant gentry toward St. Aliquis. Sire Eustace was overwhelmed with offers of assistance and has had to chase away some of the would-be entertainers almost by force.

Jongleurs are versatile people, and each of them has his specialty. Their name, "jongleur," like "charity," covers a multitude of sins. Some of them are merely expert players upon the viol, and supply music for dancers. The dances of noble folk are simple: often enough fair dames and cavaliers merely take hold of one another's hands and whirl themselves furiously in a circle, while the music goes faster and faster until the revelers cease and almost sink of exhaustion. Then there are variations when the cavaliers decorously drop from the ring and bow to their ladies; or the "dance of the chaplet," at the end of which each cavalier ceremoniously kisses his lady on the cheek—kissing between equals being quite proper if it is not on the lips. It takes rather more skill, as at present, when young Aimery dances an intricate galliard with the daughter of the Baron of Bovri. The two performers stand opposite to each other, advancing, bowing, and retiring, every step made to music; then at last the cavalier makes his bow to the lady, takes her by the hand, thanks her, and leads her to her seat. After that another noble couple dances the *tourdion,* a similar performance, but faster and with more violent action.

For all this competent musicians are indispensable. But a good jongleur is far more than a musician. He can dance himself, with intricate acrobatic figures impossible for the unprofessional; he can sing love songs, chant or recite romances; and, if he has companions, even present short farces and comedies. He is probably possessed also of series of tricks and sleight-of-hand accomplishments, which appeal more to the groundlings than do high-flown poetic recitals. If he can reach the summit of his profession he will be received at castles almost as the equal of the seigneur, and be able to retire

ACROBATS

Reproductions by the English archæologist Strutt, from various fourteenth-century manuscripts in England.

rich, after having been showered with such gifts as palfreys, furs, jewels, mantles of red cloth, and, of course, with much money. Jongleurs recall with pride their fellow-minstrel Tallefer, who gallantly led the charge of the Normans at Hastings, trolling the Song of Roland as he tossed up his sword and caught it again in the very face of the English, and who fell in the battle only after making as much havoc among the foe as would a paladin.

There is a great distance, however, between such pretentious folk and the run of minstrels. A little while since a mountebank pair called at St. Aliquis. They

called themselves by grotesque names, "Brise-Tête" and
"Tue-Bœuf." When they had disposed of a pork pasty,
the seneschal made it plain they had better pay for their
dinner. Thereupon Tue-Bœuf produced a harp, and
Brise-Tête leaped on the table, flung his arms and legs
about, and showed himself a regular acrobat. After that
his companions set the lads and girls to "ah-ing!" by
swallowing knives and by apparently eating red brands
right out of the fireplace. Next the twain joined in a
witty dialogue presenting a clutching priest wheedling
money out of a miserly burgher; and finally Tue-
Bœuf began telling stories so outrageous that Adela (not
more squeamish than most dames) bade her sister-in-law
to retire. So the two kept the whole hall laughing
through a rainy afternoon, and Conon contented his
entertainers each with a denier.[1] They slept on the straw
under the tables and were off early the next morning.
Their repertory was probably exceedingly limited, and
they must have spent their lives wandering from castle
to castle, seldom tarrying anywhere more than a single
night. Other jongleurs have appeared with trick dogs
and monkeys, and who could themselves dance through
hoops, perform such feats as tossing up two small
apples and catching each simultaneously on the point
of a knife held in each hand, or prove themselves
genuine contortionists, as is declared in the old Latin
poem:

[1] It was not unknown for jongleurs of this inferior grade to stop
at an exciting part of the story they were narrating and say (as
in the poem "Gui of Burgundy"): "Whoever wants to hear more
of this recital must haste to open his purse; for now it is high time
to give me something." The company would thus be straightway
held up. Or the entertainer would announce, "It was too near
vespers," or "He was too weary to finish that day," the result being
that he could claim hospitality at the castle of his hosts another
twenty-four hours until he could satisfy the general curiosity.

He folds himself,
He unfolds himself,
And in unfolding himself,
He folds himself!

It is often a question, indeed, to tell when a jongleur is really anything more than a roving scoundrel. Certes, they frequently seem full of thievishness, licentiousness, and lies. With them are frequently low jongleuresses, women capable of corrupting a whole monastery. The Church denounces this entire breed, male and female, as "ministers of the devil." All the vices which other ages impute to actors are charged against them, and there is an old jesting question, "Which would you rather be, a jongleur or a robber?" Answer: "A robber."

Nevertheless, God knows that people must be amused, and jongleurs are almost indispensable. Besides, as we have seen, not all are of this sinful class. The higher grade of jongleurs sometimes travel in considerable companies. They bring an orchestra of music—viols,[1] guitars, and gigues—long, slim, stringed instruments shaped like a figure eight—and, of course, including flutes, harps, and even little portable organs on which you work the bellows with one hand and press the keys with the other, something like an accordion. Horns are not lacking, nor dulcimers, nor cymbals. The Feudal Ages miss the piano, but otherwise have plenty of sweet-toned instruments.

Each member of such a troupe has his specialty, and some of the feats are wonderful. There is usually a slim girl who can perform a "Herodias's daughter's dance" so magnificently that everybody can understand how the Palestinian princess took in the gullible king by her

[1] The viol was practically like a violin, although more round and more clumsy. It was played with a bow.

acrobatic feats. She can even dance on her hands and kick her feet in the air, to the great delight of all but the more sanctimonious guests. Vainly did the holy St. Bernard inveigh against the seigneurs who receive such troupes in their castles: "A man fond of jongleurs will soon possess a wife named Poverty. The tricks of jongleurs can never please God." Certain it is that at the wedding the bishop and his priests, after a few *pro forma* coughings, seem laughing as loudly as do the barons at all the tricks of Conon's entertainers.

A great feast demands enough jongleurs to entertain many different circles. While one bold fellow is keeping the villeins roaring by the antics of his tame bear, while three others (including a woman) are dancing grossly

DANCER OF THE TWELFTH CENTURY
Restored by Viollet-Le-Duc
(Musée de Toulouse).

upon a platform before other gaping hundreds, a superior member of their mystery is attracting again many noble guests to the banqueting tent. He is no common performer. Messire sent all the way to Chalons for him, promising ample reward. Maître Edmond boasts that he is a Christian—meaning he takes his profession as a kind of lay priesthood. He is on friendly terms with great prelates. He never recites the scurrilous little *fabliaux* assailing the clergy. He knows by heart, however, nearly all the great epics and romances. His rich bliaut of green silk sets forth his impressive figure. His gestures are eloquent. He can work upon the imaginations of his audience and move it to tears, acclamations, or wild excitement. In a later age he would, in short, be a great actor or an equally great "reader"—causing all the parts of a drama to speak through one person.

Maître Edmond has consulted Conon as to what romance or epic would please the best. There is a great collection of stories of heroes, usually in a kind of sing-song verse, and claiming very largely to have a Breton origin. One whole category revolves around the doings of Charlemagne and his peers; another deals with King Artus (Arthur) of Brittany (really Britain) and his Knights of the Round Table; still another cycle tells of the Trojan War, and Sire Hector, Sire Achilles, and Sire Ulysses, making the ancient Ilium into a North French castle besieged by decidedly feudal methods; while others rehearse the mighty deeds of Alexander. In all there are at least forty well-recognized epic *chansons de geste* (songs of mighty deeds), most of them six thousand to eight thousand lines in length, besides many shorter romances. Maître Edmond knows a surprising number of them all. These bald figures give some idea of the richness of this type of feudal literature.

Of course, the famous "Chanson de Roland" constitutes the most splendid narrative. Everybody knows the story of how Roland and Olivier, the favorite peers of Charlemagne, were betrayed to the Paynim in Spain by the foul traitor Ganelon; how they sold their lives right dearly after innumerable doughty deeds; how their souls ascended to heaven; and how later Charlemagne took terrific vengeance both on the Infidels and on Ganelon. It is an epic which in later days will be rated equal, if

not superior, to its German rival, the "Nibelungenlied."
But the "Song of Roland" is now nearly two centuries
old and is very familiar. Besides, it is too long for one
afternoon, and it is hard to pick out episodes. Maître
Edmond proposes some scenes from the stories of Troy,
but the baron thinks they are not sufficiently sentimental
for the occasion. So they agree on the "Story of Tristan
and Ysolt." This is fairly well known by the company,
but is not threadbare; it gives plenty of opportunity for
the women to weep, and the jongleur says that he has a
new version not overlengthy.

Maître Edmond, therefore, strides out into the bridal
tent, accompanied by a handsome youth in a saffron
mantle, who thrums a harp with silver frets. The high
jongleur begins his story in an easy
recitative which occasionally breaks
into melodious arias. It is really a
mingling of verse and prose, although
the language never loses a certain
meter and rhythm.

The narrative runs along the
conventional lines:—King Mark of
Cornwall was a good man and wise
prince. The beautiful Ysolt was
his wife; the valiant and poetic
Tristan his nephew. These last two,

THIRTEENTH-CENTURY
HARP
From sculpture in the
cathedral of Chartres.

in all innocency, take a magic potion which compels
them to fall in love, and any sinful deeds which follow
are excused by the enchantment. King Mark suffers
for long, trying to forgive, but at last, catching Tristan
playing the lute in the queen's bower, smites him with
a poisoned dart. The unhappy youth, mortally wounded,
takes refuge in the house of his friend Dinas. While
he is still alive, King Mark magnanimously says he is

sorry for his act, while poor Ysolt announces that she will not survive her lover.

So Tristan sends for his uncle and tells Mark that he bears him no ill will; while the king (realizing his nephew is not morally guilty) laments: "Alas, alas! Woe to me for having stabbed my nephew, the best cavalier in the whole world!" After that Mark and Ysolt visit Tristan and make lamentation over his dying state. He presently causes his sword to be drawn that he may see it for the last time. "Alas! good sword, what will become of you henceforth, without your trusty lord. I now take leave of knighthood, which I have honored. Alas! my friends, to-day Tristan is vanquished!" Then, with tears, he bequeathes his sword to his comrade in arms. Next he turns to the queen. "Very dear lady," he gasps, "what will you do when I die? Will you not die with me?" "Gentle friend," says Ysolt, "I call God to witness that nothing would afford me so much joy as to bear you company this day. Assuredly, if ever a woman could die of anguish or sorrow, I should have died already." "And would you like, then, to die with me?" asks Tristan. "God knows," replied the queen, "that never did I desire anything more sincerely." "Approach me, then," whispers the knight, "for I feel death coming upon me and I should like to breathe my last in your arms." Ysolt leans over Tristan, who embraces her and presses her so tightly that her heart bursts, and he expires with her, thus mingling their last sighs.

Needless to say, by the time Maître Edmond (after much skillful prolongation and stirring of the feelings) has finished, all the noble dames are indulging in sobs, and, indeed, many of the barons blink hard. It is a delightfully tragic story! Although the minstrel is of too high a quality to cry "largesse!" when he concludes,

LISTENING TO A TROUVÈRE IN A CHÂTEAU OF THE THIRTEENTH CENTURY

When a trouvère stopped in a château, the lord, his family, and his people assembled in the great hall; the trouvère recited some long poem, accompanying himself on a musical instrument, assisted by jugglers who entertained the audience while the poet rested.

like all the humbler jongleurs, there are many deniers thrown his way (which the harpist duly gathers), the duke tells him, "Come to my court at Christmas and recite the love of Launcelot and Guinevere—it shall be worth your while," and Conon orders that a good Aragonese mule be added to the money payment originally promised.

Maître Edmond, has, however, another line of business. His opportunity opens this way. Among Conon's guests is a baron of Harvengt. This rich seigneur has spent much time in the south country. He has learned the gay science of the troubadours. Superior minstrels are always welcome at his castle; in fact, he is something of a minstrel himself. Indeed, it is claimed he is too much interested in matters which are primarily only for villeins or at best for the women, and neglects his hawks, tourneys, and even his proper feuds with his neighbors. Nevertheless, Orri de Harvengt is an extremely "gentle" man. He possesses a considerable number of books in Latin—Virgil, Ovid, Lucan, and others—although a visiting monk has grumbled that nearly all the volumes are by questionable pagans, and that this baron has almost no parchments of saints' lives and Church fathers. However, Orri spends little time over the Latin. He holds that the classical language is best for religious matters, but that for telling of brave deeds and affairs of the heart nothing surpasses romance—the tongue of North France.

A friend of Orri's was Geoffroi de Villehardouin, who has written in French an excellent history of the Fourth Crusade, in which he participated; and although the churchmen complain that "his abandonment of Latin means the ruin of all learning," the use of the vulgar tongue for all kinds of books is undoubtedly increasing. For the less formal kind of writings there is already a

considerable French literature. Conon himself has a
book of philosophers' proverbs, a collection of wise saws
and maxims that are often attributed to such ancient
worthies as Homer, Æsop, Moses, and Solomon, but
which have a flavor extremely French. Here you can
find many a saying that will long survive the thirteenth
century, although it is doubtless much more ancient.
"A bird in the hand is worth two in the bush"; "All is
not gold that glitters"; "God helps those who help
themselves"; "A friend in need is a friend indeed";
"Still waters run deep"—all are threadbare wisdom
around St. Aliquis, as well as such maxims as do not
transmit so well, such as, "Among the blind, the one-
eyed man is king"; and, "Famine drives the wolf out of
the woods."

But the bulk of this "vulgar" literature is in poetry.
The epics (*chansons*) have been growing ever since a
certain Turould is said to have composed the "Song of
Roland" not very long after A.D. 1000. We have just seen
what a wealth of romances Maître Edmond has at his
disposal. The earlier of these tales are mere recitals of
war and adventure; but in the later, though they continue in the North French dialect, the South French
(troubadour) influence appears. We have stories turning
about lawful or illicit love rather than about lance
thrusts. The troubadours of the Langeudoc language
find now compeers in the *trouvères* of the northern
Languedoil. Baron Orri is a *trouvère* himself. He has
tried his hand at making a *chanson* on the adventures
of the hero Renaud of Montauban; while composers of
less exalted rank prepare the shorter *fabliaux, contes,*
and *dits* which abound with comedy and sarcasm,
striking at all the vices and follies of society.

Baron Orri, however (who is not an original genius),

is perhaps to be classed really as an *assembleur*—that is, he adapts old romances and puts them in a new setting. He changes over stories from the Languedoc or from the Breton to his North French dialect. To-day, at a quiet interval, Maître Edmond takes him aside. "Fair baron, you know that we master jongleurs seldom wish to set written copies of the poems we chant before strangers, but how can I deny anything to so liberal a seigneur as you? I have with me transcripts of a new song concerning Charlemagne's paladin, William of Orange, and another prepared by the great *trouvère*, Robert of Borron, concerning the finding of the Holy Grail by King Artus's knight, Sire Perceval. Would you have sight of them?"

Baron Orri is only too pleased. Before he quits St. Aliquis he will have possessed himself of the precious parchments, and Maître Edmond becomes the richer by several Paris livres. A fine copy of a great *chanson* is worth its weight in silver. The monks complain that the capital letters are as carefully elaborated in gold, and the miniature illustrations are as delicately executed, as those in a copy of the Gospel; and that the bindings of embossed leather make the books so heavy that they require reading stands, before which the ladies, never-theless (neglecting holier things), seem willing to stand all day long.

However, before the wedding guests end their happy day, another entertainer than Maitre Edmond is asked to perform. It is Baron Orri himself. He has lived so long in the south country that he has caught the trou-badour gallantries. Stories run that he has left three lady loves in three different castles; that he has had a most romantic duel with a jealous husband, which ended however, in a reconciliation on proof that the friendship had been only platonic; and that he is a past master in all the thirty-four different methods of rhyming and the seventy-four different kinds of stanzas with which the expert bards of southern France serve up their sentimental ditties. At a suitable moment just before the noble guests are gathering for the supper Adela addresses him:

"We know, kind Sire Orri, that you are a practitioner of all the 'gay science' of the South. You can sing *chansons,* songs of love; *vers,* the poems of slower movement; *sirventes,* poems of praise or satire; and also are master of the *tenso,* the debate on some tender subject, carried on in courtly verse. Honor us with your skill; for our northern poetry is rude and uncourtly beside that of the Languedoc."

Barron Orri makes an elegant bow: "Ah, gracious lady," he says, "I wish I could convince you that a good refusal were worth more than a poor gift, but doubtless you would think me rude; therefore, I will obey. Though many of you, I fear, do not speak the beautiful Languedoc tongue, yet in so noble a company I am sure most of you will at least understand me. What shall it be, a *tenso* by Bernart de Ventadorn discussing most wittily, 'How does a lady show the greater affection—by enjoining her friend to win renown, or by urging him simply to love her?' or shall I attempt a short *chanson* by that other high troubadour, Arnaut de Maruelh?"

"The *chanson*—the love song!" cry the company.

"Ah! very well, my gentle mistresses and lords," answers the minstrel—"you have chosen. And now I pray Queen Venus to inspire me. Here, boy, my harp!" He takes a small lute and touches the strings. His blue mantle floats back in statuesque folds as with clear, deep voice he sings:

144

"Fair to me is April bearing
    Winds that o'er me softly blow;
Nightingales their music airing
    While the stars serenely glow.
All the birds as they have power
    While the dews of morning wait,
Sing of joy in sky and bower,
    Each consorting with his mate.
And as all the world is wearing
    New delights while new leaves grow,
'Twould be vain to try forswearing
    Love which makes my joys o'erflow. . .

Helen were not worth comparing,
    Gardens no such beauty show,
Teeth of pearl, the truth declaring,
    Blooming cheeks, a neck of snow,
Tresses like a golden shower,
    Courtly charms, for baseness hate.
God, who bade her thus o'ertower
    All the rest, her way made straight!"[1]

And so through many similar stanzas. The Baron Orri's eyes are fixed mischievously on a certain countess with whom he had talked intimately all the afternoon. Her husband looks somewhat awkward, but at the end he joins in the warm applause. So the entertainment at the wedding feast ends; and the great secular literature, which is to be the priceless heritage of later civilization, is (despite much crudeness and false sentimentality) being born.

Hitherto we have seen the life of St. Aliquis at peace; now we must gradually turn toward its grimmer aspects and the direct preparations for war.

[1] Translated by Justin H. Smith. Reprinted by kind permission of G. P. Putnam's Sons.

Chapter IX: The Feudal Relationship. Doing Homage.

OME days intervene between the wedding festivities of the sister of Messire Conon and the adubbement as knight of his brother with the tourney which follows this second ceremony. No baron can be rich enough to make presents to all the knights who frequent the tourney, if they were also guests at the wedding; on the other hand, numerous cavaliers who have no interest in the affairs of Olivier and Alienor are glad to come and break lances in the jousts and to shatter helmets in the mêlée. Most of the original guests at the wedding, however, stay on for the adubbement, and are joined by many others. Meantime there are hunts, hawkings, dances, garden feasts, and jongleur recitals. It is all one round of merry excitement. Yet gradually there creeps in a more martial note. Maître Edmond's chants have less to do with parted lovers and more to do with valiant deeds. The bride and groom recede from central gaze. Young Squire Aimery is thrust forward.

While the lists are being prepared for the jousting, one can examine the public economy of the seigneury; discover how it is a military as well as a political unit; and learn the process of education which has enabled Aimery to claim the proud status of a knight—a *miles*— a first-class fighting man.

The status of St. Aliquis is typical of that of many

baronies. Fiefs are not necessarily composed of real estate: for example, one of Conon's vassals does homage to him merely for the right to fish for a mile along the Claire, and another for the privilege of maintaining the baronial mill, with corresponding perquisites, in an outlying section of the seigneury.[1] Nevertheless, as a rule a "fief" means a section of land held by a person of noble family. He does not own this land by complete right, but pays a kind of rent to his suzerain in the form of military service, of sums of money in various emergencies determined upon, and of various other kinds of moral and material assistance. Ordinarily every feudal lordship will center round a castle; or, failing that, a fortalice, a strong tower capable of considerable defense, or a manor house not vulnerable to mere raiders. Every noble fief holder claims the right to have his own banner;

to a seal to validate his documents; and of late there have been appearing insignia soon to be known as heraldic coats of arms, which will be used or displayed by everybody of "gentle condition." Many fief holders also claim the right to coin money, even when their lands are on a very modest scale; but suzerains are gradually curtailing this privilege, base-born merchants churlishly complain that the mints of

BANNER OF THE
THIRTEENTH CENTURY
From a manuscript in the
Bibliothèque nationale
(Viollet-Le-Duc).

the lesser seigneurs strike money too full of alloy and of vexatiously variable standards; and, indeed, there is even talk that this

[1] The right to profit from certain beehives could constitute a fief, or to a fraction, say, of the tolls collected at a certain bridge.

privilege of coining is likely to be monopolized by the
king.

Feudalism, if systematized, would seem an admirably
articulated system, extending upward from the petty
nobles to the king or even the emperor.[1] The little castel-

THE COAT OF ARMS OF THE
DUKES OF BRETAGNE
(THIRTEENTH CENTURY)

lans would do homage to the barons,
they to the viscounts, they to the
counts, they to the dukes, and they
to the supreme suzerain, His Grace
Philip Augustus, at Paris. Actually,
of course, nothing of the kind oc-
curs. Not merely do many fief
holders have several suzerains (as
does Conon) and serve some of
them very poorly, but there is no
real gradation of feudal titles.
Conon, a baron, feels himself equal
to many counts and superior to most viscounts. The
mighty Count of Champagne holds his head arrogantly as the equal of the Duke of Burgundy. Of
late years, especially since Philip Augustus began to
reign (1180), the kings of France have made it clear
that they are the mightiest of the mighty, and deserve genuine obedience. Yet even now many seigneurs grumble, "These lords of Paris are only the
Capetian dukes who began to call themselves kings
some two hundred years ago. Let them wax not too
proud or we will send them about their business
as our forefathers sent the old Carrolingians." In
short, the whole feudal arrangement is utterly confused.

[1] The emperor of the Holy Roman Empire (Germany and Italy)
was usually acknowledged as the social and titular superior of the
king of France, but he was never conceded any practical power
over Frenchmen.

"Organized anarchy," despairing scholars of a later age will call it.

Yet there are some pretty definite rules about fief holding. Generally speaking a fief includes enough land to maintain at least one knight and his war horse. This warrior is obligated usually to lead out a number of armed villeins, proportionate to the number of knights. The conditions on which the estate can be held vary infinitely. The great obligation is military service. The average vassal is bound to follow his suzerain for forty days per year on summons to an offensive war. He is required to give much

SEAL OF THE DUKE JEAN OF BRETAGNE (THIRTEENTH AND FOURTEENTH CENTURIES)

greater assistance in a strictly defensive war, and especially to aid in the defense of his lord's castle. He has to wait on the suzerain at times, when the latter may desire a great retinue to give prestige to his court. At such gatherings he must likewise assist his lord in dispensing justice—a matter sometimes involving considerable responsibility for the judges. When his seigneur marries off his eldest daughter, bestows knighthood on his eldest son, or needs ransom money, if held a prisoner, the vassals must contribute, and the St. Aliquis fief holders are blessing their patron saints that Alienor and Aimery are not their overlord's children—otherwise they would pay for most of the high festivities themselves. They must also, when their lord visits them, give him proper hospitality in their castles. Of course, they must never betray his secrets, adhere to his enemies, or repudiate

149

the pledges made to him. To do so were "treason," the worst of all feudal crimes.

We have seen that holding a fief usually implies military service, and that if the estate falls to a woman the suzerain can administer the property until the maid is of marriageable age, and then give her to some competent liegeman. It is about the same if the heir is a boy. The overlord can exercise guardianship over the fief until the lad is old enough to lead out his war band and otherwise to prove a desirable vassal. Even when the vassals are of satisfactory sex and age, the suzerain is entitled to a *relief*, a money payment, whenever an old knight dies and his battle-worthy son takes over the barony.[1] This is always a fairly heavy lump sum; and is still heavier if the fief goes not to the son, but to a collateral heir. Also, when the vassal wants to sell his fief to some stranger, not merely must the suzerain approve the change, but he is entitled to an extra large fee, often as much as three years' revenue from the entire holding.

Nevertheless, when all is said, many fief holders act as if they were anything but humble vassals. Happy is many a suzerain when he is so exempt from squabbles with his feudal equals and his own overlord that he can compel his loyal lieges to execute all their promises, and when he can indulge in the luxury of dictating to them the manner whereby they must rule their lands. Some of the mottoes of the great baronial houses testify how little the feudal hierarchy counts with the lord of a few strong castles.

Boast the mighty Rohans:

> "Dukes we disdain:
> Kings we can't be:
> *Rohans* are we!"

[1] Sometimes the relief was also payable when a new suzerain came in, not merely when the fief changed vassals.

And still more arrogant is that of a seigneur whose magnificent fortress-château is in the process of erection; "No king am I, no prince, no duke: I'm just the Sire of Coucy." And to be "Sire of Coucy" means to dispose of such power that when the canons of Rheims complain to King Philip against his deeds of violence, the king can merely reply, "I can do no more for you than *pray* the Sire of Coucy to leave you unmolested."

Sometimes, in addition to money payments or personal or military service, a vassal is required to make symbolic gifts in token of loyal intentions. Thus annually Conon sends to the Duke of Quelqueparte three black horses; while for his holdings of the local abbey, every June he presents the abbot with a basket of roses and a bunch of lilies, and many other estates are burdened with some such peculiar duties.[1]

So long as he discharges his feudal obligations a seigneur can run his barony practically to suit himself. If he treats his own vassals and his peasants too outrageously they may cry out to the suzerain for justice, and sometimes the overlord will delight in an excuse to humble an arrogant feudatory. But the limits of interference are well marked. No seigneur should undermine a faithful vassal's hold on his own subjects. Every noble will feel his own rights threatened if a suzerain begins to meddle with a dependent, even if the reason for doing so is manifest. Many a baron can therefore play the outrageous tyrant if so the devil inspires him. He

---

[1] In a South Country castle a certain seigneur was obligated, if his suzerain, the Duke of Aquitaine, visited him, to wait on the duke's table, wearing himself scarlet leggings with spurs of gold. He had to serve the duke and ten knights with a meal of pork, beef, cabbage, roast chickens, and mustard. Many other obligations for payments or rendering of hospitality which were equally curious could be recorded.

has (as we have seen) to observe the vested rights of his subordinates on the fief; otherwise he may provoke a dangerous mutiny within his own castle.[1] Baron Garnier of St. Aliquis, however, has been typical of many of his class. Prisoners, travelers, peasants are subject to unspeakably brutal treatment. As has been written concerning one such seigneur: "He was a very Pluto, Megæra, Cerberus, or anything you can conceive still more horrible. He preferred the slaughter of his captives to their ransom. He tore out the eyes of his own children, when in sport they hid their faces under his cloak. He impaled persons of both sexes on stakes. To butcher men in the most horrible manner was to him an agreeable feast." Of another such baron, the trembling monks record: "When anyone by force or fraud fell into his hands, the captive might truly say, 'The pains of hell have compassed me about.' Homicide was his passion and glory. He treated his wife in an unspeakably brutal manner. Men feared him, bowed down to him and worshiped him!"[2]

Evidently, such outrageous seigneurs hold their lieges in a kind of fascinated obedience, just as do the emirs and atabegs among the Infidels. Of course, they treat

[1] One might describe the situation by saying that many a baron who would order a stranger or captive to be executed in cold blood without form of trial, would hesitate to have him hanged or beheaded save by the hereditary executioner of the seigneury, who had a vested right to perform such nice matters.

[2] What could go on in feudal families earlier, in the eleventh century, is illustrated by the tale of three brothers, noblemen of Angouleme, who quarreled. Two of them treacherously invited the third to their joint Easter festivities. They seized him in bed, put out his eyes, and cut out his tongue that he might not denounce them. The facts, however, leaked out. Their suzerain, the Duke of Aquitaine, ravaged their lands with fire and sword (thus ruining their innocent peasants), took the two criminals and cut out their own tongues and put out their eyes in retaliation.

merchants as merely so many objects for plunder. If they do not watch the roads themselves, they make bargains with professional robbers, allowing the latter to infest their seigneuries in return for an agreed share of their booty. Even noble folk are liable to be seized, imprisoned, and perhaps tortured to get a ransom. If you cannot find the deniers, you may leave your bones in a foul dungeon.

Nevertheless, St. Michael and all angels be praised! this evil is abating. In the direct royal dominions such "men of sin" have been rooted out since old Louis VI's time. The Church is using its great influence against evil sires. The communal towns are waxing strong and sending civic armies to besiege their towers and protect the roads. The better class of seigneurs also unite against these disgraces to nobility. As for Baron Garnier, he died betimes, for his suzerian the duke (weary of complaints) was about to call out the levy of the duchy and attack St. Aliquis. In other words, law and order are gradually asserting themselves after the heyday of petty tyrannies, yet there are still queersome happenings on every seigneury, and the amount of arbitrary power possessed by the average baron is not good even for a conscientious and high-minded man.

It is not the theoretical powers of a seigneur, but his actual mental and ofttimes physical ability, which determines the real extent of his power. Fiefs are anything but static. They are always growing or diminishing. A capable seigneur is always attracting new lands to himself. He ejects unfaithful vassals and adds their estates to his own personal domain land. He induces his vassal's vassals to transfer their allegiance directly to him. He wins land from his neighbors by direct conquest. He induces his neighbor's vassals to desert to

153

the better protection of his suzerainty. He negotiates advantageous marriage treaties for his relatives which bring new baronies into his dynasty. When his own suzerain needs his military aid beyond the orthodox "forty days," he sells his assistance for cash, lands, or valuable privileges.

Then, often when such an aggressive seigneur dies, his whole pretentious fief crumbles rapidly. His eldest son is entitled to the central castle, and the lion's share of the barony, but not to the whole. The younger lads each detach something, and the daughters cannot be denied a portion.[1] The suzerain presses all kinds of demands upon the weakened heir. So do neighboring seigneurs who are the new baron's feudal equals. One little quarrel after another has to be compounded after ruinous concessions. Worst of all, the direct vassals of the incoming baron refuse him homage, hunt up more congenial suzerains, or, if swearing fealty, nevertheless commit perjury by the treacherous way they execute their oaths. In a few years what has appeared a powerful fief, under a young or incapable baron seems on the very edge of ruin—its lord reduced to a single castle, with perhaps some question whether he can defend even that.

Through such a peril Conon passed inevitably when, as a very youthful knight, he took over the estates of his unblessed uncle. Only the saints' favor, his mother's wise counsels, and his own high looks and strong arm kept the fief together. But after the vassal petty nobles had been duly impressed with the fact that, even if the new baron were less of a bloody tyrant than his predecessor, he could storm a defiant fortalice and behead

[1] The absence of a strict rule of primogeniture in France and other continental countries added much to the complexities of the whole feudal regime.

154

its rebellious master, the barony settled down to relative peace. There was a meeting at St. Aliquis of all the vassals. Conon, clothed in full armor, then presented himself in the great hall.

"Will you have Sire Conon, the nephew of your late lord, as your present undoubted baron and suzerain?" demanded Sire Eustace, the seneschal.

"*Fiat! Fiat!*—So be it!" shouted all the knights. Whereat each in turn did homage; and Conon was now their liege lord by every Christian and feudal law. Next Conon himself visited the Duke of Quelqueparte, paid his relief, in turn did his own homage; and henceforth had his position completely recognized.

From that time Conon had been obeyed by his vassals with reasonable fidelity. They had never refused military service; they had fought round his standard very faithfully at the great battle of Bouvines; they had given him no reason to doubt that if he were hard bestead they would discharge the other feudal duties of defending his person at the hazard of their lives, of resigning a horse to him that he might save himself in a battle, or even of going prisoner for him to secure his release, if he were captive. On the other hand, Conon had earned their love by proving himself a very honorable seigneur. When his vassal, Sire Leonard, had died, leaving only a minor son, he administered the lad's fief very wisely and gave it back a little richer, if anything, when the heir came of age. When another vassal had fallen into a feud with a neighboring sire, Conon had afforded military help, although it was not his direct quarrel. He had respected the wives and daughters of his petty nobles as though they had been his sisters. In short, on St. Aliquis had been almost realized that happy relation mentioned in the law books, "The seigneur owes faith and loyalty to his 'man' as much as the man to his seigneur."

Nevertheless, Conon ("wise as a serpent, but *not* harmless as a dove," as Father Grégorie says, pithily) takes nothing for granted. Twice he has somewhat formally made the circuit of his seigneury, stopping at each castle, allowing each little sire to show hospitality, and then receiving again his pledges. Homage can be done many times. The more often it is repeated the more likely it will be effective.[1] Your vassal who swore fealty last Christmas is much more likely to obey the *ban* (the call to arms) than he who took his oath ten years ago. The St. Aliquis vassals have all performed this devoir quite recently, save one, Sire André of the sizable castle of Le Chenevert, whose father died last Lent, and who has waited for the present fêtes to take his vows and receive due investiture.

This ceremony, therefore, takes place some day after the wedding feast. There is nothing humiliating therein for Sire André; on the contrary, he is glad to have many of the noble guests be witnesses—they will serve to confirm his title to his father's fief.

The great hall has been cleared. Messire Conon sits in his high chair under the canopy. He wears his ermine and his velvet cap of presence. Adela sits at his side, with many cavaliers on either hand. The other St. Aliquis vassals and the noble leaders of the castle men at arms, all in best armor, stand before the dais in a semicircle. Sire Eustace holds a lance with a small red pennon. Sire André, in silvered mail and helmet and his sword girded, comes forward, steps up to the dais, and kneels. Conon rises, extends both hands, and

---

[1] Homage may be likened somewhat to *vaccination* in a later day—the more recently performed the greater its effectiveness.

HOMAGE IN THE TWELFTH CENTURY

The future vassal has put his hands in those of his lord and pays him homage; a soldier holds the lance which the lord will give to his subject as a mark of investiture in the domain.

André takes one in each of his, then repeats clearly the formula dictated by Father Grégoire, now, as so often, acting as baronial chancellor:

"Sire baron, *I enter into your homage and faith and become your man,* by mouth and hands, and I swear and promise to keep faith and loyalty to you against all others, saving only the just rights of the Baron of Braisne, from whom I hold two farms and certain hunting rights, and I swear to guard your rights with all my strength."

Whereupon Conon makes reply, "We do promise to you, vassal André, that we and our heirs will guarantee to you the lands held of us, to you and your heirs against every creature with all our power. to hold these lands in peace and quiet."

Conon then bends, kisses André upon the mouth, and the latter rises to his feet. Father Grégoire holds out a small golden box flashing with jewels, a saint's reliquary, The vassal puts his right hand upon it and declares:

"In the name of the Holy Trinity, and in reverence of these sacred relics, I, André, swear that I will truly keep the promise which I have taken, and will always remain faithful to Sire Conon, my seigneur."

The first formula has technically been the "homage." The second is the "oath of fealty"; now comes the "investiture." Sire Eustace steps forward and gives to the vassal the lance, the symbolic token of the lawful transfer to him of the fief. In other places, local custom would make the article a glove, a baton, or even a bit of straw, but some symbol is always required. This act completes the ceremony.

Sire André is now in possession of Le Chenevert and its lands, and cannot be ousted thence so long as he performs his feudal duties. Of course, if the fief had been granted out for the first time, or had been transferred to some one not a direct heir, there would be a deed of conveyance drafted in detail, and sealed by many ponderous lumps of wax attached to the parchment with strips of leather. In many cases however, no new document is needful, and, indeed, all through the Feudal Ages even important bargains are likely often to be determined merely by word of mouth—a reason for requiring many witnesses.

There is little danger, however, of a quarrel between such congenial spirits as Baron Conon and Sire André. At its best, vassalship is not a state of unworthy dependence; it is a state of junior comradeship which, "without effacing distances, created a close relation of mutual devotion"; and if vassals are often rebellious, vassals again and again in history and in story have proved willing to lay down their lives for their lord. There are few sentiments the jongleurs can repeat in the average castle with surer hope of applause than when they recite once more from the "Epic of Garin," concerning the Duke of Belin, who declared that there was something more precious than all his riches and power; for "wealth consists neither in rich clothes, nor in money, nor in buildings, nor in horses, but is made from kinsmen and *friends;* the heart of one man is worth all the gold in a country!"

Chapter X: Justice and Punishments.

ONE of the great duties of a high seigneur is to render justice. It is for that (say learned men) that God grants to him power over thousands of villeins and the right to obedience from nobles of the lower class. Indeed, it can be written most properly that a good baron "is bound to hear and determine the cause and pleas of his subjects, to ordain to every man his own, to put forth his shield of righteousness to defend the innocent against evildoers, and deliver small children and such as be orphans and widows from those that do overset them. He pursues robbers, raiders, thieves, and other evildoers. For this name 'lord' is a name of peace and surety. For a good lord ceaseth war, battle, and fighting, and reconciles men that are at strife. And so under a good, strong, and peaceable lord, men of the country are safe."

The best of barons only measurably live up to this high standard. Yet Conon is not wholly exceptional in telling himself that a reputation for enforcing justice is in the end a surer glory than all the fêtes around St. Aliquis.

Justice, of course, does not mean equality before the law. There is one legal measure for country villeins, another for citizens of the commune, another for petty nobles, another for greater nobles of Conon's own rank. The monks and priests can always "plead their clergy"

159

and get their cases transferred to a special Church tribunal.[1] The question really is: Has a man been given everything due to others of his own class? If not, there is denial of justice.

The laws enforced in the St. Aliquis region are the old customary laws in use ever since the Frankish barbarians' invasions. Many of these laws have never been reduced to writing—at least for local purposes—but sage men know them. There are no professional jurists in the barony. Sire Eustace, the seneschal, understands the regional law better than any other layman around the castle, though he in turn is surpassed by Father Grégoire. The latter has, indeed, a certain knowledge of the Canon law of the Church, far more elaborate than any local territorial system, and he has even turned over voluminous parchments of the old Roman law codified by the mighty Emperor Justinian. Up at Paris, round the king there are now trained lawyers, splitters of fine hairs, who say that this Roman law is far more desirable than any local "customary law," and they are even endeavoring (as the king extends his power) to make the Code of Justinian the basis for the entire law of France. But conditions on most baronies are still pretty simple, the questions to be settled call merely for common sense and a real love of fair play on the part of the judges. One can live prosperously and die piously under rough-and-ready laws administered with great informality.

Conon has "high justice" over his vassals and peasants. This means absolute power of life and death over any non-noble on the seigneury, unless, indeed, the baron should outrage merchants bound to a privileged free city, or some other wayfarers under the specific protection of the king or the Duke of Quelqueparte. If strange

[1] See pp. 379, 380.

noblemen get into trouble, it will depend on circumstances whether Conon undertakes to handle their cases himself, or refers them to his suzerain, the duke. The right of seigneurs to powers of justice on their own lands even over high nobles is, however, tenaciously affirmed, and it is only with difficulty the duke and, above him, the king can get some cases remitted to their tribunals.[1] If, however, the alleged offender is a monk, he will be handed over to the local abbot or, if a priest, to the bishop of Pontdebois to be dealt with according to the law of the Church.

Even the lesser sires have "low justice," with the privilege of clapping villeins in the stocks, flogging, and imprisoning for a considerable time for minor offenses; and robbers caught on their lands in the act of crime can be executed summarily. But serious cases have to go to the court of the baron as high justiciar, as well as all the petty cases which have arisen on that lord's personal dominions. If the litigants are peasants, the wheels of justice move very rapidly. There is a decided absence of formalities.

A great many disputes go before the provost's court, presided over by Sire Macaire, a knight of the least exalted class, who is Conon's "first provost." We shall see later how the baron's provosts practically control the life of the peasants.[2] One of Sire Macaire's main duties is to chase down offenders, acting as a kind of sheriff, and after that to try them. Among the brawling, brutal peasantry there is always a deplorable amount

---

[1] Of course, a seigneur who grossly molested a peaceable traveling knight, or, for that matter, a villein in lawful errand going through the barony, could be cited before his suzerain's own tribunal for "denial of justice," and might (in clear-cut cases) have his whole position put in jeopardy.

[2] See p. 380.

of crime. The seigneury has been blessed with a comparative absence of bandits, but ever and anon a Pontdebois merchant gets stripped, a girl is carried off into the woods, or even the body of a traveler is found by the roadside. All this renders Sire Macaire's office no sinecure.

Small penalties are handed down every day, but more serious matters must wait for those intervals when Messire Conon calls his noble vassals to his "plaids" or "assizes." Every fief holder is expected to come and to give his lord good counsel as to what ought to be done, especially if any of the litigants are noble, and also to give him material aid, if needs be, in executing the decision reached.[1] This last is very important, for if a fief holder is dissatisfied with a verdict, he has a technical right to declare the decision "unjust" and demand that it be settled by "ordeal of battle"—the duel not being between the defeated suitor and his adversary, but between this suitor and his judge!

All men know of what happened (according to the "Song of Roland") in the case of the traitor Ganelon. This scoundrel, who had betrayed his suzerain Charlemagne and had caused the brave Roland's death, was seized by the emperor, but he demanded "judgment by his peers." Charlemagne could not deny this claim. He convoked the high barons, whereupon Lord Pinabel, Ganelon's kinsman, announced that "he would give the lie with the sword" to any seigneur who voted for punishment. All the barons were afraid. Pinabel was a mighty warrior. They reported an acquittal to Charlemagne. The mighty emperor raged, but felt helpless

---

[1] On account of the expense and trouble involved in attending the suzerain's court, and because of the risks of acting as judge, this feudal obligation was often poorly discharged.

162

until he discovered the brave knight Thierry of Anjou, who boldly asserted that "Ganelon deserves death."

Instantly Pinabel strode forward and cried to the assize of nobles: "I say that Thierry has lied. I will fight!" and at once Charlemagne took pledges from both champions that they would stand the "ordeal." Each warrior then promptly went to mass, partook of the Sacrament, and bestowed great gifts on the monasteries. Next they met in mortal combat. After a desperate duel Thierry smote his foe "through the nasal of the helmet . . . and therewith the brain of Pinabel went gushing from his head." There was no appeal from that verdict! Well content, Charlemagne immediately caused Ganelon to be pulled asunder by four fierce stallions.

However, these noble usages are falling into decadence. Certes, it is an unknightly thing when both litigants are young cavaliers, evenly matched, and when the issue concerns honor rather than legal technicalities, for them to insist that the matter be settled merely by a peaceful verdict, as if they had been wrangling merchants. But the Church, the men of books, and the higher suzerains discourage this practice, especially when the cases are intricate, and one of the litigants cannot fight efficiently or provide a champion. As for challenging a judge after a disagreeable verdict, the thing is becoming dangerous, for all the other judges will feel bound to support him.[1]

The most likely happening is for the defeated litigant to retire to his castle, summon his followers, and defy the court to enforce its verdict. This happened with a sire

---

[1] It was clearly recognized, also, that the "right of duel" was subject to abuses, and successful efforts were made to limit it to (1) very serious offenses; (2) cases where there was no direct evidence, but only circumstantial evidence, against the accused.

of the Court of Trabey, a neighbor of Conon's. Said sire, having been ordered by his peers to give up a manor he had been withholding from his young nephew, sent a pursuivant before their tribunal formally declaring war. The entire seigneury had to arm and actually storm his castle before he would submit.

However, most St. Aliquis cases concern not the nobles, but only villeins, and with these (thanks be to Heaven!) short shrifts are permitted. The provost can handle the run of crimes when the baron is busy; but a good seigneur acts as his own judge if possible. Even during the festival period it is needful for Conon to put aside his pleasures one morning to mount the seat of justice. In wintertime the tribunal is, of course, in the great hall, but in such glorious weather a big shade tree in the garden is far preferable.[1] Here the baron occupies a high chair. Sire Eustace sits on a stool at his right, Sire André and another vassal at his left as "assessors," for no wise lord acts without council. Father Grégoire stands near by, ready to administer oaths on the box of relics; Sire Macaire, the provost, brings up the litigants and acts as a kind of state attorney.

For the most part it is a sordid, commonplace business. Two villeins dispute the ownership of a yoke of oxen. A peddler from Pontdebois demands payment from a well-to-do farmer for some linen. An old man is resisting the demands of his eldest son that he be put under guardianship: the younger children say that their brother really covets the farm. If the court's decisions are not so wise as Solomon's, they are speedy and probably represent substantial justice. But there is more serious business in hand. The news of the fêtes at St.

[1] The case of Louis IX holding court under a great tree in the royal forest at Vincennes will be recalled as typical of this custom.

Aliquis has been bruited abroad. All the evil spirits of the region have discovered their chance. Certain discharged mercenary soldiers have actually invaded a village, stolen the peasants' corn, pigs, and chickens, insulted their women, and crowned their deeds by firing many cottages and setting upon three jongleurs bound for the tourney. They were in the very act of robbing them to their skin when a party of the provost's men, coming up, managed to seize two of these sturdy rascals. Sire Macaire has also arrested a young peasant who stabbed an older farmer painfully while they wrangled over a calf.

This second case is settled summarily. The defendant is of bad reputation. He must stand all day in the pillory, and then to be branded on his forehead with a red-hot iron, that all men may beware of him. As for the alleged bandits, the case is not so simple. They keep a sullen silence and refuse to betray the lair of their comrades who have escaped. The provost intimates that they may be *halegrins*, and outlaws of the foulest type, said to violate tombs and devour human flesh. Very possibly they may have belonged to that notorious gang of brigands many of which King Philip lured inside the walls of Bourges, then closed the gates and slew them, thus capturing all their plunder. Such fellows are, of course, food for the crows, but they must not be allowed to get out of life too easily.

"Let the baron command preparatory torture?" suggests Sire Macaire, with a sinister smile. Conon nods. The two beastlike wretches groan and strain at their fetters. Preparatory torture, they know well, is inflicted both to get a confession of guilt and also to extort details about accomplices.

It is no pleasure to follow the provost, his guards,

and his prisoners to a certain tower, where in a lower vaulted room there are various iron and wooden instruments. We are given to understand that torture is a pretty usual part of criminal proceedings, unless the defendant is a noble whose alleged crime does not touch the safety of the state. It is true that wise men have discouraged the practice. What seems clearer than that which Pope Nicholas I wrote A.D. 866? "A confession must be voluntary and not forced. By means of torture an innocent man may suffer to the uttermost without making any avowal—in such a case what a crime for the judge! Or a person may be subdued by pain, and acknowledge himself guilty, though he be innocent— which throws an equally great sin upon the tribunal." Nevertheless, the Church is said now to be allowing torture in her own ecclesiastical courts, and Sire Macaire would tell us cynically that "torture is a sovereign means wherewith to work miracles—to make the dumb speak."

Torture at St. Aliquis is administered by a sober-faced man in a curious yellow dress. He is known as Maître Denis,[1] the baron's "sworn executioner." He acts as torturer, chief jailer, and also attends to beheadings and hangings. To be a professional hangman implies considerable ostracism. Hangmen's families have to marry among themselves, between fief and fief; hangmen's sons follow their fathers' calling. On the other hand, the position is an assured one, with good perquisites and not too much labor. Maître Denis is a quiet and pious man, who can exhort condemned criminals quite as

[1] Outside the barony he would probably be known by the name of the seigneury he served—e.g., "Maître St. Aliquis." Down to the verge of the Revolution the chief hangman of the capital of France was "Monsieur Paris."

sanctimoniously as a priest; but his piety never compels him to false mercy.

There are assuredly many ways of helping transgressors to make a complete confession. Forms of torture vary from region to region. In Brittany the culprit is often tied in an iron chair and gradually brought near to a blazing fire; but in Normandy the effect seems best when one thumb is squeezed by a kind of screw in the ordinary, and both thumbs in the extraordinary (doubly severe) torture. At Autun they have an ingenious method. After high boots of spongy leather have been put on the culprit's feet, he is tied near a large fire and boiling water is poured on the boots, which penetrates the leather, eats away the flesh, and vouchsafes a foretaste of the pangs of hell.

At Orléans they have another method. The accused's hands are tied behind his back, and a ring fastened to them. By this ring the unhappy fellow is lifted from the floor and hung up in midair. If they then desire the "extraordinary" torture, weights of some two hundred and fifty pounds are attached to his feet. He is hoisted to the ceiling by a pulley, and presently allowed to fall with a jerk, dislocating his limbs.[1]

There are, indeed, many simpler, more convenient methods of torture. You can inject boiling water, vinegar, or oil into the accused, apply hot pitch, place hot eggs under the armpits, thrust sharp-cornered dice between the skin and flesh, tie lighted candles to the hands so that they can be consumed simultaneously with the wax, or allow water to drip from a great height upon the stomach. This, curiously enough, is said to

[1] This method of torture by "squasations" seems to have been the one ordinarily used in the Inquisition, which began its unhappy history in the thirteenth century.

break down the most stubborn criminals, as will watering the soles of the feet with salted water, and allowing goats to lick the same.

However, the ordinary method is the rack. Then the offender is laid on a wooden trestle, cords are bound to his limbs and then steadily tightened with winches. Baron Garnier in his day took great interest in obtaining a well-made rack. It now is put to proper use in "stretching" the two brigands. Happily, these culprits break down after the first of them has undergone a few turns before his limbs are dislocated; and to the provost's satisfaction they howl out sundry details as to how their comrades can be taken. The prisoners are therefore remanded to custody until their statements can be investigated. Woe to them if they have lied! In that event there are promised them much keener tortures to make them weary of life.

While Sire Macaire is therefore leading his band after the remaining brigands, Maître Denis conducts the two captives back to prison. Really it is only a few feet from the great hall of state in the *palais,* to the cells under the old donjon. In their confinement the prisoners can hear the revelry of the baron's guests. Through their airholes drifts the jongleur's music. They can almost, at times, catch the swish and rustle of the rich dresses of the noblewomen. Conon is accounted a merciful custodian compared with his uncle, but he does not let offenders forget their sins because of kindness.

Noble prisoners are entitled to relatively comfortable quarters, to double rations of decent food, to give bail if their alleged offense is not a very heavy one, and to be released on reasonable ransom if they are captives of war. Villeins have no such privileges. They are fortunate if first they are not stripped naked as a pair of tongs

168

before the lock rattles behind them. They are usually cast into filthy holes, sometimes with water running across the floor, and with reptiles breeding in the mire. In Paris, where the king is considered more tender-hearted than the average seigneur, we hear of a cell of only eleven by seven feet in which ten people have been thrust to spend the night. Of course, these were not great criminals. The latter might enjoy the *chausse d' hypocras,* where a man had his feet continually in water, or the *fosse,* a jug-shaped round chamber let into the bowels of the rock, into which prisoners must be lowered by a pulley from the ceiling;[1] or a Little-Ease chamber, where one could neither sit nor stand. If, however, you have money you can sometimes bribe the turnkeys into letting you have a cell more private and less noisome, with the luxury of bedding and a chair;[2] but in any case he who enters a feudal prison had better invoke his patron saint.

Maître Denis has not treated the two brigands quite so badly as lay in his power. He has left them their clothes—since they are sure to be executed and he can get the raiment later. He has not put them in the *fosse* (where Baron Garnier had sometimes dropped his victims) because of the trouble later of hoisting them out. He gives them coarse bread and some meat not unfit for dogs, at the same time advising them "on his word as a Christian" to confer with Father Grégoire.

---

[1] This was one of the famous *Oubliettes* ("Chambers of Forgetfulness) or *Vade-in-pace* (Depart-in-peace) cells where the prisoners could be left to starve in pitch darkness, or perhaps be fed by a few scraps flung down from the hole in the vaulting.

[2] It was a great concession in the Paris prisons when the government ordered that the jailers in the more public wards should "keep large basins on the pavement, so that the prisoners might get water whenever they wished."

The miserable pair are not long uncertain about their fate. They have told the truth about the lair of their comrades. The provost's band surprises the spot. Six hardened rogues, in the very act of counting their plunder, are overpowered. But why weary Messire the Baron with the empty form of trying these robbers when there is no mortal doubt of their guilt and no new information is to be extracted from them? Their throats are therefore cut as unceremoniously as the cook's boy attends to pigeons. The next day, wholly casually, Sire Macaire reports his good success to his lord, and remarks, "I presume, fair Sire, that Denis can hang the two he has in the dungeon." Conon (just arranging a hawking party) rejoins: "As soon as the chaplain can shrive them." Why, again, should the prisoners complain? They are certainly allowed to prepare decently for the next world, a favor entirely denied their comrades.

If there had been any real doubt as to the guilt of the two bandits, they might in desperation have tried to clear themselves by *ordeal*. If they could have picked a stone out of a caldron of boiling water, lifted and carried a red-hot iron, or even partaken of the Holy Sacrament (first calling on God to strike them dead if they were guilty), and after such a test seemed none the worse, they might have had some claim to go free. *Ordeals* are an old Germanic usage. They seem to refer the decision to all-seeing God. But ever since Charlemagne's day they have been falling into disfavor. Great churchmen are ordinarily too intelligent to encourage them. Men learned in the law say that often they wrest justice. Brave knights declare the only ordeal worth having is a duel between two champions.

Sometimes, instead of wrangling, clerics have undertaken to prove themselves right by "passing through fire"—walking down a narrow lane between two great piles of blazing fagots, and trusting that Heaven will guard them even as it did the three Hebrew children in Nebuchadnezzar's furnace. Such tests seldom are satisfactory. Men still dispute about the ordeal of the monk Peter Barthelmey during the First Crusade. He was accused of a pretended miracle and tried to vindicate himself by "passing through fire alive." All agreed that he emerged from the flames alive; yet in a few days he died. His foes said because he was sorely burned; his friends because, although unscathed by the fire, he was merely trampled upon by the crowd that rushed up to discover his fate!

The only time one can ordinarily rely upon ordeals is in tests for witchcraft. If an old woman is so accused, she must be tied hand and foot and cast into the river. If she floats, the devil is aiding; draw her out, therefore, and burn her at the stake. If she sinks (as in a case recently at Pontdebois) she is innocent. Unfortunately, in this instance the poor wretch went to the bottom before they could determine that she was guiltless; but the saints know their own, and doubtless they have given recompense and rest to her soul.

Naturally many petty offenses do not deserve death. The criminals are usually too poor to pay fines, and it is a waste of honest folk's bread to let them spend set terms in prison. For small misdemeanants it is often enough to drive the rascals around the neighboring villages in a cart, calling out their names amid hootings and showers of offal. But in the village beyond the Claire is located the pillory for a large class of rogues. It is a kind of high scaffold with several sets of chains and wooden collars, through which the offenders' arms and heads are thrust, while they stand for hours, in hot sun or winter cold, exposed to the jeerings and **pebbles of** the assembled idlers gathered beneath.

The next stage of penalty is sometimes a public flogging. The prisoner is stripped to the waist and driven around the seigneury. At each crossroads his guards give so many blows over the shoulders with a knotted rope. We have seen how branding was ordered for one young miscreant to put on him an ineffaceable stigma; and not infrequently one can meet both men and women with a hand lopped off, or even an eye gouged out, as a merciful substitute for their true deserts upon the gallows. Old Baron Garnier once, when peculiarly incensed, ordered the "hot bowl"—namely, that a red-hot brazier should be passed before the eyes of his victim until sight was destroyed.

But if a villein has committed a great crime he were best dismissed from an overtroubled world. Dead men never bother the provost twice. All over France you will find a gallows almost as common a sight in the landscape as a castle, an abbey, or a village. Many a fine spreading tree by the roadway has a skeleton bedangling from one of its limbs. It is a lucky family of peasants which has not had some member thereof hanged, and even then plenty of rogues will die in their beds. Considering the general wickedness abroad, it seems as if there were a perpetual race between the criminals and the hangmen, with the criminals well to the fore.[1]

There are almost as many forms of execution as there are of torture. Fearful criminals, gross blasphemers,

[1] Of course, the terrible severity of the penalties made many persons who were guilty of relatively small offenses feel that they had sinnned beyond pardon. They would, therefore, plunge into a career of great crimes, to "have their fling" ere the inevitable gallows.

and the like might be killed by quartering: first their flesh might be nipped off by red-hot pinchers and hot lead poured into their wounds; then death comes as a release by attaching a strong horse to each arm and leg and tearing the victim into four parts. Witches, wizards, and heretics are, of course, burned, because they thus share the element of their patron, the devil. Most malefactors, however, find beheading or hanging the ordinary ending.

Beheading is "honorable." It is the nobleman's expiation for misdeeds. The victim is not degraded and leaves no stigma upon his children. In England the headsman uses the ax, but in France he ordinarily swings a great two-handed sword. A skillful executioner does his business at one blow—a most merciful form of mortal exit.

Hanging, however, is "dishonorable." Nobles who have especially exasperated their judges are sometimes subjected to it. Henceforth people will cry, "Their father was a felon," to their disgraced children. When a villein is ordered to die, he is ordinarily hanged, unless some other method is specified. In the village near St. Aliquis the gallows is near the pillory. It is not so large as that huge gallows at Montfaucon, near Paris, which sees the end of so many of the city offenders, and where there is a great series of stone piers with wooden crosspieces, arranged in two stories, making twenty-four compartments in all. There are permanent ladders fixed for dragging up the criminals. When all the compartments are full and additional room is needed for more executions, some of the skeletons are thrown into a deep, hideous pit in the center of the structure. The less pretentious St. Aliquis gallows has only four compartments. The structure stands close to the road, that

173

all may learn how energetic are the baron's provosts. Two compartments are now empty, however, and Sire Macaire is glad of a chance to fill them.

Because the two bandits made prompt confession they are not subjected now to a "previous" torture— that is, to a new racking as an extra punishment before execution. They are compelled, however, to perform the *amende honorable*. This involves being haled to the parish church in the village. A long candle is thrust in the hands of each victim. They are dragged forward by a noose, and at the door of the church cast themselves down and cry; "We have grievously sinned against Heaven. Our punishment is just. We beg pardon of God and man. May Heaven have mercy upon our souls!" Then they are forced back to the cart whereon they are being trundled to execution.

"Riding the cart" is a familiar phrase for going to the gallows. For a noble prisoner to be compelled to take his last journey upon a cart, instead of cavalier-wise upon a horse, is the last touch of degradation. The two bandits, securely pinioned, are placed in a two-wheeled vehicle, attended by Maître Denis and an assistant, and with Father Grégoire repeating prayers. They seem followed by all the lewd fellows of the baser sort in the entire region, and even certain knights and dames, come for the tournament, are not above craning their necks and gazing after the noisy procession. A hanging is just infrequent enough in St. Aliquis to afford a little excitement. At the gallows Maître Denis acts with a fearful dexterity. First one, next the other, criminal is dragged up the ladder with the noose about his neck, then swung off into eternity with a merciful speed. A good hangman does not let his victims suffer long. Soon a great flock of crows will be flapping around

the gallows, giving the last rites to the lawbreakers, and the ogling crowd will slink away.

The poor wretches are fortunate in that their anguish is not prolonged by such customs as obtain at Paris. There many death carts stop at the Convent of the Filles-Dieu, where the nuns are obligated to give every condemned criminal a glass of wine and three pieces of bread. This pathetic meal is seldom refused, and a great throng will stand gaping about until it is consumed. Father Grégoire, too, had mercifully refrained from a long public exhortation at the gallows as to how, literally, "the wages of sin is death," another custom ere offenders are turned off. But after the deed is over, confessor, executioner, and provost do not decline their perquisite after every such ceremony—a liberal banquet at the castle.

These proceedings have been unpleasant but not unusual interludes between such happenings as the wedding and the adubbement. It is time to return to young Squire Aimery, and see how he has been educated and "nourished" preparatory to the greatest event in his life.

Chapter XI: The Education of a Feudal Nobleman.

O the noble troubadour Bertran de Born, a congenial comrade of Richard the Lion Hearted, is attributed a little song which seems re-echoed in many a castle.

> Peace delights me not!
> War—be thou my lot!
> Law—I do not know
> Save a right good blow!

Even a seigneur who nods pious assent to all that the monks and priests affirm in praise of peace wishes in his heart that it were not sinful to pray for brisk fighting. To be a good warrior, to be able to take and give hard blows, to enjoy the delights of victory over doughty adversaries, and finally to die a warrior's death on "the field of honor," not a "cow's death" in one's bed—that is the ambition of nearly every noble worthy of his gentility.

Bertran de Born has again expressed this brutal joy in still greater detail:

> I prize no meat or drink beside
> The cry, "On! On!" from throats that crack:
> The neighs when frightened steeds run wide,
> A riderless and frantic pack,
> And set the forest ringing:—
> The calls, "Help! Help!"—the warriors laid
> Beside the moat with brows that fade
> To grass and stubble clinging:—

And then the bodies past all aid
Still pierced with broken spear or blade. . . .
Come barons, haste ye, bringing
Your vassals for the daring raid;—
Risk all—and let the game be played!

Clearly other and supposedly more peaceful ages will find in the Feudal Epoch a very bloody world.

There is at least this extenuation. Even in France the winters are cold, the days short, the nights long. Castles at best are chilly, musty barracks. Many people are living in a small space and are constantly jostling one another. Thanks to sheer ennui, many a baron becomes capricious and tyrannical. Even in summertime, hunts, hawking, jongleurs' lays, and tournaments grow stale. Often the average cavalier is in a receptive mood for war just because he is grievously bored.

The countenances of the older warriors around St. Aliquis; the great scars on cheek, chin, and forehead; the mutilated noses and ears—tell how strenuous have been most of their lives.

COSTUME OF A NOBLEMAN
(THIRTEENTH CENTURY)

The scars are badges of honor. Aimery is nigh regretful that there are no slashes on his youthful countenance, although Sire Eustace, his mentor, grimly assures him "this trouble will pass with time." Aimery is now nineteen. His brother gave him a careful training, as becoming the cadet of a great house, and then arranged that he be "nourished"—that is, taken into the family and educated as squire—by a powerful count. Unfortunately, just as Aimery was about to demand knighthood of his lord, the latter suddenly died. He therefore returned to St. Aliquis and waited some months impatiently, until Conon could give him an adubbement worthy of the St. Aliquis name.

From earliest youth Aimery has had success in arms held before him as the one thing worth living for. True, he has been taught to be pious. He understands it is well that God has created priests and monks, who may by their ceremonies and prayers enable the good warriors to enter into paradise. But the squire has never had the slightest desire to become a cleric himself. He thanks his divine patroness, St. Génevieve, that Conon has not treated him as so many younger brothers are treated, and forced him into the Church. What is it to become a lazy rich canon, or even a splendid lord bishop, beside experiencing even the modest joys of a common sire with a small castle, a fast horse, good hawks, and a few stout retainers? Aimery has learned to attend mass devoutly and to accept implicitly the teachings of the priests, but his moral training is almost entirely based on "courtesy," a very secular code indeed. Hence he acts on the advice given him while very young: "Honor all churchmen, but look well to your money."

Another well-remembered warning is never to put trust in villeins. He cannot, indeed, refuse to deal with them. He must treat them ordinarily with decency, but never trust them as real friends. The ignoble are habitually deceitful. They cannot understand a cavalier's "honor." They are capable of all kinds of base villainies. A sage man will have comradeship only with his nobly born peers, and pride is no fault in a baron when dealing with inferiors.

Literary Education of Young Nobles

Although he is to be a warrior, Aimery has been given a certain training in the science of letters. It is true that many seigneurs cannot read a word on the parchments which their scriveners interpret, draw up, or seal

GOTHIC WRITING
From a thirteenth-century chart.

for them,[1] but this is really very inconvenient. Conon is genuinely thankful he is not thus at the mercy of Father Grégoire. Another reason for literacy is that delightful books of romantic adventure are multiplying. The younger brother has, therefore, been sent over to the school at the neighboring monastery, where (along with a few other sons of noblemen) he has had enough of the clerk's art switched into him to be able to read French with facility, to pick out certain Latin phrases, and to form letters clumsily on wax tablets—writing with a stylus something after the manner of the ancients.[2]

Once possessed of this wonderful art of reading that Aimery had while yet a lad, he could delve into the wonderful parchments of romances which told him of the brave deeds done of old. Especially, he learned all about the Trojan War, which was one long baronial feud between North French cavaliers fighting for the fair Helen, imprisoned in a strong castle. His sympathy

[1] As late as about 1250 there was a "grand chamberlain of France" who seems to have been absolutely illiterate.
[2] It is risky to generalize as to the extent of learning among the average nobles. Some modern students would probably represent them as being sometimes better lettered than were Conon and Aimery.

179

was excited for Hector as the under dog. He read of many exploits which had escaped the knowledge of Homer, but which were well known to Romance trouvères. He reveled in scenes of slaughter whereof the figures are very precise, it being clearly stated that 870,000 Greeks and 680,000 Trojans perished in the siege of that remarkable Trojan fortress.

A TEACHER HOLDING A FERULE
IN HIS HAND
Restored by Viollet-Le-Duc from a
thirteenth-century manuscript in
the Bibliothèque nationale.

Almost equally interesting was the history of Alexander, based on the version of the pseudo-Callisthenes. This was very unlike the accounts which other ages consider authentic. The names of the battles with Darius were altered, strange adventures with the Sirens crept into the narrative, and finally Alexander (the tale ran) died sorely lamenting that he could not conquer France and make Paris his capital.

The story of Cæsar is also available, but it seems less romantic, although full of episodes of fairies and dwarfs.

For the history of France, Aimery has learned that the country was originally settled by exiled Trojans; later the Romans came, and some time later one meets the great Emperor Charlemagne, whose exploits entwine themselves with Charles Martel's defeat of the Saracens. Charlemagne, we gather, conducted a crusade to the Holy Land and took Jerusalem, although later the

180

Infidels regained it. Recent French history remains very mixed in the young noble's mind until the great Council of Clermont (1095), which launched the First Crusade. In the century after that great episode, however, the events stand out clearly, and of course he knows all the history of the local baronial houses down to the story of the petty feud forty years ago between two Burgundian counts.

But what is monk's or jongleur's lore compared with the true business of a born cavalier? When he was only seven or eight, Aimery was fencing with a blunted sword. From ten onward he took more regular fencing lessons, first from Sire Eustace; then from a professional master, a keen Gascon, hired by Conon. Equally early he had his horse, his hawks, and his dogs; he was taught how to care for them entirely himself, and was soon allowed to go on long rides alone into the dense forest in order to develop his resourcefulness, sense of direction, and woodcraft. Then, as he grew taller, his brother began to deliver long lectures for his betterment, even as Adela had admonished Alienor.

One day Conon exhorted him in the style of the old Count Guy advising his son Doon in the epic, "Doon of Mayence." "Ask questions of good men whom you know, but never put trust in a stranger. Every day, fair brother, hear the holy mass; and whenever you have money give to the poor—for God will repay you double. Be liberal in gifts to all, for a cavalier who is sparing will lose all in the end and die in wretchedness; but wherever you can, give without promising to give again. When you come to a strange house, cough very loudly, for there may be something going on there which you ought not to see. When you are in noble company, play backgammon; you will be the more

181

prized on that account. Never make a noise or jest in church; it is done only by unbelievers. If you would shun trouble, avoid meddling and pretend to no knowledge you do not possess. Do not treat your body servant as your equal—that is, let him sit by you at table or take him to bed with you; for the more honor you do a villein the more he will despise you. After you are married by no means tell a secret to your wife; for if you let her know it you will repent your act the first time you vex her." And with this shrewd thrust at Adela the flow of wisdom temporarily ceases.

Before he was fifteen Aimery had thus learned to read and write, to ride and hawk, to play chess, checkers, and backgammon, to thrum a harp and sing with clear voice, to shoot with the arbalist, and to fence with considerable skill. He was also learning to handle a light lance and a shield while on horseback. Then came his first great adventure—his brother sent him to the gentle Count of Bernon to be "nourished."

The higher the baron the greater his desire to have nobly born lads placed in his castle as *nourris,* to serve as his squires and be trained as cavaliers. Bernon had kept three squires simultaneously, as did Conon himself. It is a friendly courtesy to send word to an old comrade in arms (as these two seigneurs had been), saying: "You have a fine son [or brother]; send him to be 'nourished' in my castle. When he is of ripe age I will give him furs and a charger and dub him knight." Of course, it was a high honor to be reared by a very great lord like the Duke of Quelqueparte; but younger sons or brothers did not often enjoy such good fortune. Petty nobles had to send their sons to the manors of poor sires of their own rank, who could keep only one squire.

Training of a Squire

Once enrolled as squire to a count, Aimery soon learned that his master was a kind of second father to him—rebuking and correcting him with great bluntness, but assuming an equal responsibility for his training. Hereafter, whatever happened, no ex-squire could fight against his former master without sheer impiety. The Emperor Charlemagne once, in a passion, smote the hero Roland in the face. Roland turned red. His fist clenched—then he remembered how Charlemagne had "nourished" him. He accepted an insult which to him no other mortal might proffer.

It is held that no father or brother can enforce sufficient discipline over a growing lad, and that "it is proper he shall learn to obey before he governs, otherwise he will not appreciate the nobility of his rank when he becomes a knight." Aimery in the De Bernon castle surely received his full share of discipline, not merely from the count, but from the two older squires, who took pains at first to tyrannize over him unmercifully, until they became knighted, and he gained two new companions younger than himself, with whom he played the despot in turn.

In his master's service Aimery became expert in the use of arms. First he was allowed to carry the count's great sword, lance, and shield, and to learn how the older nobles could handle them. Next he was given weapons and mail of his own, and began the tedious training of the tilt yard, discovering that a large part of his happiness in life would consist in being able to hold his lance steady while his horse was charging, to strike the point fairly on a hostile shield until either the tough lance snapped or his foe was flung from the saddle, and at the same time to pinch his own saddle tightly with his knees while with his own shield covering breast and

183

head against a mortal blow. Couch, charge, recover—couch, charge, recover—he must practice it a thousand times.

Meantime he was attending the count as a constant companion. He rose at gray dawn, went to the stables, and curried down his master's best horse; then back to the castle to assist his superior to dress. He waited on his lord and lady at table. He was responsible for receiving noble guests, preparing their chambers and generally attending to their comfort. On expeditions he led the count's great war charger when the seigneur rode his less fiery palfrey; and he would pass his lord his weapons as needed. At tournaments he stood at the edge of the lists, ready to rush in and rescue the count from under the stamping horses if he were dismounted. He was expected to fight only in emergencies, when his master was in great danger; but Bernon was a gallant knight, and repeatedly in hot forays Aimery had gained the chance to use his weapons.

At the same time he was learning courtesy. He was intrusted with the escort of the countess and her daughters. He entertained with games, jests and songs noble dames visiting the castle. He learned all the details of his master's affairs. The count was supposed to treat him as a kind of younger self—intrust him with secrets, send him as confidential messenger on delicate business, allow him to carry his purse when he journeyed, and keep the keys to his coffers when at home. After Aimery became first squire he was expected also to assist the seneschal in a last round of the castle at night, to make sure everything was locked and guarded; then he would sleep at the door of the count's chamber. Beyond a doubt, since the count was an honorable and capable man, Aimery received thereby a training of enormous value. While still a lad he had large responsibilities thrust upon him, and learned how to transmit commands and to handle difficult situations. He was versed in all the ordinary occasions of a nobleman.

When he became a knight himself, he would be no tyro in all the stern problems of feudal life.

Thus Conon's brother came within four years to be an admirable *damoiseau* (little lord), an epithet decidedly more commendatory than its partial equivalent "squire" (*ecuyer*, shield bearer).[1]

Of course, his military training had proceeded apace. Soon he was allowed to tilt with his horse and lance at the *quintain*. This is a manikin covered with a coat of mail and a shield, and set on a post. The

MANEUVERING WITH A LANCE IN THE
THIRTEENTH CENTURY
Restored by Viollet-Le-Duc, from a manuscript
in the Bibliothèque nationale.

[1] The sharp distinction between the young attendants known as "pages," and the older "squires," had hardly been worked out by A.D. 1220. Such young persons could also be called "variets," but that name might be given as well to non-noble servitors. When chivalry was at its height the theory developed that a nobleman's son should spend his first to his seventh year at home with his mother, his eighth to his fifteenth in suitable training as a "page," and from that time till he was one-and-twenty serving as a squire. This precise demarcation of time was probably seldom adhered to. Many ambitious young nobles would serve much less than seven years as a squire. On the other hand, many petty nobles might remain squires all their lives, for lack of means to maintain themselves as self-respecting knights.

horseman dashes up against it at full gallop, and tries to drive his lance through shield and armor. There are many variations for making the sport harder. After Aimery could strike the *quintain* with precision he took his first tilt against an older squire. Never will he forget the grinding shock of the hostile lance splintering upon his shield; the almost irresistible force that seemed smiting him out of the saddle; the dismay when he found his own lance glancing harmlessly off the shield of his opponent, slanted at a cunning angle. But practice makes perfect. When he finally returned to St. Aliquis his own brother was almost unhorsed when they tried a friendly course by the barbican.

So Aimery completed his education. If he has failed to learn humility, humanity to villeins, and that high respect for women which treats them not merely as creatures to be praised and courted, but as one's moral and intellectual equals, he at least has learned a high standard of honor in dealing with his fellow nobles. The confidences his master has reposed in him have made it a fundamental conviction that it were better to perish a dozen times than to betray a trust. He believes that the word of a cavalier should be better than the oath of the ignoble. As for courage, it were better to die like Ganelon, torn by wild horses, than to show fear in the face of physical danger. He has been trained also to cultivate the virtue of generosity to an almost ruinous extent.

Free giving is one of the marks of a true nobleman. Largess is praised by the minstrels almost as much as bravery. "He is not a true knight who is too covetous." Therefore money is likely to flow like water through Aimery's fingers all his life. The one redeeming fact will be that, though he will be constantly *giving,* he will always be as constantly *receiving*. Among the nobles there is an incessant exchanging of gifts—horses, armor, furs, hawks, and even money. All wealth really comes from the peasants, yet their lords dispose carelessly of it even though they do not create it. Even the villeins, however, will complain if their masters do not make the crowds scramble often for coppers—never realizing that these same coppers represent their own sweat and blood.

As already stated, Aimery's master had died (to his squire's sincere grief) shortly before the latter could have said to him according to the formula, "Fair Sire, I demand of you knighthood." The young man has accordingly returned to St. Aliquis, and waited for some action by his brother. Knighthood means for a noble youth the attainment of his majority. It involves recognition as a complete member of that aristocracy which was separated by a great gulf from the villeins. Very rarely can the base-born hope for that ceremonial buffet which admits them to the company of the gentle. If a peasant has exhibited remarkable courage and intelligence, and above all has rendered some extraordinary service to a duke or king, sometimes his villein blood may be forgotten officially. But even if he is knighted, all his life he can be treated as a social upstart, his dame despised and snubbed by noblewomen, and his very grandchildren reminded of the taint of their ancestor.

True, indeed, not all men of nobility can become knights. Knighthood ordinarily implies having a minimum of landed property, and ability to live in aristocratic idleness. Many poor nobles, and especially the younger sons of poor nobles, remain bachelors, fretting upon their starving properties, or serving some seigneur as mercenaries, and hoping for a stroke of fortune so that they can demand knighthood. But they are likely to die in their poverty, jealous of the rich sires, yet utterly scornful of the peasants and thanking the saints they are above touching a plow, mattock, or other vulgar means of livelihood.

On the other hand, there are many seigneurs who, although rich and dubbed as knights, nevertheless give the lie to their honors by their effeminacy and luxury. They are worse than the baron whom we saw as a *trouvère* and collector of minstrels' romances, and who even read Latin books. The monkish preachers scold such weaklings and pretended gallants. "To-day our warriors are reared in luxury. See them leave for the campaign! Are their packs filled with iron, with lances, with swords? Not so, but with leathern bottles filled with wine, with cheeses, and spits for roasting. One would imagine that they were going to a feast in the gardens and not to a battle. They carry splendidly plated shields; but greatly they hope to bring them back undented."[1]

Such unworthy knights unquestionably can be found, but they have not tainted the whole nobility. Your average cavalier has spent his entire life training for combat; he dreams of lance thrusts and forays; and the least of his sins is that he will shun deadly blows.

At last the great day for which Aimery has waited is at hand. To-morrow Conon will dub him a knight.

[1] The words quoted are those of the Archdeacon Peter of Blois, haranguing about A.D. 1180.

Chapter XII: Feudal Weapons and Horses. Dubbing a Knight.

HE thing which really separates a noble from a villein is the former's superiority in arms. True, God has made the average cavalier more honorable, courteous, and sage than the peasant; but, after all, his great advantage is material. The villeins, poor churls, spend their days with shovel, mattock, or in mechanic toil. Doubtless, they can grow wheat, raise pigs, weave cloth, or build houses better than their masters, but in the use of arms how utterly are they inferior. How can a plowman, though you give him weapons, hold his own against a man of gentility who has been trained in arms from early boyhood. As for the peasants with their ordinary weapons—flails, boar spears, great knives, scythes set on poles, bows and arrows—suppose ten of them meet one experienced cavalier in full panoply upon a reliable charger. His armor will turn their puny blows. He will, perhaps, have brained or pinked through four of them before the other six can run into the woods. No wonder nobles give the law to villeins!

The noble is almost always a horseman. It is the great war steed that gives him much of his advantage, and a large part of the remainder comes from his magnificent armor, which enables him often to go through desperate contests unscathed, and which is so expensive that most non-nobles can never afford it. A

189

good cavalier despises missile weapons, he loves to come to grips. Bowmen are despised as being always villeins. Says a poet, "Coward was he who was the first archer; he was a weakling and dared not come close to his foe."

A KNIGHT AT THE END OF THE THIRTEENTH CENTURY

Restored by Viollet-Le-Duc, from a manuscript in the Bibliothèque nationale. He wears on his shoulders small metal plaques called "ailettes."

And many armies are reckoned by cavalry alone, even as sang another minstrel of a legendary host, "there were in it sixty thousand knights, not counting foot soldiers of whom no account is taken."

Old warriors dislike arbalists, those terrible crossbows, wound up with a winch, which enable base-born infantrymen to send heavy bolts clear through shirts of mail. They are most unknightly things. In 1139 a Lateran Council actually forbade their use against Christians. Arbalists certainly are useful in sieges for clearing ramparts or repelling attack; but they take so long to wind up after every shot that their value in open battles is limited. Crossbowmen, unless carefully protected, can be ridden down by cavalry. So for another hundred years the mailed knight will hold his own. Then may come the English long-bow (far more rapid in its fire than the arbalist), and the day of the infantry will return.

Knights are continually fighting, or at least are exercising most violently in tourneys; yet the proportion of contestants slain is not very great. This is because their armor makes them almost invulnerable. After a battle, if you count the dead, you find they are usually all from the poor villein infantry or the luckless camp followers. Yet this harness has inconveniences. It is so heavy that the knight is the prisoner of his own armor. He can hardly mount his horse unassisted. Once flung from the saddle, he can scarcely rise without help. The lightest suit of armor in common use weighs at least fifty-five pounds. Powerful knights often wear much heavier. Yet to be able to move about with reasonable freedom, to swing one's shield, to control one's horse, and finally to handle lance or sword with great strength and precision, doing it all in this ponderous clothing of metal, are what squires like Aimery must learn to a nicety ere claiming knighthood. Wearing such armor, it is not remarkable that noblemen always prefer horseback, and fight on foot only in emergencies.

The prime unit in a suit of armor is the hauberk. He who has a fine hauberk, light (considering the material), pliable, and of such finely tempered steel as to be all but impenetrable, has something worth a small manor land. On this hauberk will often depend his life.

In the olden days, before about A.D. 1000, the hauberk was a shirt of leather or quilted cloth, covered by overlapping metal plates like fishscales. Now, thanks to ideas probably gathered from the Saracens, it is a shirt of ring mails, a beautiful network of fine chains and links, in the manufacturing of which the armorers

191

("the worthiest folk among all villeins," declares Conon) can put forth remarkable skill. The double or triple links are all annealed. The metal is kept bright and "white" by constant polishing (a regular task for the squires), and Conon has one gala shirt of mail which has been silvered. These garments form an almost complete protection, thanks to long sleeves, a long skirt below the knees, and a hood coming right over the head and partly covering the cheeks. A few brightly colored threads are sometimes worked into the links for ornament, but the flashing sheen of a good hauberk is its sufficient glory. The widowed Countess of Bernon has sent to Aimery, as token of good will, a ring shirt belonging to her husband. The knight-to-be swears that he will never dishonor its former owner while he wears it.

The next great unit in the armor is the helmet. Helmets have been steadily becoming more complicated, but most warriors still prefer a plain conical steel cap

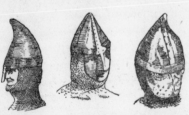

GERMAN HELMETS OF THE THIRTEENTH
CENTURY

encircled with a band of metal which may be adorned with gilt enamel. It has also a "nasal," a metal bar to protect the nose. Helmets are usually laced to the hood of the hauberk by small leathern straps. Since even a light and well-tempered helmet is an uncomfortable thing, you seldom wear it until just before going into action. "Lace helmets!" is the order to get ready for a charge; and after a knight is wounded the first friendly act is to unlace his headpiece. By the early thirteenth century helmets are beginning to have closed

visors to keep out missiles. But these visors are im-
movable without taking off the whole helm; and if
they get displaced and the small eyeholes are shifted,
the wearer is practically blind. The old-style open helm
will therefore continue in vogue until the coming of the
elaborate plate armor and the more manageable jointed
helms of the fourteenth century.

The third great protection is the shield. These have
been getting smaller as hauberks and helmets have
been improving; but one cannot trust solely to the body
armor. Besides, a shield is a kind of
offensive weapon. A sharp thrust with
its edge or a push with its broad surface
may often knock your opponent over.
Aimery's new shield is semioval and
slightly pointed at the bottom. It
covers its possessor from shoulder to
knees while sitting on his horse. The
stoutest kind of hide is used in making
it, with a backing of light, tough wood,
and a strong rim of metal. It curves
inward slightly for the better protection of the body. In the center is a
metal knob, usually of brilliant brass,

A THIRTEENTH-
CENTURY SHIELD

and the name "buckler" comes from this strong "boss"
(*boucle*). There is a big leather strap by which the
shield is ordinarily carried about the neck; but when
you go into action you run your left arm through two
strong handles.

A shield seems a simple object, but almost as much
skill goes into compacting the wood, leather, and metal
into one strong mass, not easily split or pierced, as into
making the hauberk. The front, of course, is highly
colored, and, although the heraldic "coat armor" has

yet hardly developed, every cavalier will flaunt some design of a lion, eagle, dragon, cross, or floral scroll. As for the handling of the shield, it is nearly as great a science as the handling of the sword; indeed, the trained warrior knows how to make shield and sword, or shield and lance, strike or fend together almost as one weapon.

Nevertheless, it is the strictly offensive weapons on which the noble warrior sets greatest store, and the weapon *par excellence* is the sword. Barons often love

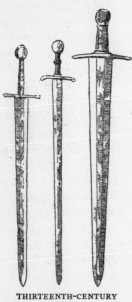

their swords perhaps more than they love their wives. They treat them almost as if they are persons. They try to keep them through their entire lives. According to the epics, the hero Roland liked to talk to his sword "Durendal," and Ogier to his "Brans." Conon swears one of his fiercest oaths, "by my good sword 'Hautemise,'" and Aimery has named his new sword "Joyeuse," after the great blade of Charlemagne.

There are many fashions in swords. You can always revive a flagging conversation by asking whether your companion likes a tapering blade or one of uniform thickness and weight. But the average weapon is about three

THIRTEENTH-CENTURY
SWORDS

inches wide at the hilt, and some thirty-two inches long in blade, slightly tapering. The hilt should be adorned with gilt, preferably set with pearls, and at

194

the end have a knob containing some small saints'
relics placed behind a bit of crystal to reveal the holy
objects. Conon's Hautemise thus contains some dried
blood of St. Basil, several hairs of St. Maurice, and lint
from the robe which St. Mary Magdalene wore after
she repented. These relics are convenient, for whenever a promise must be authenticated, the oath taker
merely claps his hand on his hilt, and his vow is instantly
registered in heaven.

The lance is the other great weapon of the cavalier.
Normally you use it in the first combats, and resort to
your sword only after the lance is broken. The average
lance is not more than ten feet long.[1] It has a lozenge-
shape head of fine Poitou or Castile steel. Care must
be taken in selecting straight, tough, supple wood for
the shaft and in drying it properly, for the life of the
warrior may depend on the reliability of his lance shaft,
and the amount of sudden strain which it can stand in
a horse-to-horse encounter. Ashwood is ordinarily
counted the best. As a rule there is no handle on the
butt. The art of grasping the round wood firmly, of
holding the long weapon level with the hip, and finally
of making the sharp tip strike squarely on the foeman's
shield (however he may slant the latter) is a matter of
training for wrist and eye which possibly exceeds all
skill in fencing. The whole body works together in
lance play. The horse must be guided by the knees;
the shield must be shifted with the left hand, the lance
with the right; the eye and nerves must be under perfect
control—and then, with man and horse fused into one

---

[1] Lances grew longer and stouter in the later Middle Ages. In
the fourteenth century they were about fifteen feet long and were
a kind of battering rams designed to dash one's opponent out of the
saddle, even if his armor were not pierced.

flying weapon, away you go—what keener sport can there be in the world?[1]

Yet there is something more important to the warrior than his panoply. What is a cavalier without his horse? Few, indeed, are the humans whom the best of barons

HORSE TRAPPINGS
Restored by Viollet-Le-Duc, from a manuscript in the Bibliothèque nationale.

will set above his favorite destrer. Your horses are comrades in hunt, tourney, and battle. By their speed and intelligence they save your life when squire or vassal avail not. When they fail, commend your soul to the saints—you will soon be in purgatory. From boyhood a cavalier has almost lived in the saddle. When in danger he knows all the capacities of his charger, and trusts him accordingly. Such a companion is to be treated with care. He is fed daintily; he is combed and tricked out like a delicate woman, and when ill he is physicked with more wisdom possibly than will be vouchsafed to most Christian deni-

[1] Another weapon not infrequently used was the mace, an iron-headed war club with a fairly long handle. In powerful hands such a weapon could fell the sturdiest opponent, however good his armor. The mace was somewhat the favorite of martial bishops, abbots, and other churchmen, who thus evaded the letter of the canon forbidding clerics to "smite with the edge of the sword," or to "shed blood." The mace merely smote your foe senseless or dashed out his brains, without piercing his lungs or breast!

Another weapon especially common in the early Middle Ages was the battle ax.

zens of a castle. Stories abound of how horses have succored their masters and stood watch over them while sleeping; and even one tale of how, when a knight returned after seven years, he was not recognized by his betrothed, but was by his faithful destrer. Another anecdote is how a knight answered, on being asked, "What will be your chief joy in paradise?" "To see Blanchart, my old horse."

Such being the case, the greatest pains are taken with horse breeding. Rich seigneurs rejoice in valuable stallions, and even monasteries keep breeding stables. A fine horse is an even more acceptable gift to a potentate than a notable hawk. Many horses are called "Arabian," but probably these come from North Africa. In France are raised horses equal to the best, especially those powerful steeds not quite so swift as the Oriental, but better able to bear a knight in ponderous armor. Gascon horses are in particular demand, and Conon takes peculiar satisfaction in a brood mare from Bordeaux. To ride a mare, however, is regarded as unknightly— "the women to the women"—probably an old Teutonic prejudice.

Aimery, while squire, found the care of the count's horses a prime duty. This was no trifle, for De Bernon, like every magnate, always kept several palfreys, handsome steeds of comfortable pace for peace-time riding, besides his special destrer—the great fierce war horse for battle. "To mount the high horse"—the destrer—is to show one's pride, not by vain boasting, but by displaying oneself in terrible weapons.[1] Of course, however, the haughty young squire did not have to bother about his

---

[1] The destrer was so called because it was supposed to be led at the knight's right hand (*dexter*) and ready for instant use, as he traveled on his less powerful palfrey.

lord's *roncins*, the ordinary steeds for the servants, or the *sommiers* for the baggage, humbler creatures still.

The favorite color for horses is white; after that dappled gray; after that bay or chestnut. Poets exhaust their skill in describing beautiful steeds, as if they were beautiful women. Wrote one bard about a Gascon horse: "His hair outshone the plumage of a peacock; his head was lean; his eye gray like a falcon; his breast large and square; his crupper broad; his thigh round; and rump tight. All beholding him exclaimed 'they had never seen a handsomer creature!'"

A KNIGHT OF THE THIRTEENTH CENTURY
From a bas-relief in the church of Saint-Nazaire at Carcassonne (Viollet-Le-Duc).

Such precious beings have names of honor. Charlemagne's destrer was the great Tencendur. Roland charged on Veilantif. Carbonel, Palantamur, Grisart are familiar names; and Conon's dearly loved companion is Regibet, whom, with all his fierceness, the baron could ride safely without bit, bridle, or spurs. The harness of the war horse is still very simple. The elaborate trappings and armor belong to a later age, but the stirrups and high saddle can be gilded and even set with pearls. More noticeable still are the dozens of little bells on different parts of the harness, which jingle merrily like sleigh bells of another age, as the great steeds pound along.

Aimery has lived where hauberks, helms, shields, swords, and lances have been the small coin of conversation since he has been able to talk. He has come to know horseflesh far better than he knows that other important mortal thing called "woman." He has now reached the age when he is extremely confident in his own abilities and equally confident that a fame like Roland's or Godfrey of Bouillon's is waiting him, provided the saints will assist. If he could have followed daydreaming, he would have been dubbed knight by the king himself after mighty deeds on the field of battle, while still covered with blood and grime; but such fair fortune comes only in the romances. At least, he is glad that he has a brother who is a brother indeed, and does not keep him in the background nor withhold from him his inheritance, as is the luck of so many younger sons.

A THIRTEENTH-CENTURY KNIGHT
From sculpture in the cathedral of Rheims.

It is a great grief that Aimery's father is not living to see his sons "come to knighthood." A good father always looks forward to that happy day; although in some disordered fiefs the seigneur will have to watch jealously lest the moment his offspring become full-fledged warriors they are not worked upon by disloyal vassals who will tell them, "Your father is old, and cannot rule the barony; seize it for yourselves." Even kings have to guard against this danger. Philip Augustus has knighted his heir, Prince Louis, only after the latter has taken a solemn oath not to enroll armed followers or perform other sovereign acts, save with his father's specific consent.

Theoretically, any knight can grant adubbement to

any person he thinks worthy; but actually a knight who dubs a villein, save in very exceptional circumstances, will jeopardize his own claim to nobility; and if he thrusts the honor on young, untried petty nobles, he will be laughed at, and their claims to the rank be promptly questioned. Fathers have often dubbed their sons, but better still, a young noble will seek the honor from his suzerain. Aimery learns with satisfaction that the Duke of Quelqueparte has consented to give the buffet of honor, for the higher the rank of the adubbing cavalier, the greater the glory of the ex-squire.

A THIRTEENTH-
CENTURY KNIGHT
From a bas-relief at the cathedral of Rheims (Viollet-Le-Duc).

The adubbement of knights is still a decidedly secular ceremony. Doubtless, the custom can be somewhat traced back to the crude rites whereby Germanic yo ths were initiated into the ranks of first-class warriors. Beyond the vigil in the church and the hearing of mass, there is not much that is religious about it. Clerical customs are indeed intruding. Young nobles like to visit Rome and be dubbed by the Pope. Others now are beginning to kneel before bishops and crave knighthood as a kind of lay consecration. Opinion, however, still frowns on this. Adubbement is a military business and churchmen had better keep their place. It will be more than a hundred years before religion and sentimentality can intrude much into what has long been a distinctly martial affair.

Easter, Ascension Day, Pentecost and St. John's day

are acceptable times for adubbements; but there are plenty of precedents for combining the ceremony with an important wedding, as it might be with the baptism of the heir to a barony. In the present case, moreover, as happens very often, Aimery, although the chief candidate for knighthood, is not alone. The duke will give the qualifying blow to five other young men, sons of the St. Aliquis vassals; and, indeed, twenty or more candidates are often knighted together at the king's court.

The night before the ceremony the whole castle is in as great a stir as before the wedding. More guests, more feasting, more jongleurs, perpetual singing, music, noise. Upon the table in the great hall Adela and Alienor (as substitutes for Aimery's mother) have laid out for public admiration the costume which he will assume the next day.

A BEGGAR

End of the twelfth century (from a manuscript in the Bibliothèque nationale).

The articles are selected as carefully as for the bridal —especially the spotless white shirt, the costly robe of ermine, and the spurs of gold. A host of beggars swarm in the bailey, for this occasion calls for an unusual recklessness of almsgiving. Even the invited guests are throwing around coppers, thereby proving their nobility.

As for Aimery, when the evening falls he and his five companions take a complete bath, not without considerable solemnity. This act has genuine significance. "It is to efface all villainies of the past life, that the bather may come out pure."[1] There are no boisterous splashing and merrymaking as the youths sit in the long wooden bathtubs. While they dress themselves, smiling sergeants appear with presents. Relatives, the suzerain, noble friends, have sent them articles of costly apparel, usually silken and fur-lined, to wear during their "vigil at arms." These are very much like the gifts that are showered upon a bride.

It is about half a mile from St. Aliquis castle to the parish church. After their bath the six candidates go hither, attended by the youths who are to become their squires. The company is joyous, but not noisy; violent mirth were unbecoming. At the church the squires-to-be leave the others. The candidates enter the great dark building. On the high altar a lamp burns, and on the side altar of St. Martin, the warrior saint, is a blaze of candles before a picture showing the holy man in the costume of a knight giving half of his military cloak to a beggar. The new weapons and armor of the candidates have been laid upon this altar. Then the vigil begins. The six knights-elect must not converse. They can only stand, or kneel at preference, for the whole ten hours—a serious physical ordeal.

During the solemn silence they are expected to pray to all their patron saints and make solemn vows to govern their whole life. It is a time for serious meditation,

---

[1] As chivalry took on its later and more religious cast, all the acts of an adubbement became clothed with allegorical meaning—*e.g.* besides the bath, the candidate must lie down (at least for a moment) upon a bed, because "it was an emblem of the rest which God grants to His followers, the brave knights." The candidate's snow-white shirt is to show that "he must keep his flesh from every stain if he would hope to reach heaven." His scarlet robe shows that he "must be ready to pour out his blood for Holy Church." His trunk hose of brown silk "remind him by their somber hue he must die." His white girdle "warns him that his soul should be stainless."

and Aimery beseeches, " Give to me honor," loyally
adding, " and to my brother long life! " He does not
ask " honor " for Conon also, for that would imply the
mighty baron still needed it. Then at last dawn creeps
through the storied windows. An old priest enters and
says mass, which the candidates follow gravely. At
six in the morning, with the summer air bright and
beautiful around them, they are all going again to the
castle, merry and talkative in reaction from the long
constraint.

Back in the castle Aimery is glad of an unusually
hearty breakfast. Not merely has the long vigil of
standing wearied him, but he will need all his strength
for the ordeal of the day. Next he goes to his chamber,
where the stripling who is to be his squire, the son of a
friendly baron, puts on his new master's gala dress.
White is the predominant color—" whiter than the
snow of the April flowers." Friends of his brother
come in to witness the process, and compliment the
candidate very openly upon his broad shoulders, healthy
complexion, and hardened sinews. These congratula-
tions become more pronounced when a bustling servitor
announces that " all is ready." Aimery strides into
the courtyard. The place seems crammed with knights
and dames, old and young, all in their best. Everybody (partly from politeness, partly from genuine enthusiasm) begins to call out: " How fine he is! A true
St. Aliquis! Right worthy of his brother! "

Immediately two loud trumpets announce the ceremony. A great orchestra of jongleurs raises a clamor.
The sight is magnificent. The castle court seems alive
with color. The women are in striking costumes, with
their long hair hanging braided on their shoulders.
The knights wear either bliauts, green, blue, or red, or

hauberks of dazzling brightness. The numerous priests present have on their finest robes. Even the monks seem less somber in their habits. All is noise, music, and animation.

The six candidates, followed by the whole rejoicing company, cross the bailey and the lists and go forth to the exercise ground by the garden. Here there is a platform covered with fine Saracen carpets. The Duke of Quelqueparte stands thereon, a majestic elderly warrior in gilded armor. The six candidates form a semicircle at the foot of the platform; then Aimery, as the brother of the giver of the fête, is the first to mount.

Immediately his " first sponsor " presents himself, a white-headed knight, a maternal uncle. Deliberately he kisses the candidate; then, kneeling, puts on his two golden spurs. As the uncle steps back, Conon and Olivier present themselves. They are the second and third sponsors. They pull a dazzling white steel hauberk over Aimery's head and adjust its cape. Upon this last they set the equally brilliant helmet, adorned with semiprecious stones. Then the fourth sponsor, the stately Count of Perseigne, girds on the candidate's sword, adding a few words of admonition how the younger man " must use it worthily "; to which the other responds by lifting the weapon and piously kissing the relics set in the hilt.

The four sponsors step back. The assembled jongleurs give a mighty crash of music. The duke lifts his clenched hand. " Bow the head! " he orders. " I will give you the blow." Aimery bows himself meekly to the greater lord, but his meekness is tested by the terrific stroke of his suzerain's fist, which sends him reeling. But the instant he recovers, the duke seizes him in comradely embrace. " Be brave, Sire Aimery. Recall that you are of a lineage famous both as seigneurs and as vassals, and do nothing base. Honor all knights. Give to the poor. Love God. Go!"

The happy cavalier replies: "I thank you, fair lord, and may God hear you. Let me always serve and love him." Then he descends the platform, and each of the other candidates mounts in turn to be knighted with similar ceremonies, although the sponsors (drawn from relatives or connections) will be different. The crowd standing round follows the proceedings with the uttermost interest, joining in a mighty shout each time the blow of honor is given. Then Conon, as master of ceremonies, waves to his marshal. "Bring in the horses!"

Immediately the new squires to the new knights appear, leading six steeds, faultlessly groomed and in beautiful harness—the gift of the baron to the candidates. The instant the horses are in front of the platform the new cavaliers break from their statuesque rigidity. Clothed as they are now in heavy hauberk and helmet, they run, each man to his horse, and try to leap to the saddle at one bound without touching foot to the stirrups. An anxious moment for them; an equally anxious moment for parents, brothers, or sisters. From the time a young nobleman is in his cradle his mother will discuss with his father, "Will he make the 'leap' when he is knighted?" It is one of the great tests of a martial education, and one that must be taken with the uttermost publicity. Truth to tell, Aimery and his friends have been practicing the feat with desperate energy for the last month. Done! All six have mounted fairly! Salvos of applause. His friends are congratulating Conon: "Such a brother!" The kinsfolk of the other young knights are similarly overwhelmed.

Meantime the happy new cavaliers hold their horses
205

montionless for an instant while their squires run to
them with their lances and triangular shields. The
lances have long bright pennons with three tails which
float down upon their riders' helmets. This act performed, the riders put their steeds through all manner
of gallops and caracoles, and next, "singing high with
clear voice," away they go, flying toward a place on the
exercise ground where the *quintain*—the wooden
manikin warrior—has been set up.[1] To smash its shield
and fling it to the ground with a single lance thrust is
another unescapable test. This ordeal also is met by
Aimery and his peers with tolerable glory for all. After
this sport the new knights are expected to *behourder*—
that is, to indulge in mock duels with blunted weapons.
These were not counted serious contests, but often
enough, if blood is high and rivalry keen, they can take
on the form of vigorous combats. To-day, however,
everybody is in too good humor for violent blows;
besides, the real tournament begins to-morrow, and it is
best to keep strength and weapons until then.

The morning is now spent. Seigneurial appetites
have been nobly whetted. The pavilions are again
ready in the garden, and the cooks have prepared
pasties, joints of meat, and great quantities of roast
poultry, even as for the wedding feast. There is another
round of gorging and guzzling, only this time the six
new knights occupy the place of honor, and the master
jongleur's story is not concerning sad Tristan, but about
how brave Godfrey of Bouillon stormed Jerusalem.

Everybody is commenting upon the admirable grace,
modesty, and proficiency in arms of Sire Aimery. A
count has approached Conon already before dinner.
"Fair Baron, you have a brother who is a credit to your

[1] See p. 185.

name. Is it true he is to receive Petitmur? I have a daughter in her fifteenth year; her dowry will be——"

But Conon tactfully shrugs his shoulders. "Fair Count, my brother will indeed receive Petitmur; but to-day he is knighted and can speak for hmself. Make your marriage proposals to him. I have no longer the right to control him."

Chapter XIII: The Tourney.

HEN Conon decided to give a tourney as a climax to the wedding and adubbement festivities, he sent out several servitors of good appearance and loud voices to course the country for some twenty leagues around. These varlets bawled their proclamation at every crossroad, village, inn, and castle gate.

"The Wednesday after St. Ancildus Day, good people! In the meadow at St. Aliquis by the Claire. The Wednesday after St. Ancildus day! Let all come who love to see or to join in deeds of valor!"

This is "crying the tourney." As soon as the news spreads abroad, every petty sire takes council with his wife whether he can afford to go. The women begin to hunt up their best bliauts and furs; the men to furbish their armor. Soon various cavaliers, arranging with their friends, undertake to form challenge parties. They write on a scroll "At the castle of A—— there are seven knights who will be ready to joust with all comers to St. Aliquis." This they post on a tree by the wayside in order that other lordlings may organize similar parties to confront them.

Tourneys are to be reckoned as "little wars themselves, and the apprenticeship for great ones." They have an inconceivably prominent place in feudal life. Vainly the Church objects to them. All nobles will tell you that without tourneys you can never train good warriors.

Early Tourneys Were Battles

Tourneys, however, bring profit and pleasure to all manner of people—no cause for unpopularity. The "joy women," who rush to ply their sinful wiles despite every attempt to restrict them; the common villeins, who drop their work to enjoy one grand holiday; and the merchants, who really hold a small fair near the lists, all are delighted. As for men of gentle blood, an English chronicler can state the case alike for France and England: "A knight cannot shine in war if he has not been prepared for it in tourneys. He must have seen his own blood flow, have had his teeth crackle under the blow of his adversary, have been dashed to the earth with such force as to feel the weight of his opponent, and disarmed twenty times; he must twenty times have retrieved his failures, more than ever set on combat." *Then* he will be ready for actual war and can hope to conquer!

In early feudal days tourneys differed from battles merely in that the time and the place were fixed in advance, and fair conditions arranged. According to the epics, at "Charlemagne's court" the nobles often got tired of ordinary sports and "demanded a tourney." The results were merely pitched battles in which many were slain and many more wounded.

There was no luxury, pomp, or patronage by fair ladies at the earliest tourneys.[1] They were exceedingly violent pastimes in which "iron men" measured their strength and rejoiced in deadly blows. Since then tourneys have been getting less brutal. An important spectacular element is intruding. The rules of combat are becoming more elaborate, fewer knights are killed,

---

[1] The earliest recorded tourney is alleged to have been about A.D. 850. In Germany they long continued to be excessively brutal. As late as 1240 one was held near Cologne at which more than sixty persons perished.

and there is an appeal to something better than mere fighting instinct. On the other hand, in the thirteenth century jousts and mêlées are far from being mere displays of fine armor and fine manners. The military element is still uppermost. Furthermore, since the vanquished cavaliers are the prisoners of the victors and are subject to ransom, or at least their horses and armor are forfeit, certain formidable knights go from tourney to tourney deliberately seeking profit by taking prisoners. In short, so dangerous are tourneys even yet, that as recently as 1208, when Prince Louis, heir of King Philip, was knighted, his father made him swear he would merely watch them as spectator—for the life of a prince royal is too precious to risk in such affairs.

The popes have long since denounced tourneys. Innocent II, Eugenius III, Alexander III, and finally the great and wise Innocent III have prohibited Christians from participating in the same under peril of their souls. But *cui bono?* Great barons who shudder at the thought of eating beef on Fridays defy the Church absolutely when it comes to a matter of "those creations of the devil" (to quote St. Bernard of Clairvaux) in which immortal souls are so often sped.

When Conon decides to add a tourney as a climax to his fête, a score of carpenters are hired down from Pont-debois to help out the levy of peasants in preparing the lists and lodges. Some of the guests have already come to the wedding and the adubbement, but many more arrive merely for the knightly contests. For these, of course, the baron affords only limited hospitality—a good place to pitch their tents, water and forage, with perhaps an invitation to the castle hall at dinner time to certain leaders. Many visitors can get accommodation in the better houses in the village, or at the monastery;

210

but, the weather being fine, the majority prefer to set out their pavilions by the Claire, and the night before the sports begin there seem to be tents enough for an army.

The visitors come in their best bliauts and armor. Certain powerful counts collect as many lesser nobles as possible, even making up bands of twenty knights, twenty squires, a great number of ladies and waiting women, also some hundreds of ignoble servitors. Except for the presence of the women and the omission of military precautions, you might think them going to an ordinary muster for war.

Meantime, in the wide exercise ground where Sire Aimery had been dubbed, the special lists are made ready. These are simple affairs, something like a race course of other days. Two pairs of strong wooden palisades are erected. The outer line is shoulder high; the inner is lower and has many openings. Between the two lines is the space for spare horses, squires, attendants, and heralds; also for privileged spectators. The humbler onlookers will peer standing over the outer palisade, but behind and above this rise the series of lodges, shaded with tentlike canopies, floored with carpets, and gay with pennons. In them will be stationed the ladies and the older, less martial knights. The space within the lists is some hundred yards long by fifty wide. That evening Conon and Sire Eustace survey the decorations, the forest of banners waving over the colored pavilions of the visitors, and listen complacently to the glad hum of voices and the jongleur's chants everywhere arising.

"Ah, fair Baron," says the seneschal, "all France will talk of this spear breaking until Christmas! It will be a great day for St. Aliquis."

At gray dawn the heralds from the castle go through

211

the avenues of tents, calling, monotonously: "Let the jousters make ready! Let the jousters make ready!"

Soon squires half dressed are seen running to and fro. There is a great saddling and girdling, neighing and stamping. A few pious knights and dames hurry to the castle chapel for a mass very hastily said, but the bulk of the company cross themselves and mutter: "We will be sinners to-day. The blessed saints are merciful!" Presently, by the time the sun is well above the trees, everybody is bound for the lists. The ladies, if possible, ride white mules and are dressed as splendidly as for their own weddings. Not in many a day will St. Aliquis see again such displays of marten, ermine, and vair, of sendel and samite, of gold thread and pearls. The common folk point and applaud loudly when an unusually handsomely clad dame sweeps by. What right have grand folk to claim the obedience of the lesser, if they cannot delight the public gaze by their splendors? As for the jongleurs, their name is legion. The whole affair is characterized by a "music" becoming deafening.

While the dames and other noncombatants take seats in the lodges, the six camp marshals—distinguished knights in charge of the contests—appear in the lists. They advance on foot, wearing very brilliant bliauts. Conon, as giver of the festivities, is naturally at their head. Behind follow the humbler born heralds and pursuivants who will assist them, and encourage the combatants with such cries as: "Remember whose son you are!" "Be worthy of your ancestry!" There is also a large squad of varlets and sergeants to keep order, bring new lances, clear away broken weapons, and rescue fallen knights. Conon's keen eye sweeps the tilt yard. Everything is ready. The baron bows politely to his suzerain, the duke and duchess, in the central lodge; then he raises a white baton. "Bring in the jousters!" he commands.

Instantly there is a great blare of trumpets from the end of the lists farthest from the castle. Four gorgeously arrayed heralds lead the procession on foot. Then comes a jongleur on horseback, playing with his sword, tossing it high in the air and catching as it whirls downward. Next come the actual contestants, some eighty knights riding two by two. They do down one side of the lists and back the other. Some cavaliers turn deliberately to ogle the ladies in the lodges, and the gentle dames (old and young) are not backward in leaning forward and waving in reply. It is a sight to stir the blood—all the pageantry of war, without as yet its slaughter; the presence of gorgeously clad women in graceful attitudes; and the air charged with the excitement of brave deeds and of genuine perils to come. Suddenly all the knights begin to sing. The women catch up the chorus of some rousing melody which makes the lists shake. The cavaliers compel their horses to prance and curvet as they go by some lady of especial favor. From many lances are hanging bright streamers—not banners, but sleeves and stockings, the gifts of friendly dames. The younger knights are rejoiced by seeing damsels, whose eye they have taken, rise in the lodges and then and there, before the cheering hundreds, fling them "gages of love." It is so with young Sire Aimery as he modestly rides near the tail of the procession. The daughter of the approving count stands boldly and casts him a long red ribbon wherewith she had braided her hair. The other new knights receive similar tokens from unabashed admirers. This process will keep up though the games. The shrieking, excited ladies will presently cast into the lists gloves, girdles, and ribbons. Many will sit at the end with only their flying hair, and their pelissons and chemises for costume.

Some combatants are intent on grim business. These are the professional jousters, determined to get as many ransoms as possible and to maintain their own proud reputation. Their armor is beautifully burnished; but it is quite plain. They have prepared for a regular battle. Other knights have painted their scabbards, lance butts, and shields with brilliant white, red, or black. On the crests of their helmets they have set outlandish figures—monsters, heads of birds, or of women. As in fancy balls of other days, their aim is to attract attention by the peculiarity of their costumes. Conon does not desire a bloody tourney and the funeral of several friendly knights as a climax to his gayety. Orders have therefore been given that all lance points are to be blunted, also that all sword edges and points be rounded. The tournament lances, too, are lighter than the battle lances and made of brittle wood.[1] Nevertheless, the blows struck will be terrible. The best leach from Pontdebois is already in the duke's lodge, and his services will be needed.

Strictly speaking, a tourney falls into two parts—the jousting always comes first, with the mêlée, which is the real tourney proper, as the grand climax to the entire occasion.

What follows might seem to men of other days somewhat monotonous after the novelty has worn away, although the first contests are exciting enough. The competing knights have been told off in pairs, partly by

[1] Often sharp weapons were used in tournaments, especially between combatants who fought *à outrance,* to clear up some desperate personal grudge. Many noblemen were thus slain—*e.g.,* in a tourney "in the French fashion" at London, the Earl of Essex was killed in 1216.

A TOURNAMENT IN THE TWELFTH CENTURY

At the back are the galleries where the ladies sit; then, near the entrance to the lists, some cavaliers wait their turn to take part in the contest; in the center, some servants and others of the combatants pick up one of the combatants who has been thrown from his horse by his adversary.

mutual consent, partly by the tactful arrangement of the camp marshals. After the procession around the lists, the contestants take their stations, some in the saddle, some dismounted in the spaces between the barriers. There is an awesome hush along the lodges and in the great standing throng of the vulgar. A herald calls in loud voice, "Let him come to joust who wishes to do battle!" Instantly two keen trumpets answer each other from opposite ends of the lists, and two pursuivants come forward. These worthies are really only jongleurs on less exciting days. They have now taken the deniers of two young barons who are anxious to make a brave appearance. The pursuivants are grotesquely dressed with bright parti-colored mantles and bliauts. Each begins bawling shrilly even while his rival is calling: "Here is the good cavalier and baron, Ferri of St. Potentin. A brave knight of a valorous house. He will teach a lesson to his enemies!" "Here is the good cavalier, Raoul, eldest son of the most puissant Count of Maurevay. Watch now his deeds, all you who love brave actions!"

Then each of the twain reviles the master of the other: "*He!* Your Sire Raoul is the son of a crow. All his friends will this day be ashamed of him. Let him find his ransom money!"

"Silence all boasts, you pursuivant of a caitiff master. Sire Ferri, if he outlives the shock, will have his spurs struck from his heels as being unworthy of knighthood!"

Meantime the two champions, rigid as statues, suffer their squires to lead them upon their tall destrers to opposite ends of the lists. When they are facing and their squires have nodded that their masters are ready, a marshal waves his white baton, calling loudly, "In the name of God and St. Michael, do your battle!"

215

All the dames, nobles, and base-born rise in the lodges and shout together when suddenly the two knights and their mighty horses spring to life. The ground quakes and the sod flies when they rush down the lists as if hurried toward each other by irresistible force. As they gallop, each bends low in the saddle—swings his shield to cover his body, lowers his helmet almost to the top of his shield, swerves his horse so as to pass his opponent on the right, and with sure grip drops his lance point before him.

"Crash!" The splintering of wood can be heard through the din from the lodges. Both horses are thrown upon their haunches and are casting out great clods of earth. Each knight is flourishing the broken butt of a lance and across the shield of each there is a long jagged mark.

"Fairly broken! Fairly broken! A noble course!" cries everyone. The two contestants wheel gracefully and canter back to their stations. Squires run up with fresh lances. Sire Raoul takes a new shield, the earlier one showing signs of splitting as well as being battered. Another course; another crash—and two more broken lances. But at the third shock Sire Ferri meets utter humiliation. He indeed meets Raoul's lance fairly on his shield and again the tough wood is splintered, but excitement, overconfidence, or the intervention of the devil makes his wrist a little unsteady. At the moment of collision Raoul swerves his body a trifle to the left. Ferri's lance misses his foe's shield entirely. It flies off in the air, and in the confusion escapes from his hand. There is hooting from the villeins; worse still, there is shrill derision from all the lodges. Sire Ferri rides back to his post, grinding his teeth and swearing blasphemously. He must now pay a ransom to Raoul for his horse and armor, despite the boastings of his pursuivant,

216

and not even have the melancholy consolation of knowing that he was unhorsed in a fair collision.

But the next duel has a more exciting ending. Two cavaliers who now engage are exceptionally experienced knights. At the first charge both horses sustain such a shock when the lances shiver that their masters can barely force them to their feet. At the second charge the more skillful rider holds his lance so squarely that, instead of its breaking, the opposing knight is fairly flung out of the saddle—dashed from his horse and sprawled headlong with a great clattering of armor. The heralds and squires run to him and find that, thanks to his hauberk, he has escaped dangerous wounds, though he coughs away several teeth. Great is the excitement in the lodges.

Several duels after this end in honorable draws. The knights have agreed to "break three lances fairly for the love of the ladies," and gallantly do so. There are no victors or vanquished. Then it is proclaimed that two seigneurs from Champagne, Sire Emeri and Sire Lourent, having an especial desire to "debate together" (their original quarrel had been over dice) are resolved to fight until one cries "mercy," and will continue their battle on foot should either be unhorsed. Three times they break lances unscathed, but the fourth time Lourent's stirrup parts and he is pitched upon the sands. Instantly he is free from his snorting, plunging destrer and on his feet, flourishing his great sword. Emeri now might lawfully ride against him, but it is no chivalrous thing for a mounted knight to attack an unmounted one. Down he leaps also, making his blade dance above his head like a stream of light. Then to the infinite joy of the lodges the two cavaliers hack and feud with each other for a good ten minutes, till the blood streams down their faces, the bright paint on their shields is marred, and the crests of their helmets have vanished in dentings. At last Emeri flings his strength into a lucky blow. His sword is blunted, but by sheer weight of the stroke the blade smashes Lourent's shield asunder, descending like a smith's sledge upon his helmet. Lourent topples like a log.

A great shout goes through the lodges. "Dead!" cry many; but, to the relief of the women, the word presently spreads that he is only soundly stunned, though the leech says that "he will not fight again till Christmas."

The duels continue all through the morning. There is an interval while cakes and wine are passed through the lodges and loaves are thrown among the plebeians. Most duels seem decidedly similar, but each is followed with undiminishing delight. The ladies no less than their brothers and husbands grasp all the niceties of the contests—the methods whereby each champion holds his lance and shield and controls his horse are wisely discussed by a hundred pairs of pretty lips. Between each tilt the heralds, besides praising the valor of the next pair of combatants, keep up their cries, "Largesse, gallant knights! Largesse!" and now one, now another baron rises in the lodges to fling coins among villeins (whose rough scrambling causes much merriment), or even to toss money to the heralds themselves—which they never hesitate to pick up.

Many knights are content with a single passage at arms, but some who have been successful once tempt fortune a second time. These are likely to be the professional champions, and they give remarkable exhibitions of perfect horsemanship and lance play. As the afternoon advances, for variation, there is a fight at the barriers. A stout wooden bar about waist high is set

across the middle of the lists, and seven knights from
one seigneury and seven from another undertake to cross
the same, while preventing the other party from ad-

KNIGHTLY COMBAT ON FOOT
(From an old print.)

vancing. They fight on foot with sword and mace. It
is desperate work; and when at last one party has
forced its way across, four of the defeated side have
broken bones, despite their hauberks, and all-but-
broken heads, despite their helmets.

Then a very arrogant baron who has already won three ransoms determines to increase his wealth. Stationing himself at the head of the lists, he bids his pursuivant challenge all comers. There is a long hush. Sire Paul has made such a trade of his prowess that assuredly there seems something mercantile about his valor, yet assuredly he is a terrible man. Suddenly the lodges begin to cry, "A St. Aliquis!" Sire Aimery himself (who earlier had broken three lances very neatly with a friend) is sending down his pursuivant.

All the older knights mutter: "A fearful risk for the lad! Let him pray to his saints." Conon demands angrily of Olivier, "Could not you keep back the boy from this folly?" But does not Heaven favor the young and brave? Perhaps it is because Sire Paul has let himself become careless; perhaps because his squire has forgotten to tighten his saddle girths; perhaps because St. Génevieve cannot allow her votary to undergo disgrace thus early in his knighthood. In any case, results confound the wiseacres. "The pitcher that goes too often to the well is broken," dryly observes Father Grégoire, when at the first course Sire Paul is ignominiously flung from the saddle. *Hé!* Sire Aimery will now have more sleeves, girdles, and stockings than can ever flutter from any one lance, and his kinsfolk are out of their wits for joy! No victory could ever be more praised and popular.

So ends the jousting, and that night round St. Aliquis blaze the great camp fires of the company, all cooking most hearty suppers (after fasting almost all day), everybody visiting from tent to tent, fighting the day's contests over again, condoling with the defeated and praising the victors. Alliances, both military and matrimonial, are negotiated between consequential barons;

220

the jongleurs produce tricks and songs; there is a great deal of dancing by the red firelight; and also, one fears, much hard drinking and most unseemly revelry.

The next day there is the climax to the festival, the mêlée. Really, it is nothing less than a pitched battle on a small scale. The details have been arranged at a council of the more prominent seigneurs at the castle. About forty knights on a side are to fight under the leadership of the Viscount of Gemours and the Baron of Dompierre. The space in the lists is insufficient. They go to a broad, convenient meadow across the Claire, where the noncombatants can watch from a safe distance. The marshals array the two companies "at least a bow-shot apart." Groups of friendly knights are set together and are placed opposite to groups of rivals with whom they are anxious to collide. The great banners of the houses of Gemours and Dompierre flutter in the center of each respective array, and all the little banderoles of the various knights wave with them.

A COMBAT IN THE TWELFTH CENTURY
From the manuscript of Herrade of Landsperg (Schultz).

When all is ready, Conon gives the signal, "Charge them in God's name!"

Each baron is expected to charge a particular foe, but all are liable to be swerved in the great rush of men and horses. The two flashing squadrons of cavalry come together like thunderbolts. All the danger of the jousts is present, and another more terrible—that of being trampled to death, if once down, by the raging horses. There is no real leadership. Gemours and Dompierre

221

merely try to set examples of valor and to push their banners forward as rallying points. At first the fighting is good-humored, but when the lances are broken and everyone is smiting one another with sword or mace, the contest becomes desperate. A fearful cloud of dust rises, almost blinding to the combatants, and rendering their blows more reckless.

After the fight has progressed some time, certain of the less adventurous knights begin to drop out. The squires dive into the murk of warriors and horses and drag to safety now this, now another fallen cavalier. At last, just as Conon is considering whether he should not proclaim a "draw," the Gemours banner is observed to topple. A desperate attempt is made to right it, but it sinks again amid a rending shout from the victors. The uplifted hands fall. The frantic horses are brought under control. "A Dompierre! A Dompierre!" bawl all the heralds. And so the mêlée ends.

No one, thanks to excellent armor, is dead, although one heir to a barony is in a desperate condition and several shoulders and thighs are broken. It is futile to count the shattered collar bones and ribs. "A very *gentle* passage at arms!" says the Duke to Conon, congratulating his vassal on the fête and its climax. All the other seigneurs join in similar praises. That night there is another round of festivities and of visiting. The next dawn the whole company scatters. The jongleurs' music has ceased at last. There is no more dancing. After over two weeks of intensifying gayety St. Aliquis suddenly returns to sober, normal life.

Alienor, after tearful farewells, departs with her husband for Burgundy. Aimery rides over to his little castle at Petitmur, which he will hold as his brother's vassal. Adela lectures her maids on the need of catching up with their weaving, while Conon holds anxious conferences with his chief provost on the costs of the celebration.

Doubtless the affair has brought glory to the seigneury. More than a hundred knights and two hundred squires or unknighted nobles have attended, along with thousands of villeins. But how costly have been the furs, drinking cups and fine weapons presented the guests, the destrers given the new knights, above all the vast quantity of provisions devoured! Just God! If Conon had realized the entire expense he would hardly have embarked on the whole undertaking. The worst is that the peasants of the whole barony are so demoralized that it will be two weeks more ere they return to work. Money must be borrowed from Jew Simon in Pontdebois to tide over the crisis. The baron must give up his usual visit to the king's court at Paris. He must also dismiss certain cherished schemes of picking a quarrel with the Sire of Rideau and forcing a private war. Thanks be to Our Lady, however, François need not be knighted these ten years, when (being an eldest son) an "aide" can be levied on all the vassals to help cover the cost.

Chapter XIV: A Baronial Feud. The Siege of a Castle.

E have visited St. Aliquis in days of peace, and at peace the seigneury remains while we tarry. But peace and pageants no more deadly than tourneys are seldom the continuous state of things. "Rumors of wars" there are every day; actual wars every few years. Let the saints be praised if such contests are largely local, are not bitterly fought out, and are composed before they have caused worse things than the harrying of certain villages of helpless, innocent peasants.

In spite of the efforts of clergy and of kings it will be truthfully written of feudal France that "war was practically a permanent scourge almost everywhere. *In the society of that day war was the normal state.*" When these wars are waged by mighty kings one can at least take the comfort that perhaps they are settling long-standing questions concerning many people, and, however dreadful, may pave the way for lasting peace. Such a war has lately found its climax in the decisive battle of Bouvines, whereof more anon. But most of the wars are for miserably petty stakes. Time was when every insignificant sire holding a feeble tower considered that he had the right to declare war on any neighbor with whom he argued the rights to a trout stream. Yet the case is changing. Suzerains are insisting that the lower class of vassals arbitrate their quarrels and not embroil the neighborhood. Nevertheless, the superior type of barons still claim war as their "noble right." The amount of local fighting can hardly be computed.

There is something abnormal about a powerful seigneur who (if blessed with a long lifetime) does not have at least *one* war with each of his several suzerains, a war with the bishops and abbots with whom he has contact, a war with each neighboring noble of equal rank, unless their houses are unwontedly friendly, and a war with at least some of his own vassals. A war can start out of a dispute about a bit of land, an ill-defined boundary, or the exact obligations of a feudal tenure. Theoretically, the suzerain can interfere between wrangling vassals. Practically, he had better let them fight it out, at least till there seems real danger that their fiefs will be permanently injured. Then he can sometimes compel a truce.

Unfortunately, however, God often permits the bitterest wars to be fought within the fief itself. Sons fight with fathers—"the Old Man" will not let his grown boys rule the seigneury to their liking.[1] Younger brothers battle with elder brothers over the inheritance. Nephews attack uncles who seem prolonging their guardianship. Sons even attack a widowed mother to seize her dower lands. These are only some of the things which make the devil rub his taloned fingers.

Nevertheless, certain limitations are intruding, customs that have nearly the force of law.[2] For example, if a vassal attacks his suzerain, none but his own family

---

[1] Primogeniture did not exist on the Continent as in England. The elder son was entitled to the largest share of the estate, but by no means to the whole.

[2] They became formal law by about 1260, in the days of Louis IX.

(among his noble followers) can aid him. Also, in any case, at least a week's notice must be given ere the war is commenced. After the war does begin, forty days' respite must also be granted your foe's relatives ere attacking them. In the interval they are entitled to proclaim their neutrality and so to become safe. Again, one is supposed to respect priests and women and minors. Finally, if a truce is made the suzerain is bound to punish the violators. Such understandings rob warfare of part of its horrors, but do not prevent infinite blood and misery.

As for that motive which prevails in other ages for waging wars—*patriotism*—often it does not seem to exist so vitally. Certainly Frenchmen ought to make a common front against Germans, Italians, English, etc., but lapses from this obligation are not always condemned as morally outrageous. Quite recently the Count of Boulogne, being at odds with King Philip, took money from both the King of England and the Emperor of Germany to raise up enemies against the King of France; and the count evidently felt that this was a proper measure against an obnoxious suzerain. The great significant tie is that of *personal loyalty*.[1] It is horrible to betray the prince to whom you have sworn fealty. A suzerain will call out his host by a summons to "my vassals," he will seldom think of appealing to "my fellow countrymen."

We have said that wars are incessant; yet there is one strange thing about them—*pitched battles are very rare*. The campaigns abound in petty skirmishes— valorous duels, surprises of small castles, occasional clashes of cavalry, and, above all, in the pitiless ravaging

[1] French opinion, of course, condemned this count, not for being a traitor to his country, but for breach of fealty to his personal lord.

of the lands, farms, and villages of the helpless peasantry. What better way to put pressure on your foe than to reduce his villeins to such misery that they can render him nothing in money or kind and that he thus be brought to poverty? If you have the weaker force you will not think of meeting an invader in battle. You will shut yourself up in your castles when you see the burning villages, stifle your pride, remain passive, and trust that after the "forty days' service" of your enemy's vassals is expired they will weary of the operations and not venture to besiege your strongholds. Then when the foe's army is beginning to disperse you can employ some neutral baron or abbot to negotiate peace.

Even when kings are in the field, with really large armies, somehow the opposing forces seldom risk a decisive encounter. They maneuver, skirmish, and negotiate underhandedly with the uncertain elements in the hostile camp. The upshot often is that the invading army, having devoured all the provisions in the open country and not daring to besiege strong cities with a powerful enemy close at hand, retreats homeward.

Of course, sometimes there are great battles with great results. Such in the eleventh century was Senlac, when Duke William the Norman won all England. Such, more recently, was the famous day at Bouvines. Such marked several of the Crusades against the Infidels, particularly the great and successful First Crusade, and the Third Crusade, when Richard the Lion Hearted seemed to come nearer than any other feudal general to being a really able tactician, if not a great strategist.

These battles are few and far between—and even the mighty Richard's ideal style of fighting was rather that of a headlong cavalier followed by only fifteen knights and with his ponderous ax hewing a bloody lane through

227

a host of Infidels, than that of a careful commander
coolly directing a mighty army. Besides, most of the
wars between second-class barons involve very small
forces. They are only affairs for hundreds. If matters
come to grips, the best captain is he who orders "Advance, banner bearer! Follow me, vassals!" and leads
the headlong charge.

Enormous pains have been taken in training the individual warrior. For personal prowess the French
cavalier is as formidable an individual as ever shared the
sins of mankind. But he is trained only in simple
evolutions when maneuvering in companies. He dis-
likes taking orders. He wearies of long campaigns. His
camps are very unhygienic and subject to pestilence.
Wars, in short, are to him superb games, exciting, spiced
with danger, and played for large stakes—which give the
zest; but, save in the Crusades and certain other rare
cases, the higher objects which supply wars with their
sole justification escape him entirely. "Warfare," in
the true scientific sense of the word, is something whereof
your baron is usually in complete ignorance.

Earlier in this recital it has been seen that Baron
Conon, soon after he obtained the seigneury, engaged
in a brisk feud with the Viscount of Foretvert. This was
so like many other feuds in the region that it is well to
obtain an authentic history thereof from Father Grégoire,
who knows all the circumstances.

The origin of the quarrel (he tells us) was commonplace. Doubtless the viscount had a contemptuous
opinion of his then young and untried neighbor. There
was a wood betwixt the two seigneuries which had been
haltingly claimed by Foretvert; but all through terrible
Baron Garnier's time none but St. Aliquis peasants had

been suffered to cut fagots there. Now suddenly Huon, one of the forester's helpers, appeared before Conon in a piteous plight. His thumbs had been hewn clean off. He had been chopping timber on the debatable land, had been seized by the viscount's men, haled before their master, and the latter had ordered this treatment, adding, with a grin: "This is the drink penny for touching a twig in my forests. Tell your young lord to spread these tidings among his villeins."

When Conon had heard this taunt, his squires trembled at the workings of his face. Then and there he pulled out his sword, placed his hands on the hilt, pressing upon the reliquary, and swore "By God's eyes!"[1] that he would make the viscount and all the spawn of Foretvert swallow enough of their own blood to be drunk to damnation.

"Certes," says Father Grégoire, "he could not as a Christian baron do less; for the lord who lets another seigneur oppress his villeins is no lord; and if he had failed to resent such an insult none of his vassals would have obeyed him."

That same day one of Conon's squires rode to Foretvert. He bore a "cartel," a bunch of fur plucked from his master's pelisson.[2] He was only a young squire, but carried his head high. There was some danger in being such a messenger. The squire had to be as insolent as possible without actually provoking Foretvert to violate the protection due to a herald. Into the great hall of the offending seigneur strode said squire, carrying a bough of pine in his left hand, the bunch of fur in the right. His coming had been anticipated. The

[1] The terrible oath of Henry II of England and other great chieftains.

[2] Later custom would probably have sent a fur-trimmed glove.

greetings, as he was led up to the dais where the viscount presided, were cold and ceremonious. Then the squire straightened his slim form and shook out his long mantle.

"Sire Viscount, my master, the Baron of St. Aliquis, demands of you satisfaction. If you do not make good the wrongs you have done to him and his, I loyally defy you in his name."

And down he flung the cartel.

"It is fitting," returned the viscount, mockingly, "a mere boy should be a squire for a lad. Tell your very youthful master that I will soon teach him a lesson in the art of war."

So with a few more such exchanges the squire rode homeward. Meantime at St. Aliquis things were stirring. The great bell on the donjon was ringing. Zealous hands were already affixing the raw hides to the projecting wooden hoardings upon the battlements, All the storehouses for weapons in the bailey were being opened for a distribution of arms. From the armory forge came a mighty clangor of tightening rivets. The destrers must have caught the news, they stamped so furiously in the stables. In the great hall Conon sat with Adela (a wise head in martial matters), Sire Eustace, and the other knights in serious debate.

Simultaneously, messengers were pricking away to all the little villages and to the fortalices of the vassals. To the villeins they cried: "The baron proclaims war with Foretvert. Bring your cattle and movables near to the castle for protection." To the vassals they announced, "Come with all the men you are bound in duty to lead, seven days from to-day, to St. Aliquis, armed and provisioned for service; and hereof fail not or we burn you." This right to burn the dwellings of vassals who failed to obey the summons to the ban was one of long standing in feudal lands. Other messengers proclaimed the ban by blowing the trumpet at every crossroads in the barony. To have disobeyed this call would have been the depth of feudal depravity. None of the vassals ventured to hesitate. On the contrary, most of them, like good liegemen, affected to show joy at this chance to follow their seigneur, crying at once, "My horse! My horse!" and ordering out all their retainers.

The abbot of the monastery now, as duty bound, visited both leaders and vainly tried to negotiate peace. He met with courteous thanks and prompt refusals. While he was thus squaring with his conscience, Conon was notifying all his outlying relatives. He was also sending to several powerful barons who had received armed assistance from St. Aliquis in the past, and who were now tactfully reminded of this fact. He likewise sent an especially acceptable messenger to his suzerain the duke, to convince the latter that Foretvert was entirely wrong, and that the duke had better not interfere. Thanks to this energy and diplomacy, by the end of the week the whole countryside had been roused, the peasants had driven most of their cattle so close to St. Aliquis castle that they could be protected, and many villeins, deserting their hovels, were camping in the open (it being fine summer weather) in the space between the barbican and bailey. As for Conon, with pride he mustered his "array"—one hundred knights or battle worthy squires; two hundred sergeants—horsemen of non noble birth; and some seven hundred footmen—villeins with long knives, pikes, arbalists, big axes, etc.—of no great value in open battle, but sure to have their place in other work ahead.

From Foretvert reports came in of similar preparation. But the viscount had quarreled with some of his relations.

He had broken a promise he once made to help a certain sire in a feud. His immediate vassals responded to his call, but they felt that their lord ought to have consulted them ere provoking St. Aliquis so grossly. In a word, their zeal was not of the greatest.

Nevertheless, the viscount, an impetuous and self-confident man, having hastily assembled his forces, the very day the week of intermission ended invaded Conon's territory. He expected to find his enemy's peasants still in the fields and the St. Aliquis retainers in the process of mustering. To his amazement, he discovered that the villages were almost empty and most of the cattle driven away. Nevertheless, he foolishly allowed his men to scatter in order to ravage everything left at their mercy. Soon hayricks were burning, standing crops were being trampled down, and the thatch on the forsaken huts was blazing. Here and there troopers were driving before their spears oafish peasants who had lingered too long. The hands of these wretches were tied behind their backs. Beside them trudged their weeping wives and children. Every sheep, pig, and chicken discoverable was, of course, seized.[1] The ravagers soon had enough booty to load their horses to such a degree that one of Foretvert's more experienced knights warned him his men were becoming dangerously encumbered in case of an encounter.

The viscount laughed at these fears, yet was about to sound trumpets to recall the foraging parties; when, lo! down a wood road, through a forest that had been imperfectly scouted, came charging the whole St. Aliquis

---

[1] Such plunderings were common enough, though the best knightly sentiment was against participating directly in them. Says a bard, Geraud de Borneil, "O fie on the knight who drives off a flock of bleating sheep—and then appears before a lady!"

levy, with Conon's great banner racing on ahead. Half of the viscount's men were dispersed; the other half barely got into a kind of order when their enemies were upon them, thrusting, slashing, and laying about like fiends. Such being the case, Foretvert had cause to bless the Virgin that he got safely from the field. He only did so because his squire most gallantly stabbed the horse of Sire Eustace just as he was closing with the viscount. The squire himself was brained by the seneschal's mace an instant later. Five of the Foretvert knights were slain outright, despite their armor. Four more were pulled from their horses and dragged off as prisoners for ransom.

Of the foraging parties, the leaders got home by putting their horses at speed, but the miserable footmen were intercepted by scores. Many of these were slain while dropping their sinful booty. About forty were taken prisoners, but, being only villeins (from whom no ransom was to be expected), Conon promptly hanged ten as a warning against further ravaging of his lands, and took the other thirty back to his castle to be hanged later in case this first hint should not prove effective.[1]

This unusually decisive engagement ought, in the opinion of many, to have ended the war. Conon now invaded the Foretvert domains and with proper precautions sent out *his* ravaging parties, who soon taught their foes a lesson as to how to devastate a countryside. But the viscount, although sorely shaken and deserted now by many, arrogantly refused to make those concessions which Conon declared "his honor required ere

---

[1] These prisoners were lucky if they finally escaped without at least mutilation. To "give your captives [of villein blood] the empty sleeve or the wooden leg" seems to have been direfully common in feudal wars.

he could think of peace." The war thus promised not to terminate until, by incessant raids and counter-raids, the peasants of both seigneuries had been brought to the edge of starvation.

The viscount, of course, reckoned that at the end of their ordinary "forty days' service" Conon's vassals and allies would leave him. Most feudal levies were wont thus to melt away, after a very short campaign, and leave their leader bereft of almost all save his immediate retainers. Foretvert could then regather his men and resume the contest. But the saints so ordered it that Conon had been a thrifty seigneur as well as a popular suzerain and neighbor. He now offered his allies and vassals good deniers if they would serve until the autumn rains. He also hired the services of some fifty horsemen and two hundred footmen, led from Lorraine by an iron-handed soldier of fortune, Ritter Rainulf of the Moselle, who would put his German mercenaries at the beck of about any baron offering good silver. Mercenaries did not serve for "forty days," but for as many months as they received steady wages—a great advantage.

Conon likewise hired a base-born fellow, Maître Jerôme. The knights complained that the baron gave him too great pay and confidence, but Maître Jerôme had been one of the king's best engineers in the siege of the great castle, Château Gaillard, on the Seine, when Philip Augustus took that supposedly impregnable fortress from John of England in 1204. Now the castle of Foretvert itself was almost as strong as St. Aliquis, and no siege thereof was worth considering. But the viscount had a smaller fortalice, Tourfière, which lay closer to Conon's lands and was not so formidable.

Tourfière consisted merely of a single curtain of walls

234

around the courtyard of a central keep, with, of course, a palisaded barbican before the gate. There was a moat, but not deep, and flooded only in wet weather, and the foundations of this stronghold did not rest, apparently, on solid rock—a matter upon which Maître Jerôme laid great stress after a discreet reconnaissance. Suddenly, to the amazement of many, Conon with all his forces appeared before Tourfière and summoned its castellan, Sire Gauthier, the viscount's nephew, to surrender—a demand refused with derision.

Sire Gauthier commanded some twenty knights, squires or sergeants, also at least ninety armed villeins—a sufficient force, it seemed, for a small castle, especially as the women in the place could drop stones, throw down burning pitch hoops, pour boiling water, and help twist back the casting engines. The defenders thus prepared to resist with energy, confident that Conon could not keep his heterogeneous levies together much longer and that the siege would break up ignominiously. But, despite his villein blood, Maître Jerôme ordered the siege in a marvelously skillful manner. No chess player could have moved his pieces better than did he. First he persuaded the baron to resist his impulse to attempt the walls by a sudden rush with scaling ladders, pointing out that Gauthier, besides his arbalists, had four great trenchbuts (stone-hurlers worked by counterweights) and also two catapults, giant bows mounted on standards and able to send a heavy arrow clean through a man in full armor.

"We must take Tourfière by the crowbar and spade, and not by the sword, fair Seigneur," said Jerome, smilingly; whereupon a great levy of Conon's serfs began cutting timber and building a palisade all around the besieged castle, to stop sorties or succoring parties.

Meantime Jerôme was directing the making of trench-buts and catapults for the besiegers. With these they soon smashed the wooden hoardings which had protected the battlements, making it impossible for the garrison to mount the walls, save at a few places or in great emergencies, lest they be picked off by the attackers' arbalists. The trenchbuts also cast small kegs of "Greek fire" (a compound of pitch, sulphur, and naphtha) inside the castle court. These terrible fire balls could not be quenched by water, but only by sand. By desperate efforts, indeed, the defenders prevented decisive harm, but some of the buildings in the courtyard were burned and Sire Gauthier's men became wearied in their efforts to fend off disaster.

A CATAPULT

A sort of sling which one tightened with the aid of a windlass and which threw heavy projectiles.

In bravado the defenders took two prisoners and hanged them on the highest tower. Conon retaliated by immediately hanging four prisoners just out of bowshot of the castle, and causing his largest trenchbut to fling a dead horse clear over the battlements and into the court. Meantime a remarkable energy of the assailants, just outside their palisades, was observable by Sire Gauthier. The castellan took counsel with his most experienced men, for the besiegers seemed shaping very many timbers.

His advisers were divided in opinion. Some said that

Conon was planning to build a *beffroi*. This was a most ambitious undertaking ordinarily used only in great sieges. A *beffroi* was a movable tower built of heavy timbers and raised to at least the height of the wall attacked. Its front was covered by rawhides to repel arrows and fireballs. It was worked forward on rollers or clumsy wheels until close to the hostile parapet. Then, when almost touching, a swinging bridge from the summit was flung across to the wall, a host of assailants swarmed up a ladder in the rear and over the bridge to the battlements. The defenders then needed all their valor to keep their castle from speedy capture.

Others in the garrison, however, derided the idea

AN ATTACK WITH THE AID OF A TOWER
(From Viollet-Le-Duc); the moat has been filled up, the tower covered with skins to protect it from fire and rolled up to the wall.

that a *beffroi* was projected. It would be winter ere such a complicated structure could be completed. They said that the baron was preparing battering rams and a "cat." The battering ram was simply a heavy timber with a metal head, swung by chains from a kind of wooden trestle. Set up close under a wall it was pulled back and forth by ropes, and by repeated blows knocked down the masonry. The "cat" was a long, narrow,

237

tent-shaped structure of heavy timbers covered with hides or iron to turn missiles from the parapets. One end of this was built out until it came into contact with the walls, when skillful miners under its protection quarried their way through the masonry with pickaxes.

A MANTELET IN WOOD

These methods were easier to prepare than the *beffroi*, although not so effective. The defenders felt sure they would be used when the attackers were seen making *mantelets,* large wooden shields mounted on small wheels, to protect the cross-bowmen when they crept up to clear the walls—a needful preliminary to advancing either the cat or the ram. Their certainty increased when one night, by a sudden rush, Conon's men stormed through the weak palisade of the barbican and, forcing their way near to the walls, began filling up the moat with *fascines*—bundles of fagots. By using his trenchbuts and catapults to best advantage, Sire Gauthier felt confident, however, that he had prevented them from leveling the moat sufficiently to make a firm foundation for siege engines. The Tourfière men, therefore, shouted arrogantly: "Take your time, St. Aliquis hirelings! Your 'Madame Cat' will never gnaw our rats." [1]

Presently, after a couple of weeks, the besiegers were seen in great activity, as if arraying themselves for an assault. Gauthier was convinced they were about, in desperation, to try to scale his walls with ladders. Then

[1] Similar taunts were delivered at the well-known siege of Carcasonne in 1240.

of a sudden a panic-stricken sergeant ran up to his watch-tower. Wafts of smoke were escaping near the foundations of the curtain wall near the gate!

Gauthier instantly realized what had happened, but it was too late. Under an elaborate feint with other preparations, Maître Jerôme had taken advantage of the soft ground beneath the castle and had driven a mine, beginning at a safe distance in the rear and cunningly concealing the entrance and the earth excavated until it was fairly under a vital section of the wall. Then a large chamber had been cleared and wooden posts soaked with tallow had been put under the masonry to keep it from falling on the miners. As the last of them retreated, a torch was set to the woodwork, the whole chamber having been crammed with inflammables.

ATTACK ON A WALL WITH
THE AID OF THE SAP
At the top of the wall the scaffolding can be seen (theoretical figure from Viollet-Le-Duc).

Presently the fire ate away the posts. With a thundering crash a vital section of the wall collapsed.

The besieged had not realized the situation in time to drive a countermine or to erect a second wall inside the danger point. The moment the St. Aliquis men saw the wall topple they rushed forward. The defenders met them bravely in the breach and there was bloody swordplay, but the thrust of numbers was irresistible. Gauthier and part of his men fled, indeed, to the donjon and barred the entrance, but they were utterly demoralized. All the women and children, packed into the tower, were shrilly lamenting the dead and were otherwise frantic. Most of the provisions had been in a storehouse outside the donjon. The end, therefore, was certain. At the end of the next day the garrison in the donjon surrendered on promise of life and limb for all, and courteous treatment for the knights.

The storming of Tourfière ended the war. Conon might, indeed, have ruined Foretvert utterly, but now the duke intervened. It was not for his interests to have any vassal rendered unfit to meet his feudal obligations. Conon, however, was able to exact very high terms. For evacuating Tourfière he obtained the cession of a village whose peasants paid very large dues, and two of the viscount's best vassals also transferred their homage to St. Aliquis. The contending parties swore to peace upon the most precious relics at the abbey, and exchanged the kiss of amity. Henceforth Foretvert, a sadder and wiser seigneur, has been outwardly friendly with his powerful neighbor and even came as a sulky guest to Alienor's wedding.

Chapter XV: A Great Feudal Battle—Bouvines.

SO ended the feud between St. Aliquis and Foretvert—a less exhausting and more decisive baronial war than were many, and causing correspondingly less misery to the helpless peasants. But it has also been Conon's fortune to fight in a really great battle, one that will hereafter be set down among the most famous engagements in the annals of France.

It is a sunny afternoon. Young François and Anseau have wearied of hunting frogs beside the outer moat. Under the garden trees, Sire Eustace, tough old warrior, is meditating over a pot of hippocras. They demand of him once more the story of "the battle." For them there is only one battle—Bouvines. The seneschal, ever the slave of his youthful masters, after suitable urgings, begins.

"Now you must know, my fair damoisieux, that all this took place six years since, in the year 1214, upon the seven-and-twentieth day of July. For our sins it was extremely hot that season, so that all of us have, I trust, obtained some remission from purgatory. God grant that next time we have a great battle it be in the pleasant spring or autumn, though otherwise the saints showed to us French a great mercy. But now to commence.

"That year King John of England, having, by his evil

241

rule and folly lost nearly all his Anjou and Norman lands to our good King Philip, sent large money and skillful ambassadors into Flanders and Germany to stir up trouble. The great counts of Flanders and Boulogne nursed grievances against their liege lord our king, and to them joined many other seigneurs of those parts, notably the Dukes of Brabant and Limburg, the Count of Holland, and chiefest of all the German Emperor Otto IV himself, who came with a huge levy of Saxons. With those rode the English Earl of Salisbury with a great band of Flemish mercenaries who took King John's ill-gained penny. Never since Duke Charles Martel smote back the Paynym had so terrible a host menaced our gentle France; and when at last, in July, the whole array under Emperor Otto came together at Valenciennes to take the road to Paris, even brave knights trembled for the king and kingdom.

"Never had the call for the royal ban and rear ban gone out more urgently than that summer. The king's messenger came to St. Aliquis with the 'brief of summons' bidding Messire Conon ride with every man and lad that could stride a horse or trudge with a spear; and so went the command through all North France. But in the south country John was making a formidable diversion from his remaining dominions in Gascony, and we of the Languedoil lands had to meet the northern shock alone.

"When Messire your Father received the summons, there was even greater furbishing than when old Foret-vert defied us. Sire Conon had in the abbot and wrote his last wishes, arranged that if he fell he should be buried in the abbey church by the altar where St. Bernard had once said mass, and he left to the monks **five hundred livres** in return for perpetual masses for his soul. The remainder of us made vows according to ability. I say nothing of the parting, or how your mother bravely promised to guard the castle.

"So the ban was answered all through the land, and the king's great host came together. Never again shall I see so fine a mustering of knights as gathered at Peronne. It far surpassed any tournament. Every hour the banners came in, to the sound of tabors, horns, and drums. There was an enormous baggage train, so that I believe there were more mules than horses, for many barons brought their great tents, with many coffers of extra arms and fine clothing. In the rear were gathered a second array of jongleurs, peddlers and very evil women, whom not all the commands of the king, somehow, could disperse. Verily in that army there were twice as many mouths to fill as there were men to fight; likewise, short as was the campaign, there was much sickness, thanks to bad food, bad water, and, so certain even averred, to overmuch filth. The comfort was that in Otto's camp matters were, if anything, much worse.

"In any case those tumultuous days of assemblage were soon at an end. Tidings came that the Germans and Flemings were advancing, and on the twenty-fifth of July we marched into Tournai on the edge of Flanders. Messire Conon, who was at the royal council-tent, told me that the king's barons debated as to the purpose of the enemy. Would he offer fair battle in the plain near Cambrai, as we much desired, or would he strive to slip past our army and go straight toward Paris? I have been told of books concerning the ancient Roman captains, Julius Cæsar and his peers, and it would seem as if to them the moving of armies had been a business of deep sagacity, advancing your columns by careful rules, somewhat as you move your men on a gaming board. No one, however, is so sage as that to-day, and I think it was either mere fortune or (speaking as a Christian) the kind St. Denis, who guards our beautiful France, that brought the hosts together when and where they presently came.

"It was at break of day on that seven-and-twentieth of July that we quitted Tournai, intending to pass the little river Marque, to get to the town of Bouvines and thereby to be covered by certain marshes so we might be protected from surprise, and yet be able to strike the foe's rear if he should take the road to Paris. But Otto and his lords, swollen with their German and Fleming pride and confident in their great host of infantry, were determined to attack, and so kept hard after us. It is only nine miles from Tournai to Bouvines, but our long trains of baggage crawled along like snails. Therefore it was almost noon when the sumpter mules and the infantry had crossed the bridge. We of the cavalry were still on the nearer side, covering the march, when our scouts came racing in. 'The Germans! The Germans!' And there assuredly, over the rolling slopes of the cornfields beyond Bouvines, we saw the long lines of horsemen flying in a great dust cloud.

"Now there was with the king the Bishop Garin of Senlis. He was an old knight hospitaler, one of those holy brethren who, despite churchly vows, rejoice to fight in just causes, and Bishop Garin at once clapped spurs to his destrer to reconnoiter. Soon he dashed back, having discovered quite enough. He found our Lord Philip sitting under an ash tree close to the bridge eating dinner, with many great nobles, Messire Conon among them, sitting on the grass. 'Tidings, fair Sire!' cried Garin. 'The Germans will fight. Their knights are in panoply, and behind them march the infantry!'

"It was no pleasant moment for the king. His own infantry were beyond the river, but his cavalry were on this side. He could not get his horsemen across the single bridge without grievous loss; but there was, perchance, still time to bring back the foot. Therefore, with what speed we might, every man of us fell into the array, and some brave sergeants of Champagne made such charges upon Otto's vanguard that, though outnumbered and pressed back, they delayed the foe until our men could take their places and present a gallant front. As for the attackers, when they saw that we were ready to do battle, like prudent men they halted and arrayed their own lines. So for an hour both sides waited, just out of bowshot, many of us very nervous and cursing the delay—the more as the sun beat down pitilessly—although the more pious confessed hastily to the priests, who were always moving up and down the files, or at least we said our *mea culpas* for our sins.

"Presently you could see the whole array of the enemy spread out like some fair picture on a long tapestry. On their right, facing our Counts of Ponthieu and Dreux, were the mercenaries under Salisbury, and the men of that foul traitor Boulogne. On their left were the long lines of Flemish horsemen over against our cavaliers of Champagne and Burgundy. But we from Quelqueparte, with so many other companies, were in the center battle where flew King Philip's great oriflamme, a mighty scarlet banner of samite, surrounded by chosen cavaliers. We horsemen were in the rear. In front of us spread the French footmen—the burgher levies of the towns who answered the king's summons. 'Shame that burghers should stand before knights!' cried some of us; but the King and Bishop Garin, who seemed to know everything, understood their business, as you will see.

"It is told that just before the hosts charged King Philip prayed aloud before his bodyguard: 'Lord, I am but a man, but I am also a king. Thine it is to guard the king. Thou wilt lose nothing thereby. Wherever thou wouldst go, I will follow thee!' Also I heard that close behind the king there stood, as long as he might, the royal chaplain, William the Breton, who all through the battle, with another clerk, kept singing psalms such as 'Blessed be the Lord my strength, who teacheth my hands to war and my fingers to fight.' But Bishop Garin sang no psalms. Up and down the lines of horsemen he rode, thundering: 'Extend yourselves, lest the enemy outflank you. One knight should not make another his shield!' So he put all our knights in the first line of the cavalry. In the rear lines he put the mounted sergeants. We had perhaps two thousand knights and five thousand sergeants. Our infantry were over five-and-twenty thousand, but the foe had even more footmen than we, though their horse was a little inferior. Thus the battle was very fair, two lines of men and horses a mile and a half long, and the fields smooth and open enough for a jousting. There never was better place for an honorable battle.

"After we had sat in our saddles a long time, thinking of our sins and admiring in a fearsome way the splendor of the great press of the foe opposite, a party of our sergeants suddenly charged out on our right against the Flemings. Their attack was too weak, and the Flemings drove them back and charged in return, their leaders crying, 'Think on your ladies!' as if in a courteous mêlée. Whereat, nothing loath, our Burgundian and Champagnois knights dashed out on them, and long engaged in an uncertain battle, every cavalier selecting a foe and riding against him. Here one side prevailed and here another, and some warriors even dropped to the rear to recover breath and tighten harness, then spurred back to the charge. For a little while we of the center watched them thus; then nearer things engrossed us.

"I have told you that King Philip and his footmen, as well as many of our knights, held the center battle. Facing them was the dense array of Flemish and German infantry, with Emperor Otto himself, accompanied by chosen horsemen, in their rear, and we could see in the middle press the great imperial banner, a silken dragon, white and green, raised upon a pole capped with a golden eagle. It was not borne by a cavalier but flew from a tall car drawn by four horses. As we gazed at this vast hostile array, lo! the whole mass seemed surging forward against our infantry. Never was there a sight like it, spear points, hauberks, and helmets all flashing in the sun. The ground shook with the trample of thousands of feet. Countless war horns sounded, and we heard the deep '*Hoch! Hoch!*' of the German infantry coming down on us like thunder.

"Then the emperor's great masses struck our footmen from the communes. Doubtless our poor knaves meant bravely, and always had plenty of courage when defending their walls, but never would France and King Philip have been saved by townsmen. Soon we saw all those base-born infantry breaking toward the rear, and for a moment our skies looked black. But, 'Open the ranks,' called Messire Conon and our other leaders, 'and let the villeins run through.' So we opened the lines in the cavalry and let these timid friends escape. Then came a last tightening of buckles and pushing down of helms. Right before us, thousands upon thousands, were surging the emperor's infantry. All together we raised the glad '*Montjoie St. Denis!*'[1] the royal battle cry of France. Whereupon followed such a coursing as never in all my life I can hope again to see. With our eyes on Otto's great banner, straight into that press of Germans and Flemings we French cavaliers rode like mad, the knights in front and all the squires and good sergeants raging behind us. The horses knew their hour. They flew at speed with no touch of spur. Though I am blessed with all the joys of paradise, never, after ten thousand years of bliss, shall I forget the wondrous rapture I felt when we struck that hostile line!"

(Sire Eustace's eyes are gleaming now like sparks of fire. François and Anseau are hardly breathing as he speaks).

"Through that caitiff infantry we went as a hot knife cleaves through cheese. I had the St. Aliquis banner, and kept close behind Messire Conon with all our men hallooing and smiting behind. *Hé!* what chance had those villein footmen against *gentle* Frenchmen, who all had known horses and lance since they ceased from mother's milk? So one and all we charged, and, like castles rising out of the plain, soon you could see here, there, and yonder the banners and squadrons of our cavaliers on their tall horses, looming above

---

[1] This famous battle cry of French royalty probably meant "*Follow the banner of St. Denis!*" Its exact origin, however is obscure.

In feudal battles, armies often used merely the names of their leaders, "*Burgundy!*" "*Coucy!*" "*Bourbon!*" etc. But many regions had a special war cry. Thus the Normans cried "*Dex ais!*" the Bretons, "*Malo! Malo!*" the Angevins "*Valée!*" Imperialists were likely to cry "*Rome!*" and Crusaders "*Holy Sepulcher!*" To "cry one's ensign" was a great object in all mediæval battles.

the snarling, striking footmen, who closed in all around them, and yet could not keep our knights from charging forward, always forward.

"After that, all the battle was broken up. For when Emperor Otto and his knights saw their infantry being cut down like sheep, they also charged, giving us the honest joy of crossing swords with men of nobility. So for a long time it was horse to horse and man to man. You have heard the jongleurs tell of the great deeds done. But as for us of St. Aliquis, just as we were close to hewing our way clear through the whole German line, lo! a great shouting rose on our left—"The King! The King!" And we saw the royal standard being tossed up and down, as in distress, by Sire Wado de Montigny, who bore it. Then back we charged, with many cavaliers more—just in time. For King Philip, while attacking gallantly like any other knight, had been separated from most of his friends, and a swarm of knavish Flemish pikemen had striven to drag him from his horse. His good armor turned their pikes, yet a soldier caught the hook of a halberd in the chain mail round his throat and pulled him to the ground. But the king sprang up as briskly as a young squire, and all the French knights at hand spurred to his aid. Then it was that Sire Peter Tristen leaped from his own horse and mounted his lord upon it; and Messire Conon, being among the very first to ride up and scatter or trample the Flemings, later received no small praise and thanks.

"Therefore, in that part of the field God prospered us; and then came the signal mercy when Emperor Otto fled the field. For as our knights charged and his cavaliers gave way, our men slew Otto's horse, and when he fell they almost seized the emperor. However,

his Saxons, selling their lives right dearly, got him another
horse. But herein was the German emperor different from
our good French king. For when Philip was remounted
again he raised once more his clear *'Montjoie St.
Denis!'* and pressed the charge; but Otto (nigh out of
his wits, perhaps, and somewhat wounded) fled from
the field with only three knights, leaving his great banner
and all his brave vassals to their fate; and they say he
never drew rein till he reached Valenciennes.

"The German knights, though deserted, still fought
bravely, but the Netherlanders and Flemings soon were
fleeing in droves. Besides, on the two wings of the
conflict we Frenchmen were already proving victorious
and from right and left our knights were charging in to
help the center, cutting their way so far to the rear
that when at last the German cavaliers knew that all
was lost, and now began to flee, they often found themselves surrounded and were pulled from their horses and
so made captive.

"Thus ended the day's work, save on the right wing
of the enemy. Here had fought the great rebel Reginald
of Boulogne, who knew there was naught left for him
save victory or ruin. He formed some seven hundred
Brabantine infantry into a circle. With their pikes
and axes they beat off for long the charges of our cavaliers. From behind this living wall Boulogne, with a
few brave knights, time and again charged out, performing high deeds of valor, and then, as it were, retreating
into their fortress to get breath. But now that the
remainder of the field was cleared, King Philip brought
up his whole power of cavalry. He formed three thousand of us into three great columns of mounted men
and, charging in on every side, by sheer weight we broke
the Brabantine circle down. So we dragged the Count

of Boulogne from his horse, fighting to the last, and the king holds him close prisoner unto this day.

"This was the last mêlée of a battle the like whereof has not been in France these many years. Of course, the slaughter of the footmen was great, some thousands of both ours and theirs. The field was a sorry sight that evening and the groans of the dying rang in my ears, for all that we were so happy. But it pleased the saints that, thanks to good armor, we cavaliers got off quite safely. I have heard that 'only three French knights were slain,' although I am sure that number is too few. Of the Germans and Flemings they say one hundred and seventy knights were killed outright; but better still, we took five German counts, twenty-five barons, and some hundred and six lesser knights as prisoners. It was the ransom of that Baron of Imgerfels whom we unhorsed which presently went far to pay for your aunt's wedding and uncle's knighting.

"As for the manner in which we all returned to Paris joyous as the angels, and how the church bells rang and all the fat burghers hung the streets with tapestry, and with the clergy and scholars in the university we had seven days of illuminations, feastings, and rejoicings, which is a story repeated every day. But there will never be another Bouvines."

So spoke the seneschal. If we would comment on his narrative, we would say that Philip manifestly conquered because his very unepiscopal chief of staff, Bishop Garin, drew up his army with greater skill than Otto's leaders arranged the German-Fleming host, and also because when at last the hosts engaged in a series of innumerable duels, the French knights on the average proved superior. King Philip, after the fight was started, showed himself a valiant cavalier personally, but hardly figured as a commander. Otto contributed to shake the morale of his men by premature flight, but his great host of footmen were almost worthless, despite their pikes and halberds, against the terrific shock of the French cavalry, charging on perfectly smooth ground, where mailed horsemen could fight at their best. Missile weapons played no part. When the English yew bow shall appear, the situation may change. Till then the mounted knight, in all his ponderous armor, charging with lance at rest or with his great sword dancing in his hands, will appear as the monarch of the battlefields. Bouvines has marked the apogée of the feudal cavalry.

Chapter XVI: The Life of the Peasants.

HUS have been seen Messire Conon and his familiars in their pleasures, feasts, and wars. The gentle folk seem to monopolize all the life of the barony. Yet at best they number scarce one in a hundred of all the Christians who dwell therein. Assuredly the poor and humble seem much less interesting and command less attention. They have no splendors, no picturesque fêtes or feuds. A life of monotonous poverty seldom detains the chronicler; nevertheless, it is time to visit the village of huts so often seen spreading beyond the bridge to the west of the castle.

The St. Aliquis peasants are told that they have naught whereof to complain. They have a kindly seigneur who "renders justice." Since the Foretvert feud, no war has ravaged them. The saints of late have sent neither short crops nor pestilence. To repine against their lot is ingratitude toward God.

There is abundant class consciousness in the Feudal Ages. Clerks, knights, peasants—every man knows to which of the three great categories of humanity he belongs, and acts accordingly.

A monkish preacher[1] pictures the world as a vast body whereof the clerics are the eyes, for they show

[1] This cleric, Jacques of Vitry, may have written a few years later than the presumable date of this narrative, but it represents entirely the orthodox viewpoint of A.D. 1220.

to all men the way to safety; the noble knights the hands and arms, for God orders them to protect the Church and the weak and to promote peace and justice; finally the common people (*minores*) form the lower parts of the body—it is their business to nourish the eyes and limbs. More bluntly still, as long ago as about A.D. 1000, Bishop Adelberon of Laon had divided mankind into two great divisions—first, the clergy who prayed and the seigneurs who fought; second, the toilers; adding that "to furnish all with gold, food, and raiment—such is the obligation of the servile class."

Since these classes are clearly ordained of Heaven, to rebel against one's status is manifestly questioning the justice of Providence—a damnable impiety.

Few of the St. Aliquis peasants ever dream of being anything but villeins. They regard gentlefolk somewhat as good Christians regard angels—as beings of another sphere. All they hope for is kindly treatment and modest prosperity within the limits providentially assigned them. Therefore, they are not too unhappy.

If we go up and down France we shall find the rural population decidedly dense.[1] One little village usually follows another closely and every collection of huts swarms with human bipeds. There are, indeed, vast forests and marshes which might with better management be put under the plow, but the extent of arable land is great. Heaven surely loves the peasants, it has made so many of them. Seemingly their number is limited merely by the question of food supply.

[1] It has been estimated that the rural population of France in the thirteenth century was almost as great as in the twentieth. There was probably a decided falling off, in the fourteenth century, thanks to the Black Death (1348) and the ravages of the Hundred Years' War.

If the condition of the peasantry often seems bad, it is comforting to know that for the last two centuries it has been improving. Not for many years have matters

GROUP OF PEASANTS AND OF SHEPHERDS
(Twelfth century), from a window in the cathedral of Chartres.

in the St. Aliquis region been as they were in some parts of France during the terrible famine of 1030–32. At that time we are told that the poor devoured grass, roots and even white clay. Their faces were pale, their bodies lean, their stomachs bloated, "their voices thin and piping like the voice of birds." Wolves came out of forests and fed on children. Strangers and travelers were liable to be waylaid in solitary spots and killed simply that they might be eaten. Near Macon a "hermit" at last was seized who had lured wayfarers to share the hospitality of his cell. The skulls of forty-eight victims were there discovered, after which they burned the wretch alive.

You can go on multiplying stories about famines—

how human flesh at times was sold in markets; how starving children were lured by the offers of a bit of food to places where ghouls could kill and feast on them; how a measure of corn rose to sixty sous in gold; and how even the very rich "lost their color." These days, thanks be to the saints, seem disappearing; yet the danger of pinching hard times is still a real one, even in fortunate St. Aliquis.[1]

The peasants of Messire Conon are free. The serfs of the barony had been manumitted about a hundred years earlier, by a baron who (after an extremely iniquitous life) was admonished on his deathbed by his confessor that he must do something extraordinary for the salvation of his soul.[2] As a result the St. Aliquis peasants were no longer bound to the soil and could quit the seigneury—as serfs assuredly could not do. They could also marry any women they wished without asking their lord's consent or paying him a fee. They could bequeath their goods without having him sequester an outrageous part. All this, of course, improved their status, yet they were still subject to numerous imposts in money and kind, and to various forms of forced labor. Although they had now the legal right to quit the barony, only with the greatest difficulty could they sell their little farms and chattels thereon, so they could take a decent share of their possessions elsewhere; and

[1] By 1220 these wholesale famines were really becoming matters of tradition, thanks to better transportation and better methods of agriculture. Very lean years, almost ruinous to the peasantry, remained, however, as extremely grim possibilities.

[2] In Brittany, and, somewhat less generally in Normandy, most of the peasants at this time were free. In Champagne and central France there were still so many serfs that very possibly the peasants of St. Aliquis were more fortunate than the majority of the villeins on neighboring baronies. The advantages of the free peasants over the serfs have, however, been somewhat exaggerated.

if they wandered to distant parts, the local authorities were likely to call them "masterless men" and assume that if they had forsaken their old lord they must somehow be criminals.

Nevertheless, it is much better to be a free peasant than a serf. The majority of the French lower classes are now becoming free, although in other Christian lands, notably Germany, serfage will prevail for a weary day hereafter.

But even though one becomes free, he is a villein still. The taint of ignoble blood clings like a shirt of pitch, even after achieving prosperity and wealth. Knightly opinion is expressed by that great troubadour, Bertran de Born: "I love to see the rich churl in distress if he dares to strive with nobles. I love to see him beg his bread in nakedness."

Even a well-disposed lord looks on a peasant largely as a source of income. In time of peace the taxes and forced labor squeezed out of him yield that which presently turns into destrers, silvered hauberks, furs, hawks, fair dames' luxuries, dowries, adubbements, tourneys. In time of war he exists to be pillaged and massacred, in order to impoverish his master by ruining the latter's revenues. The burghers of the towns are a little more respected. Their industrial products are needful. They can better protect themselves. But the richest syndic of a commune cannot really hold up his head socially with the unknighted bachelor who drags out life in a tumble-down manor house.

At every turn the peasant finds himself exploited. He must pay a direct tax supposedly proportioned to the size and yield of his farm. That is only the beginning. When his wife has bread to bake, it must be taken to the lord's oven. One loaf in so many goes as the fee.

The flour must be ground up in the lord's mill—again for a fee. The grapes must be pressed out in the lord's winepress. The sheep must be driven into the lord's sheepfold every night, that he may get the manure. Every dispute must be arbitrated before the lord's provost or the great man himself—more fees. In short, the whole régime aims to compel the peasant to go to his seigneur for everything he needs, so that he will have extremely little business to transact away from the seigneury. Doubtless it is a convenience often to find things commonly needful always at hand. There is a certain return for many of the exactions. But the seigneur does not act out of benevolence. If the peasants wish, for example, to set up their own ovens, they must pay the seigneur the equivalent of the baker's fees of which he is deprived. If they then wish to bake their own bread, he is now quite indifferent.

Besides the imposts and numerous fees (*banalités*) the peasants owe the *corvées,* payments by labor. A large part of every seigneury is "domain land"—for the lord's own personal use. The peasants are obliged to give a certain number of days to keep this plowed and tilled, mow the meadows, bring in the hay, dress the vines. They must also see that the castle has its firewood and fodder; clean out the moat; help keep the fortifications in repair; and assist on many extraordinary occasions.[1] For this they get no pay, although they may be given their rations during the days of labor.

---

[1] The list of curious *corvées* required of peasants on various seigneuries is a long one. On one fief they were expected to beat the water of the castle moat to stop the noise of the frogs whenever the mistress was sick. Or on certain specified occasions they had to perform some absurd service: to hop on one leg, to kiss the latch of the castle gate, go through some drunken horseplay in the lord's presence, or sing a broad song in the presence of his lady.

In time of war they do almost everything from helping to defend the castle to marching on offensive campaigns as part of the ban—serving, as we have seen, as grooms, baggage attendants, diggers, and engineers, and also as the despised, but sometimes useful, infantry pikemen.

Such are the burdens of the St. Aliquis peasants. They burn holy candles of thankfulness, however, that Baron Conon does not multiply their troubles by intrusting the collection of his imposts and the administration of his forced labor to outrageous officers. Sire Macaire, the provost, is harsh toward real offenders and strict in exacting the last *sol* or sheaf in just debts, but he is no blackmailer, as is Foretvert's general factotum. In old Baron Garnier's day, of course, there had been a provost who not merely levied abominable imposts, diverting a share thereof toward his own pocket, but who would accuse poor men falsely of theft and then take bribes for condoning their alleged offenses, all the time that he was dividing the profits of real bandits whom he protected.

Even more obnoxious can be the forester who controls the hunting preserves and grazing grounds. He decides how the peasants' pigs may be turned out in the oak forests, how and when firewood may be cut, and he battles incessantly with the multitudinous poachers. A few years ago even Conon was deceived by a fellow in his employ, one Maître Crispin. He was "a very handsome man with fine carriage and well armed with bow and sword." No one could *congé* more gracefully to Madame Adela, or do more to help messire to discover a great boar, but all the while he was filling his own chest. For example, he seized lame Georges' oxen on the pretext that he had cut three oaks and a birch in the seigneur's forest—yet he would forget the crime if

Georges could find him one hundred sous! Fortunately Sire Macaire discovered the evil ways of his lieutenant, and Conon, exceedingly incensed, had the smooth Crispin turned over to Maître Denis and his halter after abrupt formalities. The present forester, taught by example, is more honest, although of course, all the real poachers curse him.

A great part of the peasant's time is spent neither in working nor in resting, but in walking. Few are so lucky as to have all their land in a single compact plot. Even a rather poor peasant has his farm scattered in several tiny holdings, possibly at the four quarters of the neighborhood. When a peasant dies, his children all divide the paternal estate, and if a separate piece of ground cannot be provided for each heir, some lots must be subdivided smaller still. The St. Aliquis lands

PEASANTS AT WORK
From a manuscript of the thirteenth century (Bibliothèque nationale).

thus present a curious sight—innumerable little parcels scattered everywhere, each carefully fenced off and each growing its own separate crops. Meantime their owners begin in the morning toiling with their heavy mattocks, on one of their holdings, then on to the next, and so on until sundown. Thus they trudge several miles, and yet are seldom far from their village, whither they must all return at dusk.

Primitive Agricultural Methods

Men of more fortunate days will be astonished when they survey the agricultural methods of even the least stupid peasants. Everything is according to traditions—"so it was with our fathers." In the abbey library there are some Latin books about agriculture. They deal with conditions in ancient Italy, however, not feudal France. The most benevolent monk hardly dreamed of examining his Cato or Columella to learn how to better the lot of the peasantry, though in fairness it should be said that the abbey farms enjoy on the whole a much superior cultivation. Not all peasants can own plows; they borrow or hire from their neighbors, or break the ground with the clumsy mattocks. What plows exist have only wooden plowshares. The wheat in St. Aliquis is beaten out by flails, although a little farther south it is trodden out by cattle. The soil is often impoverished, and it is usual to leave one-third fallow all the time to recuperate. Such a thing as "rotation of crops" is still a matter of vague talk save on some of the monastery lands.

Under these circumstances, even in the best of years, there is not much surplus of food. A short crop means misery. Men pessimistically expect a famine on the average of one in every four years. If there has not been one of late in St. Aliquis, it is because the saints are rich in mercy. "In 1197 a countless throng died of hunger," significantly wrote a chronicler in Rheims. Naturally, the villeins seldom get enough ahead to be able to learn the practices of thrift. If the year has been good, with an extra supply of corn in the barns, and plenty of pigs and chickens fattening, the winter will be spent in gorging and idleness. By spring the old crop is exhausted almost to the seed corn; then perhaps the new crop will be a failure. The next winter these

261

same peasants may be glad to make a pottage of dead leaves.

Lame Georges, who had his oxen sequestered, is, despite his misfortunes, one of the most prosperous peasants in the village. He limps because in his youth a retainer of Baron Garnier's twisted one of his feet while trying to extort money. Georges is really only forty-five years old, but to see his gray head, gnarled face, and bent back you would think him sixty. His wife Jeanne is four years younger than he, but looks as aged as her husband. "Old Jeanne," the children call her. The pair have been blessed with at least fifteen children, but four of these died in childbirth, and five more before they could grow up. The other six are, all but the youngest, married already and Jeanne has been a grandmother for several years.

Georges' house stands near the center of the village. To reach it you pick your way down a lane usually deep in mud. In front of each fenced-in cottage there is an enormous dungheap, beloved by the hens and pigs, which roam about freely. Georges' one-story dwelling is an irregularly built, rambling structure of wood, wattles, and thatch, all of dirty brown. This "manse" stretches away in four parts. The rearmost contains the corn cribs, the next mows for hay and straw, then the cattle sheds; and nearest, and smallest, the house for the family.

Pushing back the heavy door, after lifting the wooden latch, one enters a single large room; the timbers and walls thereof are completely blackened by soot. There is really only one apartment. Here everything in the household life seems to go on. The floor is of earth pounded hard. Upon it are playing several very dirty, half-naked children, come over to visit "grandmother," and just now they are chasing two squealing little pigs under the great oak table near the center. One makes no account of a duck leading her goslings in at the door in hopes of scraps from the dinner. A hen is setting on eggs in a box near the great fireplace.

Jeanne has just kindled a lively fire of vine branches and dry billets. She is proud that her house contains many convenient articles not found with all the neighbors. By the fireplace is an iron pot hanger, a shovel, large fire tongs, a copper kettle, and a meat hook. Next to the fireplace is an oven, in case she does not wish to use that at the castle and yet will pay the baron's fee. On the other side of the fireplace is an enormous bed, piled with a real mountain of feather mattresses—we do not discuss their immunity from vermin. In this one bed a goodly fraction of Georges' entire family, male and female, old and young, have been able to sleep; of course, with their heads usually pointing in opposite directions. If a stranger chances to spend the night, it will be hospitable to ask him to make "one more" in that selfsame bed!

If the goodman takes us about his establishment we shall find that, in addition to various stools and benches, he owns a ladder, a mortar and pestle for braying corn, a mallet, some crudely shaped nails, a gimlet, a very imperfect saw, fishing lines, hooks, and a basket. He is fortunate enough also to own a plow, and, in addition, a scythe, an iron spade, a mattock, a pair of large shears, a handy knife, and a sharpening stone. He has replaced the stolen oxen with another pair and owns a two-wheeled wagon with a harness of thongs and ropes. Besides the oxen, there are three milch cows in his barn, and he has a hennery and pigpen. The place seems also to abound with long, lean cats, very wild, who gain a living by hunting the numerous rats and mice which lurk in the dense thatch of the roofs.

Georges himself wears a blouse of dirt-colored cloth, or sometimes of sheepskin, fastened by a leathern belt. In cold weather he has a mantle of thick woolen homespun, now also dirt color, to his knees. He has a pair of very heavy leathern boots, although not seldom he goes on short walks barefoot. The lower part of his body is covered by a pair of loose woolen trousers which once were blue. Very seldom, save in storms, does he wear any headdress; then he produces a kind of cap of the same dirty woolen as his coat. As for gloves, he never wears them except when hedging. Jeanne's costume is much the same, with a few changes to make it suitable for women. In her chest she has,

A LABORER, THIRTEENTH CENTURY
Restored by Viollet-Le-Duc, from the manuscript of Herrade of Landsberg.

however, a green bliaut of Flanders wool made somewhat in imitation of those she has seen at the castle, and it even is beautified with red and purple embroidery. This bliaut she wears with pride on great festival days, and in it, despite the envious hopes of her daughters and daughters-in-law, she expects at last to be buried.

Georges' house is considerably better than many others. Some of his neighbors live in mere cabins that are barely weather tight. They are made of crossed laths stuffed with straw or grass, and have no chimney.

The smoke from the hearth escapes through a small hole in the roof (where the thatch is very liable to take fire) or merely through the door.

None of these houses has glass windows. Georges fastens his few openings with wooden shutters, but poor Alard near by has to close his apertures by stuffing them up with straw, if it is too cold to leave them open. Alard, too, is without a bed. His family sleep on thin pallets of straw laid on the ground, with a few ragged blankets. There are plenty of peasants who have not even the straw.

PEASANT SHOES
Twelfth century (abbey church of Vézelay)

A REAPER
From the doorway of the cathedral of Amiens.

Alard inevitably has no cows, no oxen or cart, no plow, and only a few rude tools. He and his are barely able to satisfy the provost's men by grinding field labor, and have still enough grain laid up to carry them till the next harvest. If it is a little too dry, a little too wet, if, in short, any one of a number of untoward things happen, by next spring he, with his bent and bony wife and his five lean children, will all be standing at the castle or abbey gate with so many other mendicants to cry their "Bread! For the love of Christ, a little bread!"

The peasants marry as early as do the nobility. Of the moral condition of many of them it is best to say little. Good Father Étienne, the parish priest, spends much of his time first in baptizing infants of unacknowledged paternity, and then in running down their presumptive fathers and forcing the latter to provide for their children's upkeep. But a girl can often indulge in amazing indiscretions and later find some self-respecting peasant willing to marry her.

Every girl looks forward to her marriage as the climax of life. If she hopes to find a husband in the coming year, she will dance around a bonfire, then cast some pins into a bubbling fountain. If these are thrown to the surface it is a sign the right swain will come along. When drawing water from a well, if she can throw into it an egg cracked upon the head of some companion, she can see in the water the image of her future husband. As for the young men, when one of them decides he wishes to marry a certain girl, he often comes to her parents,

A MARRIAGE IN THE
THIRTEENTH CENTURY
From a manuscript of the
Bibliothèque nationale
(Bordier et Charton).

presenting a leathern bottle of wine. If they drink of the same his suit is accepted. However, if he is uncertain of his reception by the maiden herself, he invites himself to dinner at her home. If at the end she serves him with a dish of walnuts, it is a clear token that he is rejected. He had better slink away.

On the wedding day, if the bride has always been sage and modest, the neighbors present her with a white hen, but her mother gives her a piece of fine cloth, to make a gala dress which will serve ultimately for a shroud. At the ceremony itself the great question is, "How will the wedding ring slip on?" If easily the bride will be docile. If it goes on tightly she will rule her husband!

The peasants need every kind of public and private holiday. On ordinary days toil begins at gray dawn and usually continues until dusk. There are no eight-

A PLOW

Restored by Viollet-Le-Duc, from a manuscript of the thirteenth century at the Seminary of Soissons.

hour laws; even the "nooning" is short, although sometimes there is time taken out in hot weather for a siesta during the afternoon. The women labor in the fields as hard as do the men. Children begin weeding, digging, and carrying when very little. Their help is so important that many peasants look on large families as assets of so much unpaid field labor, rather than as liabilities which they must clothe and feed until the children reach maturity. Education is almost unknown. One or two very bright boys from the village somehow have been caught by the churchmen and trained for the priesthood. There is even a story of a lad born in a neighboring seigneury who thus rose to be a bishop! But such cases are very exceptional. In the whole village by St. Aliquis, Father Etienne is the only person who understands the mysteries of reading and writing, except two assistants of the provost, who have to keep accounts for the baron.

It is very hard for great folk to understand such teachings of the Church as that "all men are brethren." "Doubtless it is true," Adela and Alienor have often told each other, that "God created man in His own image," but how is it possible that God should have the image of most of the villeins on the seigneury? Are not so many of them like the peasant described in the epic "Garin"? "He had enormous hands and massive limbs. His eyes were separated from each other by a hand's breadth. His shoulders were large, his chest deep, his hair bristling, and his face black as a coal. He went six months without bathing. Nothing but rain water had ever touched his face."

The manners of these people are equally repulsive. Countless ballads as well as monks' sermons and treatises represent your typical villein as incessantly discontented, scolding about the weather, which is always too wet or too dry, treating his wife like an animal, hauling her about by the hair. Lately at the castle a jongleur told this anecdote: "A certain peasant showered his wife with blows on principle. 'She must have some occupation,' said he, 'while I work in the field. If she is idle she will think of evil things. If I beat her she will weep the whole day through, and so will pass the time. Then when I return in the evening she will be more tender.'" According to other stories, however, many peasants are clever, aggressive, and insolent—well able to care for themselves.

The castle folk and the burghers are none too careful in sanitary matters, but even to them the peasants are disgustingly filthy. They relate in Pontdebois this story: "Once a villein, leading some donkeys, went down the lane of the perfumer's shops. Instantly he fainted at the unaccustomed odor. They brought him to, however, by holding a shovel full of manure under his nose." Another story (told at the monastery) has it that the devil has refused to receive more villeins into hell because they smell so vilely!

In the village you soon find many typical peasant characters, and nearly all of them are bad. There is the surly fellow who will not even tell a traveler the way. There is the malcontent villein who mutters enviously whenever he sees a knight riding out hawking; there is the mad fool who reviles God, saints, Church, and nobility; there is the talkative villein who is always arguing bad causes before the provost's court and inciting his neighbors to senseless litigation, there is the honest simpleton who wandered up to Pontdebois and got his pockets picked while gaping at the sculptures on the portal of the cathedral; finally, there are the misers, the petty speculators in grain (who pray for a famine), and all the tribe of poachers. Certainly there are also a great number of hard-working, honest folk who bow respectfully when Messire Conon rides by and who pay their taxes without grumbling. Such give prosperity to the seigneury; but it is the rascals who ever thrust themselves into prominence.

The St. Aliquis villeins seem doltish and dirty enough, but they are nothing to those existing in Flanders. Some monks have recently returned thence after doing business for their order. They tell with horror that in summertime Flemish peasants are seen around their villages, taking their ease, with no more clothes on than when they were born. When the monks remonstrated, the rough answer was: "How is this your business? You make no laws for us." It is pitiful (say the monks) that any seigneur should tolerate such things on his fief, for the peasants are such sodden creatures they cannot of themselves be expected to know better.

If the knights exploit the peasants, the clergy do so hardly less. It is notoriously hard for the bishop's tithe collector to secure the quota of pigs, hens, eggs, wheat, vegetables, etc., which everybody knows that the villein owes to the Church after or upon the same time he satisfies the collectors for the baron. Indeed, certain impious villeins complain, "The tithe is worse than the imposts and the *corvées*." The monkish preachers have to be constantly threatening these sinners who pay their tithes slowly. The Church tithe is the property of God. "It is the tax you owe to God, a sign of his universal dominion." Those who withhold it not merely imperil their souls, but God will send them "drought and famine," punishing them alike in this world and the next.

Villeins too often wickedly insist on working on Sundays and holy days. The peasants complain there are so many saints' days that it is hard to keep track of them, but if only they would go to Church on Sundays when the priest announces the next holy days they could avoid this sin. Worse still are the peasants who, when they see their fellows going dutifully to mass, hide under the hedges, then slip away to rob the unguarded orchards.

It seems certain, therefore, that God has no such love for villeins as he has for gentle knights and their dames. The knights display their superiority by always reminding their peasants of their condition. With some barons, to flog their villein for most trifling offenses is about as common as for them to eat their dinners. Even Conon has plenty of use for his riding whip. Unless the blows are very brutal the average peasant takes this as all in the day's work. He merely trades out his own blows upon his wife and children. Indeed, it is commonly said that most villeins are so numb mentally they never can comprehend the simplest orders unless they are driven home with stripes. In time of war the fate of the peasants is, as we have seen, far worse than this. Whatever a feud means to the contending parties, to their villeins it means houses and crops burned, fruit trees girdled, young girls dragged off to a life of infamy, and probably the massacre of many peasants in cold blood. One of the reasons the nobles delight so in war is because it is seldom that they have to endure its real anguish and horror; but in the churches the non-nobles pray, *"Grant us to peace"* quite as fervently as they beseech, "Save us from famine"—and with equal justice.

The monkish preachers who make a business of scolding sometimes denounce high-born oppressors of the villeins. One monk thus cries out, "All that the peasant amasses in one year of stubborn toil, the noble devours in an hour. Not content with his lawful revenues, he despoils them by illicit exactions. As wolves devour carrion while the crows croak overhead, awaiting their share of the feast, so when knights pillage their subjects the provosts [their agents] and others of the hellish crew rejoice at the prospect of devouring the remainder." Or again: "Ye nobles are ravening wolves; therefore shall ye howl in hell," for you "despoil your subjects and live on the blood and sweat of the poor." (Jacques of Vitry.) Nevertheless, the selfsame preachers accuse the peasants of the cardinal sins of avarice and of shunning labor. Only rarely are the villeins comforted by being told that if they work faithfully and bring up

271

a proper family they are morally on equality "with a cleric who chants all day in a church."

On the St. Aliquis fiefs, and, indeed, on many others, these grosser abuses do not obtain, but nowhere are the villeins exempt from one evil which they must meet with dumb resignation—the seigneurial hunts.[1] Conon and his guests never hesitate at going with horses and hawks or hounds straight across plowed and seeded fields or even over standing grain. This is the lord's absolute right, and protest is impossible. The hunters, too, are entitled, if far from home, to stop at the peasants' huts and demand food and fodder, perhaps for a large party. If payment is made, it is merely out of charity. Greater evils still may come from the depredations of the wild game, if the fields are close to the hunting preserves. Villeins cannot harm any deer nibbling the young sprouts. They can only scare them away—and the cunning creatures soon grow daring. A wild boar can root up a dozen little farm plots before the baron can find leisure to chase him down. Upon some fiefs the peasants can arrange to pay an extra fee to their lord, in return for which he keeps only rabbits near their fields; but the hunt of a single rabbit, if the flying wretch doubles in among the corn, may ruin a family.

On the other hand, the penalties for poaching, for "killing messire's game," are terrible. It is probably safer on St. Aliquis'—as on any other fief—to risk killing a traveler than killing a fawn or even a hare. The law is pitilessly enforced by the foresters. Maître Denis will tell you he has hanged more stout fellows for poaching than for any other two crimes put together.

Do the villeins ever revolt? Sometimes, when they are driven to desperation by extreme misery; when they

[1] See page 67.

find a clever leader; when circumstances are peculiarly favorable. Then may come the sudden burning of manor houses and small fortalices; the massacre of their inmates; and other brutish deeds of tardy retaliation. The rebels are likely to boast, as did some insurgent peasants in Normandy in the eleventh century: "We have been weak and insane to bend our necks for so long. For we are strong-handed men, and solider and stouter limbed than the nobles will ever be. For everyone of them there are a hundred of us!"

Such revolts always have a single end. The ignorant peasants submit to no discipline. They cannot use the knight's weapons if they capture them. They cannot organize. If they seize a castle, the liquor in the cellars lays them out helpless through a week of orgy. The seigneurs instantly rally and with their great horses hunt down the rebels as creatures worse than wolves. The vengeance then taken on the insurgents is such that every ear that hears thereof must tingle. Perhaps along a league of roadway a corpse will be swinging from every tree. Such measures effectively discourage rebellion save under most exceptional circumstances. Even with atrocious seigneurs it is usually best to bow to the will of God and merely to pray for deliverance.

Georges' and Alard's mental horizons can be imagined. They have on rare occasions been as far as Pontdebois, although some of their neighbors have passed a lifetime without even that privilege. They have only the most limited, one might say only the most animal, hopes and fears. Their ideas of such things as the king's court, Paris, and the various Christian and Infidel lands are a jumble of absurd notions. "Religion" means a few prayers, a few saints' stories, as told in the church, the miracle plays at Christmas, and a fear lest

273

by failing in proper respect to monks and priests they will be eternally tormented in worse torture chambers than old Baron Garnier's.

The villeins, of course, have their own rustic holidays, full of rough sports—wrestling, throwing weights, archery, and also cockfighting and bull baiting. The best of entertainment is when two blindfolded men, each carrying a cudgel, try to kill a goose or pig let loose in an inclosure. The whole village roars to see them belabor each other. During the wedding festivities, to show their dutiful esteem for Alienor and Olivier, the peasants had arranged a special ceremony in their honor. Four blindfolded men were led about the neighborhood, preceded by two men, one playing an oboe, the other carrying a red banner whereon a pig was painted. After this noisy merrymaking a real pig was produced, and before an august company of most of the castle folk the four champions "attacked the pig." They hit one another so hard, that one was picked up almost dead. The pig became the property of the villein who had managed to pound the life out of the creature just as in mercy Alienor was about to beg that the contest end.

Despite grievances and grumblings, the average peasants are loyal, somewhat after the manner of dumb dogs, to their seigneurs. Conon and Adela command the real affection of their villeins because of acts of charity, but even Baron Garnier had been treated with an astonishing faithfulness. Many a knight has owed his life or honor to humble dependents whom he has not treated so well as his horses or hounds. It is the toiling thousands in the little thatched huts that make possible the wedding feasts, the adubbements, the tourneys, and the spectacular battles. Some day the exploitation will cease—but not in the thirteenth century.

Chapter XVII: Charity. Care of the Sick. Funerals.

EVEN upon a well-ordered seigneury the number of the poor, disabled, and generally miserable is great. Despite the contempt displayed by the great for the lowly, the Feudal Age is not lacking in pretty abundant charity or rather in almsgiving. The haughtiest cavalier feels it his duty to scatter copper obols when he goes among the poor, though doubtless he tells his squire to fling the coins merely to "satisfy this hungry rabble." Among the virtues of Conon and Adela is the fact that they throw the money with their own gentle hands. This somehow adds to the donative's value.

The present season is prosperous at St. Aliquis. Furthermore, there has just been such an open house at the castle that one would expect even the most luckless to be satiated for a while. Nevertheless, the very day after the guests have departed Adela is informed that there are more than thirty people before the drawbridge, chanting their "Alms! For the sake of Christ, aims!" The baroness, suppressing a sigh, quits her maids, to whom she is just assigning their weaving, and goes to the bailey. With her attends lay-brother Gensenius, an assistant to Father Grégoire, who acts as castle almoner. The crowd contains many familiar faces. Yonder old man on one leg, the blind woman led by a little girl, the lad with a withered arm, the woman disfigured by

275

goiter, the widow whose husband was slain in a brawl, leaving her with eight children, the harmless idiot—all these Adela immediately recognizes. But the excitement of the fêtes has attracted others whom she and Brother Gensenius scan closely. This melancholy fellow on crutches possibly can run very fast if he sees that the provost's men are after him. His companion, who seems covered with sores and who claims to be on a pilgrimage to a healing shrine, is clearly a scamp and malingerer. Right before the baroness a strange woman falls down foaming at the mouth, as if she had epilepsy. Gensenius shakes his crafty head. "She is the same impostor," he whispers, "who tried her trick with a bit of soap yesterday in the village."

So the sheep gradually are separated from the goats. Some of the charlatans are chased away. Some of those who receive loaves of bread and broken meat are perhaps no more deserving than the rejected. But dare one really be too critical? After all, the reason why great folk give to beggars is to cancel sins. If the beggars are undeserving, that hardly diminishes the credit with the saints for Conon and Adela. It would be calamitous if there were suddenly to be no poor, worthy or unworthy, for how then, by parting with some of their abundance, could the rich buy peace for their souls? Fortunately, however, there is no such danger. Our Lord has directly said, "The poor ye have always with you," a most comforting word of Scripture. Poverty, then, is a blessed institution even for the fortunate in this world; it enables them to procure entrance to heaven by acts of charity. As for persons who are needy, of course, if they bear their lot with Christian resignation they accumulate a blessed stock of indulgence which will cut short their durance in purgatory.

The morning dole is a regular feature at St. Aliquis, as at every other castle and monastery. The amount of food given away is really very great. But there is next to no attempt on the part of the average seigneury really to remedy this mendicancy—to devise honest work within the capacities of the blind or the lame; to give systematic relief to the widow; to put the idiot lad in some decent institution. Every premium is placed upon the idlers, the impostors, and the low-browed rogues who prefer anything to honest toil. In the times of real famine, even, the temptation to cease prematurely struggling against hard times and to lapse into beggardom is very dangerous. Despite, therefore, much genuine kindness on the part of many donors, charity in the Feudal Age is allowed more than ordinarily to cover a multitude of sins—alike those of the givers and the receivers. Upon the St. Aliquis barony there is an astonishing number of unabashed drones and parasites.

These miserable folk, however, have some excuse. Conditions of life in the Feudal Age, even for the cavaliers, are very severe. Men and women begin the duties of life young, mature young, grow old young. Henry II of Anjou and England was only forty-seven when they began to call him "old." Philip Augustus was only fifteen when he was capable of assuming the actual duties of a responsible monarch. Many a baron is gray headed at forty. When he is fifty his sons may often be intriguing to supplant their superannuated father. If this is true of the nobility, what of the toiling peasantry? We have seen how Georges and Jeanne are aged before their time.

Grinding toil by weakening the body, of course, leaves it exposed to many ordinary diseases. But certainly conditions in castle and village open the doors to extraordinary plagues as well. The age is happily ignorant of sanitary precautions which more sophisticated mortals will consider a matter of course. The peasants "almost live on the manure heap." The clergy (though not themselves so uncleanly) seldom preach the virtues of bathing; indeed, their discourses on "despising the body" apparently discourage the practice. It is hard to keep meat any length of time unless it is salted, and the vast amounts of salt meat consumed everywhere are direct promoters of scurvy and gangrene. We have seen that nearly all the clothing worn close to the body is woolen. This retains filth, is hard to wash, and irritates the skin, another cause for frequent dermal diseases—scrofula, the itch, and things even worse.

A LEPER

Holding in his hand the bones with which these unfortunates were compelled to signal their approach from a distance. From a window in the cathedral of Bourges (thirteenth century).

Leprosy is a terrible scourge. Its nature is misunderstood. Often severe but curable cases of eczema are confounded therewith, and harmless victims are condemned to a death in life—perpetual banishment to filthy cabins in the woods. Cholera and smallpox every now and then break out in a neighborhood, and they are almost always fatal. Nothing really can be done to check them except to pray to the saints. Such diseases are (say the best informed) communicated "in the air"; consequently any ordinary isolation is useless. On the whole, they ravage the villages more than they do the castles, though hardly

278

because the castle folk are able to take more effective physic. Yet often enough a baron and his entire family may be swept away. Very seldom is it suggested that pure water, cleanliness, and rational schemes of isolation can accomplish much to defeat the apparent desire of heaven to devastate an entire duchy.

Other diseases are fearfully common. The sufferers from nervous complaints make up small armies. The general terrors and wars of the times, the brooding fears of the devil, hell, and the eternal torment, the spectacle of the fearful punishments, and, on the other hand, the sheer ennui of life in many castles and in certain ill-ruled convents, drive men and women out of their wits. Such sufferers are lucky if they are treated with kindness and are not, as being "possessed of devils," clapped in a dungeon.

Finally, it should be said that lucky is the mother who does not have one-third to one-half of all her offspring die in the act of birth. Every entrance of a babe into the world is a dice throwing with death, even if the mid-wife is clever. Once born, the children are likely to be so injured in the initiatory process that they will be physically imperfect or dangerously weakened. This is true even in the royal families; how much more true in the peasant huts! It is not surprising that the average man of the Feudal Ages can give and sustain hard blows. Only the strongest have been able to survive the ordeals of birth and childhood.

To fight these dangers, one must invoke both human and divine aid. Good Christians usually feel that the healing saints avail more than do physicians or wise women. If you have indigestion, invoke St. Christopher; if dropsy, St. Eutropius; if fever, St. Petronila; for the pest, St. Roch; for insanity, St. Mathurin; for

kidney complaint, St. René; for cramps, St. Crampan—
and so with many other ills. Nevertheless, one need not
trust solely to prayers. Only great people, however,
employ regular physicians (*mires*). Villeins commonly
have in a "good woman," much better than a sorcerer.
The breath of an ass drives poison from a body. The
touch of a dead man's tooth cures toothache. If you
have a nosebleed, seize the nose with two straws shaped
like a cross. If the itch troubles you, roll yourself naked
in a field of oats. Georges, the peasant, will tell you
that such remedies seldom fail.

A local professor of the healing art is Maître Denis, the
executioner. Since he knows so well how to mutilate
bodies, he ought to be able to understand the converse
process of curing them. He has wide reputation as a
healer of broken bones, and he often sells his patients a
panacea for multifarious ills—"the fat of a man just
hung."

There is at least this to be said for the peasants: the
science of *their* healers will agree almost as much with
that of later physicians as does that of the contemporary
"physicians" themselves. The Church has not given any
too great encouragement to medicine. The mighty St.
Ambrose has said that the proper healing is by prayers
and vigils. Only clerics of the inferior orders are allowed
to study medical science, and the dissection of dead
bodies is decidedly discountenanced.[1]

At the castle the ordinary functionary to abate bodily
ills is Maître Louis, the baron's barber. When not
scraping chins, he was very likely giving the castle folk
their monthly bleedings, without which it is very hard

[1] As a result of this attitude, such a distinguished and genuinely
learned scholar as Albert the Great is said to have confounded
tendons and nerves.

to keep one's health. The bleedings take place, if possible, in the great hall near the fire, and are undergone regularly by both sexes. When the St. Aliquis forces are called to war, Maître Louis goes with them as barber-surgeon, and he really has considerable skill in setting fractures and cauterizing and salving wounds, as well as with a few powerful drugs—mostly purgatives—which probably help those of his patients who have the strongest constitutions to recover.

When one of the baron's own family is seriously sick, it is usual to send to Pontdebois for a professional physician. About two years ago Conon himself fell into a fever. They brought to him Maître Payen, who claimed to have learned his art as *mire* by travel among the schools of medicine—at Salerno in Sicily, at Montpellier in the Languedoc country, and even at Cordova among the Infidels, although the baron swore angrily (after he was gone) that he had never been nearer any of these places than Paris.

A THIRTEENTH-
CENTURY DOCTOR
Restored by Viollet-
Le-Duc, from a manu-
script in the Biblio-
thèque nationale.

Maître Payen was sprucely dressed half as a priest, half as a rich burgher. He wore elegant furs. He talked very learnedly of "febrifuges" and "humors," and kept repeating, "Thus says Avincenna, the prince of Spanish physicians," or, "Thus says Albucasis, the infallible follower of Avincenna." If Conon had suffered from some easily discoverable malady, probably Maître Payen could have suggested a fairly efficient means of cure. He was not without shrewdness,

281

and in his chest was a whole arsenal of herbs and drugs. He had also efficient salves, although he had never heard the word "antiseptic." But the baron had picked up one of those maladies which baffled easy diagnosis. Maître Payen, therefore, fussed about, clearly betraying his bewilderment, then struck a professional attitude and announced oracularly, "The obstruction to health is in the liver."

"Nay," groaned the baron, "it is in the head that I feel so wretched."

"That is foolish," retorted the *mire*, crushingly: "Beware of that word 'obstruction,' because you do not understand what it signifies."[1]

He next muttered certain cabalistic words; said that the baron should be glad that his liver was affected, because that was the seat of honor, and that upon recovery his honor would be enlarged. The spleen was the seat of laughter, while the lungs fanned the heart. Payen then talked of remedies. Perhaps the urine of a dog would be best, or the blood of a hegoat; but these were only villein remedies. Messire, the patient, was a great noble and needed noble remedies, suitable for his rank. He would therefore (since the liver was affected) give him the dried and pulverized liver of a toad. And so he left his medicines, took a gold piece, and departed.

That night Conon was delirious, but Adela, who, like every mistress of a castle, had perforce learned much of nursing, applied cold cloths to his body, while Father Grégoire prayed to the saints. The next morning, because of the cloths, the saints, or toad's liver, the fever abated. Perhaps it had merely run its natural course.

---

[1] A mediæval medical treatise deliberately advises the use of this argument to silence patients when the physicians cannot make a diagnosis, yet must say something.

After the baron recovered he would curse terribly at mention of Maître Payen. He would be ready enough to cry "amen!" to the saying of the monk Guy of Provins, "they (the physicians) kill numbers of the sick, and exhaust themselves to find maladies for everybody. Woe to him who falls into their power! I prefer a capon to all their mixtures!" The monk concedes, indeed, that certain physicians are useful, but that it is because of the confidence which they inspire rather than thanks to their medicines that they effect cures.

When next Conon falls sick, he vows that he will trust simply to Maître Louis or even to Maître Denis, although he may consent to send for a Lazarist monk, a member of the great monastic order which makes a specialty of healing the sick. For although these truly noble monks (who combine worldly wisdom with an equal amount of piety) treat especially leprosy, they are gradually turning their attention to diseases in general. If he cannot get a Lazarist, he will be likely to hire in an astrologer to discover a remedy by consulting the stars; or Father Grégoire may organize a "healing procession" of all the monks, clerks, and pious laymen whom he can muster. With solemnity they will carry the whole stock of saints' relics in the neighborhood to the sick seigneur, and lay them devoutly upon his abdomen. This remedy was tried in Paris some time ago to cure Prince Louis, the king's heir, and he recovered promptly. Similar assistance is available for a great seigneur like Conon.

Not always, indeed, will even the saints' relics avail. When the time had come for the good Lady Odelina, Conon's mother, they postponed extreme unction to the final moment, because after that ceremony the sick

person has really no right to get well. The hair falls out
and the natural heat is diminished. The moment breath
quitted the noble dame's body, the servants ran furiously
through the castle, emptying every vessel of water lest
the departing soul should be drowned therein. The
dead body was also watched carefully until burial, lest
the devil should replace it in its coffin with a black cat,
and likewise lest a dog or cat should run over the coffin

A THIRTEENTH-CENTURY BURIAL SCENE
From an English manuscript (Schultz).

and change the corpse into a vampire. Conon and
Adela are not convinced of these notions, but do not
dispute them with the servitors.

Next the body was carefully embalmed. The heart
was removed, to be buried at a nunnery whereof Lady
Odelina had been the patroness. A waxen death mask
was made of the face, and the body was laid out on a
handsome bed with black hangings. A temporary altar
was set up in the apartment that masses might be said
there, and one or two of Conon's vassals or squires remained on guard night and day, fully armed, while
round the bed blazed two or three scores of tall candles.

The interment took place in the abbey church, in the

transept where rested so many of the St. Aliquis stock. They laid upon the Lady Odelina's breast a silver cross engraved with the words of absolution; and in the heavy stone casket also were buried four small earthen pots, each of which had contained some of the incense burned during the funeral ceremony. Finally, when the rites were over, Conon employed a cunning sculptor to make a life-size marble effigy of his mother, to rest upon the slab covering her tomb—an effigy which, by the dignity and genuine peace of form and face, was long to express how truly noble had been his gracious mother.

Common folk cannot have marble caskets and effigies, but even poor peasants are graced with decidedly elaborate funerals. When a person of the least consequence in the village dies, a crier goes down all the lanes, ringing a bell and calling out the name of the deceased, adding, "Pray God for the dead." Peasants of quality are likely to be laid away in plaster coffins, although the poorest class of villeins are wrapped only in rags and tossed into shallow pits.

Still worse is the fate of those who die excommunicated by the Church or of suicides. These unfortunates cannot even be buried in holy ground. Their bodies are often exposed, to be torn by the dogs and crows. Sometimes, however, a hardened sinner repents sufficiently on his deathbed to be restored to the graces of religion. But in this case his body is frequently burned, all laden with iron or brazen fetters. The idea is thus to mortify the body, even after the breath of life has departed, and so to abate those fires in purgatory assuredly awaiting for all save great saints, who can pass straight to heaven, or the numerous reprobates whose guilt requires not temporary, but eternal torment.

Chapter XVIII: Popular Religion. Pilgrimages. Superstitions. Relic Worship.

LL the folk of St. Aliquis are Christians. Nobody, far and wide, except a few Jews in Pontdebois, openly dissents from the Catholic religion, denies the validity of the creeds, or refuses a certain outward conformity to the Church practices. The age is not greatly interested in improving the general moral and social condition of the common people. The common people even are not always interested in this themselves. Each peasant prays for "just treatment" and for good luck. Otherwise, castle and village alike accept as a kind of natural law the immutability of society. God has established the various orders and gradations. All that one can ask is that each man shall accept the condition assigned to him and live in it efficiently and happily.

Conon, like every other knight, has no temptation to unbelief. The doctors of the Church know all about religion, just as the king's falconers know all about hawking. It is sensible to trust the expert. If you ask idle questions, you merely risk your soul, as do the followers of Mahound, the false prophet. The baron frequently denounces the arrogance and covetousness of the clergy and resists their pretentions, but he nevertheless trusts them to supply him with the Sacraments and bless his death and burial so that his soul may pass promptly through purgatory into paradise—where exist-

286

ence presumably is one grand admixture of a marriage feast in a fine garden and of a magnificent tournament. Plenty of knights are lax and blasphemous, but they hardly are deliberately unbelieving.[1] Good knights ought to hear mass every morning; venerate holy objects and places; hate Jews and Saracens; worship the Virgin and the saints; also keep most of the major fasts and other special occasions of the Church. Conon does all these things. He is "a good Christian." But he is exempted from any serious thinking for himself upon mysterious matters.

A GROUP OF PRIESTS, THIRTEENTH CENTURY

The one who is near the altar is wearing a chasuble and the second and third are clad in the dalmatica, or deacon's gown. The second carries the consecrated wafer and the third a sort of fan. (From a manuscript in the Bibliothèque nationale.)

When Conon prays in the morning, if not hurried he lies down with his head turned toward the east, and his arms stretched out like a cross. He recites the favors which God has shown him in the past, beseeches Heaven to continue favorable. Often he adds a Credo and a certain paraphrase of the Lord's Prayer then very common—"Our Father, who desirest that we all be saved,

[1] In the well-known romance of *Aucassin and Nicolette,* Aucassin complains that if he cannot have his beloved he cares not to go to paradise. "For there go those aged priests, and those old cripples and the maimed, who, all day long and all night long, cough before the altars . . . who are naked and barefoot and full of sores. . . . *But to hell will I go!* For to hell go the fair clerks and the great warriors. . . . And there go the fair and courteous ladies, who have friends, two or three together with their wedded lords!" This was blasphemous enough, but it was not atheistical.

grant that we acquire Thy love even as have the angels who do thy pleasure on high; and give us our daily bread—for the soul the Holy Sacrament, and for the body its needful sustenance." Yet if his mood is not unusually humble and contrite, he is likely to conclude patronizingly, "And I confide also in the strength of my heart, which thou hast bestowed, in my good sword and my fleet horse, yet especially in Thee!"

Many a cavalier breaks into blasphemies when things go wrong. Such men are like William Rufus of England, who cried, "God shall never see me a good man—I have suffered too much at His hands!" Or Henry II, who, on learning that his son Henry had revolted, cried aloud, "Since Thou, O God, hast taken away from me that which I prized the most, Thou shalt not have what Thou prizest most in me—my soul." And even Conon, once when hard beset, had exclaimed, like a certain crusading lord: "What king, O Lord, ever deserted thus his men? Who *now* will trust in or fight for thee?"

Nevertheless, one should deal mercifully with such sinful words, for, after all, is not the world very evil and the temptation to rail at God extremely great? It is true that things are not as they were in the year A.D. 1000, when even the wisest felt very sure the Last Day was at hand. Eclipses, comets and famines had then seemed foreshadowing this. People crowded the churches in agony, expecting to hear the Seven Trumpets announce Antichrist. Repeatedly since then, when the years have been calamitous, monks and old wives have stirred multitudes by vehement predictions that the plagues of the Apocalypse and the other preliminaries to the millennium are not to be delayed. As late as A.D. 1200 the monk Rigord, at the abbey of St. Denis, wrote: "The world is ill; it grows so old that it relapses into

288

infancy. Common report has it that Antichrist has been born at Babylon and that the Day of Judgement is nigh."

Fears like this restrain even reckless seigneurs and sodden peasants from proceeding to inconceivable crimes. The agonies of the damned will be so dreadful! The preachers understand very well that it is of little use to try to restrain the wicked by talking of "the love and mercy of God." If King Philip had only used love and mercy upon his vassals he would be now a king without a kingdom. It is the dread of the eternal burning which apparently keeps a large part of all Christendom tolerably obedient to the more essential mandates of morality and of the Church.

When a great criminal deliberately defies the Church there is a ceremony which makes even the righteous inquire as to their own salvation. A few months ago a certain impious baron robbed a parish church of a chalice. Instantly at Pontdebois the bishop took action. The great bell of the cathedral tolled as for a funeral; and such it was, though of the soul, far more precious than merely the body. The bishop appeared in the chancel with all his clergy. Each cleric held a lighted candle. The building was hung with black tapestry. Amid a terrible hush the bishop announced the name of the offending knight to the crowded nave, then proclaimed in loud voice: "Let him be cursed in the city and cursed in the field; cursed in his granery, his harvest, and his children; as Dathan and Abiram were swallowed up by the gaping earth, so may hell swallow him; and even as to-day we quench these torches in our hands, so may the light of his life be quenched for all eternity, unless he do repent!" Whereat all the priests dashed their torches to the pavement and trampled them out. One could almost see that sacrilegious baron writhing in the flames of Gehenna.

After a scene like this there is no reinstatement for the sinner save by some great act of penance and mortification. An excommunicated person is next door to an outlaw. He may find sundry companions in crime, but most people will shun him as they would a leper. This particular baron, after vain boasts and defiance, at last was so conscience-torn and forsaken that he made an abject peace with the bishop. First, he gave ruinously costly gifts to the cathedral; then he presented himself barefoot and in the robe of a pilgrim at the chancel. He prostrated himself and for a day and a night remained in prayer before the high altar, eating and drinking nothing. After that he knelt again while some three-score clerics and monks present each smote him with a rod, he crying aloud, "Just are Thy judgments, O Lord!" after every blow. Not till all this was accomplished did the bishop raise him, pronounce the absolution, and give him the kiss of peace. It was very dreadful.[1]

For lesser offenses against the Church there are lesser but effective penalties. In Pontdebois there was once a religious procession in Lent. A certain woman marched therein with pretended devoutness, but then went home and in defiance of the fast-time dined upon some mutton and ham. The odor escaped into the street. The woman was seized, and the bishop condemned her to walk through the town with her quarter of mutton on the spit over her shoulder, the ham slung round her neck, and with a ribald crowd, of course, trailing behind. After that penance the fasts were well kept in Pontdebois.

[1] This was very much like the penance imposed on Henry II after the murder of Thomas à Becket at Canterbury.

Yet one must not think of the religion of this Feudal Age as in general sad. On the contrary (by one of those abrupt contrasts now grown familiar) clergy and people get vast joy, not to say amusement, even out of the sacred ordinances. "Men go gayly along the road to salvation." For example, the great pilgrimages (pardons) are often festive reunions with merchants chaffering and jongleurs playing or doing their tricks while the whole company proceeds to some shrine.

Even in the church building solemnity is not always maintained. The choir, indeed, belongs pretty strictly to worship, but in the nave all sorts of secular proceedings can go on, even the meetings of malcontent factions and of rioters. The church bells ring for markets, for musters, or for peaceful gatherings almost as often as they ring for the holy services. As for the sacred festivals, good bishops complain that they are so numerous that the secular element intrudes utterly, and disfigures them with idleness and carousing. The peasants may go to early mass; after that they will drink, chatter, sing, dance (in a very riotous fashion), and join in wrestlings, races, and archery contests until nightfall.

Besides these ordinary abuses of holy things, every parish seems to have its own special Reign of Folly, although the name of the celebration varies from place to place. Even the younger clergy participate in such mock ceremonies. In Pontdebois the subdeacons elect a Pope of Buffoons, give him a silver tiara, and enthrone him with much dignity, electing at the same time several "cardinals" to help direct his revels. There are noisy processions, cavalcades, and even scandalous parodies of some of the most sacred services of the Church. The mock pope issues "bulls" enjoining all kinds of horse-play, and actually strikes a kind of lead money with such

291

legends as "Live merrily and rejoice," or, "Fools are sometimes wise." It seems next to impossible to confine such proceedings to the streets, the market place and the church porch, although decent bishops fight against instrusions into the holy building. The canons of the cathedral have finally induced the junior clergy and the lay rabble to refrain from the more extreme parodies and from such pranks as stealing the church bells by giving the "Pope" and all his noisy rout a grand dinner. Pious churchmen groan on such days, but they comfort themselves by saying that these proceedings make religion popular and give an outlet for "the flesh," which if restrained too much, will succumb before even worse temptations of the devil.

In St. Aliquis village the parish priest actually participates in a ceremony equally calculated to astonish another age. On a certain Sunday the folk celebrate the virtues of the ass which bore our Lord and the Holy Virgin when St. Joseph fled with them into Egypt. The peasants take the best ass in the neighborhood, caparison it gayly, and lead it through the streets to the church, all the children running along, waving flower wands and shouting, with the older folk almost equally demonstrative. At the holy portal the priest meets them and announces in Latin "This is a day of mirth. Let all sour lookers get themselves hence. Away with envy! Those who celebrate the Festival of the Ass desire jollity!"

Then the ass is led straight up into the chancel and tethered to the altar rail. A solemn Prose, half Latin, half French, is chanted, setting forth the virtues of the faithful, stolid beast which enabled our Lord to escape the wicked Herod. Ever and anon the cantor stops and all the crowded church rings with the refrain, "*He! haw!*

sire ass—he! haw!" everybody trying to pull down his nose and bray as lustily as possible. Finally, when the ass has been led decorously back to his stall, the choristers, with many friends, indulge in a bountiful repast. This Festival of the Ass is celebrated in° very many French cities and villages.

One must also comprehend that certain saints are the particular patrons of given regions. St. Martin is a potent saint through all France, but St. Denis is the especial guardian of the royal domains; St. Nicholas of Lorraine, St. Andre of Burgundy, and of course St. George of England. St. Michael, too, may assist French knights sooner than he will foreigners. There are also many local saints of incalculable sacredness in their own small regions, yet hardly heard of elsewhere. Thus, if you travel very far, you are likely to lose all trace of good St. Aliquis, and, indeed, peevish visitors have suggested that he has never been canonized at Rome or properly accepted by the Catholic Church. For all that, he is venerated locally, perhaps with greater fervor than any other holy one, saving always our Blessed Lady herself.

There is no saint with whom it is possible to compare the Virgin. She is the "Lady of Heaven," the "Queen of the Holy City," the "*Dame débonnaire.*" God the Father and God the Son seem perhaps to be inaccessible celestial emperors, but the Holy Virgin, who understands the needs of toiling men, will transmit their pleas and exert her vast influence in their behalf. Therefore, on her statues she is dressed like a feudal queen with rich stuffs, a crown glittering with jewels, and she bears a royal scepter and an orb of the world. All the saints are her vassals and do her liege homage.

There is another set of joyous celebrations legitimate

and uplifting. At Christmas time, on *Noël* eve the good folk will install a heifer, an ox, and an ass in the parish church "to warm the holy babe with their breath." Torches are lighted everywhere and fires are lit upon the hills. Groups of people march about dressed like shepherds bound for the Christchild's manger and led by pipes and viols, while all sing joyously:

> "Good sirs, now hark ye!—
> From far lands come we,
> For it is Noël."

Then in the church are sung long responses, telling the story of Christmas in the vernacular and interspersed with comments by the animals in Latin, because (as says the hymn)

> All the beasts in other days
> Spoke French less well than Latin.

So the cock crows out his satisfaction, the goat bleats, the calf bellows, the ox lows, the ass brays. It is all done simply, reverently, and for the benefit of simple, loving souls.

In Pontdebois, however, they have a more elaborate performance. Twelve clerks, representing six Jews and six pagans, present themselves in the cathedral choir, declaring they wish to examine the evidence that the babe newly born is truly the Redeemer. Whereat appear in stately sequence all the prophets who have fore-warned the coming of Christ, besides Moses with his horn, Balaam with his ass, the three Hebrew children of the fiery furnace, the pagan sybils, and the twelve apostles. Each responds with canticles in sonorous Latin, until the twelve doubters declare themselves satisfied and fall down to worship the Infant King.

Mystery Plays

At Easter there are other mystery plays telling the story of the divine Passion and of the Resurrection; and still others come at intervals through the year. Some of the participants are priests, but many others laymen, both men and women.[1] All the more important episodes in the Bible are acted out with considerable detail and with much comedy interspersed. The crowds howl with glee when Ananias, like a shrewd Jew, chaffers for the sale of his field, or when hideous devils leap up from hell to seize Herodias's daughter the instant she has accomplished her wicked will with John the Baptist. There is no attempt to represent ancient times. Herod is dressed like a feudal duke, and before him is carried a crucifix. The numerous devils are always black; the angels wear blue, red, and white; "God" appears wearing a papal tiara; and the "souls of the dead" appear covered with veils—white for the saved, red or black for the damned. It is a source of great delight for the people to take part in these plays, and even the great folk are not above joining in them. One need not comment on how completely such proceedings impress the imaginations of the unlearned with the stories of the Old and New Testaments. The Bible can be *read* only by the few, but an essential part of it is *seen* and reasonably comprehended by the many.

So much for ordinary religious beliefs and occasions. But there are plenty of people who find their sins are so terrible that they must resort to some great penances, often consuming the remainder of their lives, in order to propitiate Heaven. Besides the monks and the nuns dwelling in convents, there exist a great many hermits

[1] These plays might be guild or even civic affairs, with the secular element predominating among the actors.

and "religious solitaries," who abide in little huts in the woods, perhaps maintaining a tiny chapel for travelers, and being fed on the offerings of forest rangers and peasants. Not all these hermits live, however, in genuine solitude. Right in St. Aliquis village there is something everywhere common—a female recluse.

Many years ago, a certain peasant woman, Elise, murdered her husband. She was promptly condemned to the gallows, but Baron Garnier, with unusual mercy, pardoned her on condition "that she be shut up within a small house in the cemetery, that she might there do penance and so end her days." A stone hut was accordingly built, and the unhappy woman conducted thither with a regular procession, two priests blessing the hut and giving Elise a kind of consecration. She was put inside. Every aperture was then built up except a narrow chink to admit air, a little light, and a small dole of food from her relatives.

Elise has been vegetating in this hut for now twenty years—living in filth and darkness, but talking most piously to visitors standing outside. Seemingly, she does little except to mutter almost incessant prayers. Already her crime is forgotten. The peasants speak of her as "that holy woman" and even wonder whether, after she dies in her cell—for she will never leave it—she cannot be enrolled among the saints. There are many other much more innocent recluses, male and female, who have been walled up voluntarily—either out of piety or of sheer love of idleness, possibly because of both.

Nevertheless, ordinarily the best way to discharge the load of a guilty conscience is by pilgrimage. Confessors often impose this means of penance upon penitents, as the best way of winning the divine mercy. Since death is about the only judicial penalty for great crimes, a penance of pilgrimage for six, ten, or twelve years—going from shrine to shrine all over Christendom—is really a substitute for a term of imprisonment. Pilgrims of this pronounced type are required to go barefoot, with head shaved, to quit their families and wives, and to fast continually—that is, never to touch meat more than once a day.

Even exalted nobles thus spend the remainder of a lifetime expiating their iniquities. Everyone has heard of Count Fulk the Black of Anjou, who heaped up misdeeds even to the murdering of his wife. Then at last he realized the awful peril to his soul. Three times he made the long pilgrimage to Jerusalem, the third time letting himself be dragged upon a hurdle through the streets of the Sacred City, while two varlets smote him with whips.

Such great criminals often carry passports issued by bishops, certifying that they are expiating by pilgrimage specified evil deeds—and requesting Christian folk to give them lodging, food, and assistance. These penitents, if knights, are likely to wear chains upon their wrists and neck, forged of their own armor, as witnesses at once of their social position and their genuine repentance.

Most pilgrims, however, have no such fearful things weighing down their souls. They are simply ordinary erring men who are moved by a genuine piety, possibly admixed with a willingness to find excuse for "seeing the world." Every day they appear at the gate of St. Aliquis castle to ask a share in the supper and a bed on the rushes in the hall, and they are respectfully treated, although Conon sometimes complains that their trailing robes of brown wool, heavy staffs, and sacks slung at belt are merely the disguises for so many wandering rogues. Unwashed and unkempt though many of them are, it never does to repulse them, lest you lose the Scriptural blessing for those who received strangers and so "have entertained angels unawares."

Pilgrims, too, are good newsmongers. They supply you with tidings from Italy, Germany, Spain, or even the Holy Land. They will carry letters also to foreign parts and transmit verbal messages to kinsmen. They do not always travel alone, but by twos, fives, or even tens. Recently at Dunkirk, where the peasants revolted, the bishop laid upon twenty-five of their leaders the penance that they should spend a year going about in a body to different holy places and joining in religious processions "in twenty-six churches," wearing no clothing save their trousers, going barefoot, and carrying the rods with which they had been disciplined.

Innumerable are the shrines where sinners can profit their souls by a visit. Every important abbey claims to be a pilgrimage resort, and the monks will tell of remarkable miracles wrought by all the saints whose relics they chance to treasure. Probably there are more than a thousand such places whose claims have been somewhat recognized by the Church. Many of these shrines have some famous image of the Madonna, frequently brought from the East by Crusaders, but often very old and, to carnal thinking, ugly, perhaps only a "black virgin," a clumsy doll carved of wood. This matters not, provided it is holy and efficacious. "Our Lady of the Fountain" at Samour, "Our Lady of the Osier" near Grenoble, "Our Lady of Good Hope" at Valenciennes, Our Lady of Chartres, of Liesse, of Rocamadour, of Auray, of Puy—these are merely examples.

The greater the distance the pilgrim must go, the greater his merit ordinarily. Happy the pilgrim who can venerate the bones of an actual apostle, as at Rome. Happiest of all is he who can go to Jerusalem and pray at the Holy Sepulcher. Nevertheless, God has provided very efficacious shrines nearer home. Right at Paris there are the seats of St. Génevieve and the great St.

Denis. You can pay your devout homage at Tours to the puissant St. Martin, the ideal of pious warriors. In Normandy, where Mont St. Michel looks across the sands to the tumbling ocean, one can pray best to the mighty archangel nearest to God. It avails much, also, to visit St. Martial of Limoges, St. Sernin of Toulouse, and more still to visit

A SHRINE IN THE FORM OF AN ALTAR (THIRTEENTH CENTURY) IN THE CATHEDRAL AT RHEIMS

Spain and at Compostella beseech the intercession of St. James the Apostle.

Assuredly, however, Rome is best (always barring Jerusalem), and on the way thither the pilgrim can lighten his spiritual load by visiting many excellent Italian shrines—such as "Our Guardian Lady" at Genoa, and, at Lucca, "Our Lady of the Rose." In the city of St. Peter itself, time fails to enumerate the three hundred churches worthy of a devout visit. Besides the majestic cathedral of the Prince of the Apostles and the tomb of St. Paul, even the most hurried pilgrim will not fail to repair to St. Maria Maggiore, where is the actual manger in which Christ was born; and St. John Lateran, where are the holy stairs Christ ascended while wearing the crown of thorns; St. Peter in Montorio, where Peter himself was .crucified, St. Lawrence Without the Walls, where the blessed martyrs St. Stephen and St. Lawrence are buried; not to mention others. A man must be a master criminal if he cannot deliver his soul by suitable visits to these invaluable shrines in Rome.

As is well known, the blessed saints both in this life and after death wrought many miracles through their relics. These wonders continue to-day, although the iniquities of mankind render them infrequent. Every now and then Heaven still permits some holy man to work undoubted miracles. Thus only recently it is said that when the venerable abbot of St. Germer preached the Fourth Crusade in England, he need only bless a fountain, lo! its waters made the dumb speak, the blind see, and the sick recover. Once (so a pilgrim related in the castle only the other day) when this abbot reached a village which wanted a supply of water, he gathered all the folk in the church. Right in the presence of the people he smote a stone with his staff and water flowed forth—not merely potable, but healing for all maladies.

God also speaks to us in dreams as he did to Pharaoh and Nebuchadnezzar. He caused St. Thomas à Becket to visit the late king Louis VII and warn him to make a pilgrimage to St. Thomas's new shrine of Canterbury to pray for the recovery of his son Philip, later "Augustus." Henry II of England was Louis' foe, but the king made the solemn pilgrimage unimpeded, and the crown prince duly recovered.

Omens of calamity, too, appear often, although it is

not always clear whether sent from God or the devil. A few years ago the wolves in the forest near the monastery of St. Aliquis howled steadily all through the day of the feast of St. Honore. "A clear sign of trouble," announced the prior; and four days later the feud began betwixt Conon and Foretvert, which convulsed the whole countryside. Many a man is warned to prepare for death by seeing a will-o-the-wisp in the marshes, a shooting star, or a vulture hovering above his house. If thirteen people chance to sit at one table, or if one chances to dream of a physician, it is proof positive some one in the house is about to die. The same is true if a man inadvertently puts on a clean white shirt on Friday; while if the left eye of a dead man will not close promptly the deceased will soon have company in purgatory. Any woman, also, who thoughtlessly washes her clothes in lye during the holy week is not long for this world. It is needless to explain how sinister are eclipses and comets. In July, 1198, there was a great comet visible. Sage people wagged their heads with melancholy satisfaction when Richard the Lion Hearted died very soon after.

Time will fail to list all the strange beings, neither human, angel, nor exactly devil, that Providence permits to infest the world. These creatures possess no souls, and when they perish are gone like cattle, although they live long and are very hard to kill. Probably they are more numerous in wild and solitary places, yet towns and crowded castles are not free from them. Thus there are *fées* (fairies) good and bad—creatures relatively like human beings; undines in the waters, who by their perfidious beauty lure unwary knights to destruction; ogres who lie in wait to devour small children; ghouls who disinter the dead and gnaw their bones; vampires who rise every night from the tombs and suck the blood; wolf-men (humans turned into beasts) who attack lonely travelers; dracs, who carry off little children to their subterranean realms; will-of-the-wisps in the marshes, who are the souls of unbaptized dead infants; also many rather friendly spirits such as the *soleves,* who sometimes overnight do a weary laborer's work for him. It needs much knowledge to tell the good spirits from the bad—to know, *e.g.,* whether you are dealing with a goblin who will only display harmless antics, or an *estrie,* a real imp of darkness, who may hug you like a bear, to suffocation.

The Church does not forbid the belief in these creatures, nor of such pagan monsters as giants, pygmies, cyclops, satyrs, tritons, sirens, etc., although it plainly teaches us that they are only ministers of the devil. The existence of the devil is as certain as that of the Holy Trinity. As has been said already, the fear of falling into his clutches has often a more excellent effect upon the sinner than the love of God. Countless legends and sculptures in the cathedrals tell all about the master-fiend. The monk in his convent, the peasant in his hut, yes (for all his brave words and his long sword), the baron in his castle, all tremble lest they meet him.

The devil produces all kinds of misery, and he can actually take possession of the living bodies of men. It is affirmed that once, not far from St. Aliquis, a knight was sitting peaceably at table when suddenly the devil entered into him. The fiend spoke through the poor man's mouth. He raved and uttered blasphemies. The priest brought his book of exorcisms. When he recited them, the devil screamed horribly. Yet for some days he resisted the holy formulas, and then departed, leaving his victim utterly exhausted.

RICHARD CŒUR DE LION

From Capefigue's *Histoire de Philippe-Auguste*

Bargains with the Devil

It is much worse when you make a direct pact with the devil. Some time ago, it is affirmed, there was a young scholar at Paris. He was much troubled because he progressed slowly in his studies. Then Satan visited him, saying: "Do me homage. I will make you excel in wisdom!" He gave the youth a stone, asserting that, "So long as you hold this stone in your hand you will know everything." Soon the lad astonished the schools by his erudition, but, on falling sick, confessed his crime, threw away his stone, and at once forgot all his learning. Speedily he died. At once the devils began to torture his soul, but God promptly sent an angel ordering them "to let alone this soul which you have tormented." Immediately the soul flew back into the body, which sprang to life even as the Paris students were celebrating the funeral service. The revived scholar, however, at once entered a convent and took no more chances with carnal studies.

Very many people, however, have compounded with the devil and been less fortunate. The fiend apparently will not come unless one is in a desperate plight and willing to promise everything. Then usually the unhappy mortal must deny the Christian faith, repudiate the saints, utter blasphemies, and, it is even asserted, kiss the arch fiend upon the buttocks. Next a horrid oath must be taken, standing inside of three magic circles and burning incense. After that the devil will, it is true, give his votary great worldly prosperity and especially riches through a long life, but in the end the fiend never fails to claim his soul for an eternal possession. It is even said that Satan made such a bargain with the great ecclesiastic Gerbert, who became Pope Sylvester II. He was very wise[1] or very wicked, probably both; and

[1] His real "wisdom" probably lay in a superior knowledge of mathematics.

in the opinion of many he rose to be Pope by the aid of "a hierarchy of demons and a brass idol which uttered oracles." But on the day of his death (A.D. 1002) Satan demanded his own; and whenever a pope lies near his end the bones of Sylvester II rattle in the tomb. The Church discredits this scandalous story, but it is widely believed.

Since the recent trial of a witch and a wizard before the bishop at Pontdebois, the folk near St. Aliquis have gained a much more precise knowledge of the black art. Magicians usually begin their ceremonies by creating a magic smoke of various inflammables and spices, also by burning such fiend-compelling ingredients as the brain of an eagle, the blood of a black cat, and plenty of hellebore. The smoke thus created is so dense and foul that uninitiated customers are readily convinced there are demons rising in the vapor and talking to the wizard. Thanks to such assistance, the magician, and his even more sinful wife, the witch, were able to instruct how to find a pot of gold and how to rob the house of a rich Jew, but especially they could prepare philters—some of them intended to inspire love and others hatred. Wives could buy fearful compounds made of substances from "the three domains of nature"—the entrails of animals, scales of fishes, parings of nails, human blood, pulverized loadstone, and such powerful drugs as mandragora—which, if duly brewed and beaten up together, then put in an unfaithful husband's goblet, would win back his affection. Other such potions, a little changed, however, would make sworn lovers separate.

These dealers in the black art at Pontdebois could also sell magic rings which had power over demons, thereby protecting the wearer from sudden death, illness, or dangers of travel, and enabling him to drive good bargains. The witch and wizard also possessed, undoubtedly, the "evil eye"—which, if resolutely fixed on an ox or sheep, would cause it to perish and was almost as dangerous to human beings. However, the twain were presently ruined (thus showing how fickle a protector is the devil) because a certain silly nobleman got them to "overcast" a knightly enemy against whom he lacked the courage to press an honorable war. After the wizard had burned much incense, the witch had proceeded to shape a puppet of virgin wax as much like the victim as possible. Then, with a shameless parody of the baptismal service, she christened the doll with the name of her patron's enemy. Next the wizard placed the livers of swallows under the armpits and upon the place where the heart of the puppet ought to be. Finally, he and his wife pierced the wax image with red-hot needles, then cast it into a blazing fire, chanting all the while cabalistic words—probably beseeching the special help of the devil.[1]

Inevitably, soon after this the knight thus assailed would have sickened and died had not, by the mercy of God, the whole proceeding been discovered. The knight was saved by the powerful exorcisms of the bishop. The wizard—after proper tortures to get confession—was buried alive. His wife, the witch, was burned. The foolish cavalier who had plotted murder saved his life, for he had powerful relatives, but was condemned to go on a pilgrimage to Rome. Certain fatuous women who had bought love philters were publicly rebuked in the church and spent an unhappy afternoon in the pillory. Good Christians hope that it will be a long day before

---

[1] This wizard and witch evidently used almost exactly the same means to "overcast" their victim as did Robert of Artois' wizard, when (in 1328) that great nobleman tried to destroy his aunt Mahaut.

the black art is again practiced so iniquitously in this part of France.

Nevertheless, there are some forms of divining which the Church counts as innocent. Any time you desire you can consult the holy books. With proper prayer and circumspection you should open the Bible at random and note the tenor of the first passage that meets your eye. Is it favorable to your condition, or unfavorable? The pious Simon de Montfort thus consulted the "sacred lots" ere taking the cross for the Albigensian crusade. Chapters of canons use this method to see what the omens are concerning a candidate for a bishopric. According to jongleurs' tales, even popes thus seek for an oracle ere taking any important step in the government of the Church, although these stories are wisely doubted. A more precise method of augury is the "*Sortes Apostolorum*." Fifty-six sentences (expressing sentiments good or bad) are written on parchment; a string is attached to each and allowed to protrude while the sentences are covered up. You say a prayer, seize a string at random, then follow it down to read its sentiment. In this way the saints and not the devil will reveal the future to you.

Undoubtedly the peasants carry their belief in bad omens or unlucky actions too far. Conon and Adela laugh heartily at some of their notions. To avoid bad luck, Georges, when weaning a calf, always pulls it away from its mother by the tail backward. He never begins plowing until he has walked thrice around the plow with a lighted candle. Jeanne never spins or sews on Thursdays or Fridays, lest she make the Virgin weep. In the springtime a bone from the head of a mare should be set out in the garden to drive off the caterpillars. Time fails to list these rustic beliefs; besides, they vary from village to village. But what peasant has not as many thereof as he has hairs in his head?

There is one pious matter shared in alike by great and humble and highly approved by the Church, although the wiser ecclesiastics deprecate some of its excesses— the worship of holy relics.

Saints' relics abound. Where is the monastery, church, or even castle without them? Sometimes they rest in golden caskets in the very place where the holy personages departed this life. Sometimes they have been brought from Rome or Palestine by pious pilgrims; very often they come as gifts. The direct purchase of relics is somewhat sacrilegious, but you can present a king, duke, or great ecclesiastic with a good relic just as you give him some hawks or ermine skins—as a reward for favors past or expected. The Pope is always sending desirable relics to bishops and abbots whom he wishes to honor; and, as all know, after the Latins sacked Constantinople in 1204 there was hardly a shrine in all France which did not get the skull, a few ribs, or even the entire body of some Eastern saint. The booty in relics in fact, was almost as important as that of gold and jewels.

Possessing relics is most desirable. Prayers said near them have extra efficacy. Oaths taken upon their caskets are doubly binding, but sometimes the holy objects are surreptitiously removed when the pledge is being given; it is then no perjury to break the promise. In dealing with slippery individuals one must, therefore, beware. On the other hand, who is ignorant of the manner in which William the Norman inveigled Harold the Anglo-Saxon into taking a great oath of fealty? The slow-witted Englishman swore to the pact, believing the casket on which he rested his hands contained relics of very inferior worthies, who could never punish him if he perjured himself; but the instant the words were said the priests opened the sacred box, showing it full of the bones of the most powerful saints imaginable. Harold turned pale with horror, realizing how he had been trapped. When later he broke his oath, beyond a doubt it was these angered saints who wrought his death at Hastings.

Good relics also imply a source of income, provided that they are properly advertised so as to make the church or abbey possessing them a pilgrimage resort. Sometimes, indeed, one fears lest overzealous monks exaggerate the miracles wrought by the relics at their abbey church. The tale runs that when the Abbey of St. Vanne was deeply in debt, the abbot asserted: "Our debts will all be paid with the red tunic of St. Vanne [a relic]. I never doubt it."

The monks at St. Aliquis are proud of their collection, although by no means the largest in the region. They have two teeth of the prophet Amos; hairs of St. Martin and St. Leonard; finger-nail parings of the martyrs of the Theban legion; bits of the robe of St. Bernard; finger bones of Saints Saturnin, Sebastian, and of the Patriarch Jacob; a fifth rib of St. Amond; a skull of one of the Holy Innocents; a chip of the stone on which Christ stood when He ascended to heaven; the jaw bone of St. Sixtus; some of the hay from the manger of Bethlehem; and, last but not least, a fair-sized splinter of the true Cross. The mere adoration of such things cancels many grievous years in purgatory.

It is advantageous to the whole region to have such a collection. If there is need of rain, the relics can be carried in procession around the thirsty country and relief is sure to follow. If there is a public assembly, the holy relics can be brought in before the contending knights or burghers—wise counsels will ensue. If you are going on a journey, a visit to a shrine with such relics almost guarantees a safe return. We have already seen how Conon (as did other knights) kept certain relics always in his sword hilt, to confirm his oaths and to lend efficacy to his actions.

The enormous value of such sacred things often makes them the booty of thieves. Thus in 1219 a band of robbers stole the remains of St. Leocadia from the Abbey of Vic, and when pursued cast the holy bones into the Aisne, whence they were rescued with serious difficulty. We need not multiply records of similar crimes. Profligate noblemen will sometimes seize and keep very sacred relics in their castles, as talismans against long-delayed justice.

Not less miraculous is the manner in which the relics have been preserved when less sacred objects have been lost. This is, indeed, a divine mystery, not lightly to be inquired into. When, however, two identical relics of the same saint are displayed in France, how are worldly questionings to be silenced? For surely the holy men of old had only one head and two arms apiece. Not long since, the monks of St. Étienne exhibited a skull of St. Denis. But the monks of St. Denis claimed *they* had the skull of their own patron saint already. What lack of charity ensued! The backbiting did not cease till the great Pope Innocent III tactfully silenced the controversy without actually deciding which relic was the more authentic. Many say that such relics can miraculously duplicate themselves—so that *all* are equally genuine; and undoubtedly God has worked far greater wonders than this.

Nevertheless, such is the sinfulness of men that spurious relics are often imposed upon the faithful. Good churchmen do zealous work in exposing these sacrilegious frauds. Not long since, Father Grégoire had Conon give a terrific flogging to a pretended pilgrim who was trying to sell the credulous peasants "a bit of the sail of St. Peter's boat and a feather of the Angel Gabriel." It is more serious when a spurious shrine is set up. Near Lyons recently the peasant women insisted in venerating "the tomb of St. Guinefort." It was discovered to be only the spot where a lady had buried a favorite greyhound. In another case, many years ago, the great St. Martin found near Tours a chapel where the people worshiped a supposed martyr. The saint stood on the sepulcher and prayed, "Reveal unto me who is really here!" Soon a dark form arose and the specter confessed to Martin: "I am a robber. My soul is in hell, but my body is in this sepulcher." The saint, therefore, destroyed the chapel, and saved many from wasting their prayers and substance.

It is a dangerous business, however, to be over-skeptical concerning popular relics. Even great churchmen, such as the late Bishop of Orléans, are liable to be mobbed if they call an alleged and much-venerated skull of St. Génevieve "the head of some old woman"— as once did that astute prelate. Nevertheless, the authorities try to do their duty. Pope Innocent III has issued a formal warning to the French clergy against accepting spurious relics, and the monks of every monastery never hesitate to dispute the authenticity of almost every kind of a relic provided only it is deposited in a neighboring and rival abbey!

If, however, relics are genuine, it is impossible to exaggerate their desirability. They are produced on numerous holidays; and often a special holiday is proclaimed when they are "translated." Then you may see the relics of some saint being carried through the streets of a village or town, the holy objects themselves borne in their golden boxes under a canopy, accompanied by all the local clergy, with perhaps the barons and the duke of the entire region being allowed to assist the highest prelates in carrying or at least in escorting the sacred casket.

Thus has been explained certain features of the religion of the laity, humble and exalted. At length we can approach one of those great institutions which have built up the strength of Catholic Christianity. A league from the castle lies the other great center for the countryside—the monastery of St. Aliquis.

Chapter XIX: The Monastery of St. Aliquis[1]: Buildings. Organization. An Ill-Ruled Abbey.

HE great St. Bernard has written thus of the convent: "Good is it for us to dwell there—where man lives more purely, falls more rarely, rises more quickly, treads more cautiously, rests more securely, dies more happily, is absolved more easily, and is rewarded more plenteously."

Every now and then they say in the castle of St. Aliquis: "Such and such a cavalier has become a monk!" Then there are cries of astonishment and probably slurring remarks, but even Conon in his heart wonders, "Has he not, after all, chosen the better part?" at the very moment when he storms about the "greedy monks" before his sons. The monastery is the great interrogation point thrust before the castle. The castle says: "The hunt, the tourney, the excitement of feudal war are the things for man. Who truly knows about the hereafter?" The monastery replies: "There is a kingdom not of this world, where baron and villein must spend the æons. Prepare ye for it!" Very probably the monastery is right.

The monastery of St. Aliquis has existed for centuries.

[1] In these chapters the terms "monastery," "abbey" and "convent" are used synonymously. Of course, the term "convent" (from "conventus," or "meeting") might also be used for "nunnery." A "priory" was usually a smaller type of institution, ruled by a prior and not an abbot (see p. 322 note) and dependent on some greater "abbey."

312

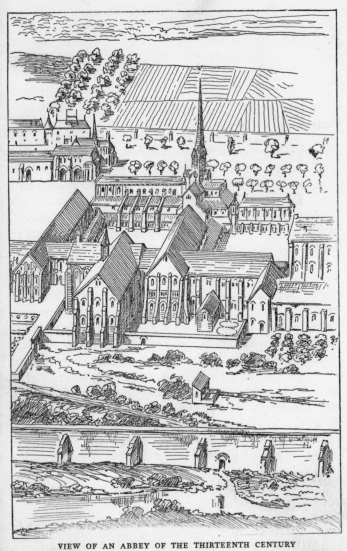

VIEW OF AN ABBEY OF THE THIRTEENTH CENTURY

At the left of the structure the building for guests and in front of it the church;
beyond the two cloisters the buildings reserved for the monks; in the foreground
the gardens of the abbey and the outside wall.

It is a Benedictine monastery—that is to say, its rule (system of government and discipline) comes from the famous St. Benedict of Nursia, who lived in Italy in the sixth century. Many new orders of monks have been founded since then, but none more holy than the Benedictines when they really live up to the ideals of their founder. Barons of St. Aliquis and other rich people have endowed the monastery from time to time with ample lands. It is a passing wealthy institution.

Ignorant folk of other ages may think of a monastery as a collection of idlers meditating on heaven and living on charity. Such groups once perhaps existed in Eastern lands, but never in a Benedictine monastery. Each is the scene of a very busy life. Many industries are carried on. The monks are almost self-supporting. The monastery, in fact, contributes more to the economic life of the region than does the castle; and Abbot Victor, its head, is hardly less important, even in a worldly sense, than Messire Conon, with whom, happily, he is now on cordial terms.

The monastery, however, is an establishment distinctly set off by itself. It is in the world, but not of it. As you travel from the castle, you presently enter fields unusually well cultivated. These are part of the abbey lands. Then you come to a small village, comparatively clean and well built, where the lay servitors of the monks live with their families. Then straight ahead there rises a strong battlemented wall of wide circuit surrounded by a water-filled moat. Beyond this wall appear the spires and pinnacles of pretentious buildings. The wall is needed to stand off attacks of bands of godless men who dream even of plundering convents. There are a drawbridge, portcullis, and strong gate. Inside you are within a little world. The center

is not the donjon, but the new monastery church, an
elegant pointed-arch structure almost equal to a small
cathedral. Grouped around it are numerous buildings—
usually long, high, and narrow. These are the dormi-
tories, the refectory, the cloisters for the monks' walks
and study, as well as many less handsome barns, storehouses and workhouses. There is a good-sized garden
where rare herbs and flowers are tended with loving
care, and an orchard where fruit trees are grafted with
unusual skill. One even sees a slaughterhouse in a
convenient corner, a tannery (at a safe distance from
the garden!) and a building where the monks' garments
can be spun and woven out of flax and wool produced
on the abbey lands. The monks of St. Aliquis are,
therefore, anything but droning hermits.

Some monasteries really comprise small towns. The
famous establishment at Cluny harbors four hundred
monks; that at Clairvaux, seven hundred; that at
Vezelay, eight hundred. St. Aliquis is content with
one hundred and fifty brethren, but that number
(plus the lay servitors) is enough for a busy community. As has been said, the focus for its entire life
is the abbey church. Without a church building a
monastery is almost impossible. The choir is constantly
needed for the recitation of the canonical hours; many
altars are required so that the monks who are in holy
orders may celebrate mass frequently; while the great
processions around the nave are part of the routine,
especially on Sundays. Abbot Victor, like all his
predecessors, is straining every nerve to gather funds
to beautify his church. In it are deposited invaluable
saints' relics. It is hard, however, to convince the laity
that they are extremely sacred unless they are lodged
in a splendid edifice. The monks of rival monasteries

are always comparing their churches enviously. Victor
has set his heart upon widening the transepts and
putting in a new rose window. If only a certain pious
heiress in Champagne would be called to heaven!

In the choir is a long array of stalls, one for each
monk in order of seniority. The abbot sits in a chair of
state on the southern side; the prior, his chief lieutenant,
faces him on the north. Connected with one transept
of the church is the cloister. It is a rectangular court.

THE GALLERIES OF THE CLOISTER OF THE ABBEY OF MONT-SAINT-MICHEL
(THIRTEENTH CENTURY)

Its four walks are roofed in, the walls nearest the court
being pierced with open arcades. The pillars upholding
these arcades are beautifully carved with floreated
capitals, each separate pillar forming an individual work
of art, lovingly executed, and differing slightly from its
neighbors. The three walks of the cloister which do not
touch the church adjoin very needful buildings—the

chapter house, where the brethren congregate, the refectory on the side opposite the church, and the dormitory. The walk nearest the church is where the monks are supposed to spend the time allotted for pious meditation. It faces the south, and the great structure behind cuts off the chilling winds. It is, therefore, a pleasant place in cold weather. On the inner side of this part of the cloister are many little alcoves let into the massive walls; here monks can study or even converse without annoying others.

Looking down upon the cloister court is a remarkable object. If holy brethren did not possess it, the peasants would declare it was possessed by a devil, although these mechanisms are now becoming more common. It has a dial marking the twelve hours, and by an ingenious system of pulleys and weights indicates when it is noon or midnight without reference to the shifting of shadows or movement of the stars. It even has bells that ring every hour—a great convenience.[1] The monks are almost as proud of this device as of some of their less important saints' relics.

The books which consume so much of the monks' time are kept in cupboards in the cloister alcoves, since this is not a Cistercian monastery, which always has a separate library. From the cloister one is naturally led to the chapter house. Almost as much care has been taken with this large oblong chamber as with the church. The ceiling is beautifully groined and vaulted. The abbot sits on a raised seat at the east end, with all his officers at right or left. The remainder

[1] Clocks run wholly by weights were known as early as Charlemagne's time, and the famous "magician" Pope Sylvester II (see p. 303) studied their mechanism. By the thirteenth century they were slowly coming into general use. Of course, at first they had only one hand—showing merely the hours.

of the brethren are on stone benches ranged around the walls, while in the center of the floor stands a desk, whence the daily "lection" is read from the lives of the martyrs, or the chapter (hence the name of the room) from St. Benedict's holy Rule—a document only a little less authoritative with the monks than the actual Scriptures.

Then come other rooms. The cloisters are *supposed* to be extremely quiet for study and meditation. But sinful flesh requires an outlet. Go then to the parlor (the place of *parle*), a good-sized room where merchants can bring their wares. The subprior can discuss the sickness of certain pigs on the farms, and the saints know how much personal gossip can be tossed about. Next is the dormitory, a large open apartment with the beds of the monks standing against the walls between the numerous windows, so that the feet of the sleepers point in two long rows toward the center line of the room. A quiet place, but at night, with several score of brethren all

THE REFECTORY AT THE ABBEY OF MONT-SAINT-MICHEL (THIRTEENTH CENTURY)

snoring together, what repose is left for the stranger? In any case, there is very little privacy, for few of the monks have separate bedrooms.

318

Close by the cloister is the refectory—an aisleless hall with a wooden roof. Across the east end is a high table for the officers—the whole place resembling the great hall in a castle. Most of the brethren sit at very long tables running up and down the apartment; and near the high table is a still higher pulpit mounted by a winding stair. Here a monk will droningly read a Latin homily while his associates are expected to eat and hearken in silence.

The kitchen with its great fireplaces adjoins the refectory. At the entrance to the dining hall, just as in the castle, there is the lavatory, a great stone basin with many taps, convenient for washing the hands. Since some brethren are sure to be sick, there is a separate infirmary, a well-arranged suite with places for sleeping, dining, and even a little chapel for those too feeble to to get to the church.[1] The abbot has lodgings of his own where he can entertain distinguished visitors, although he is expected to mingle freely with his fellow monks and not to assume solitary grandeur. The less exalted guests are put in a special *hospitium* in the court. The monastery never turns away any decently

---

[1] By its very nature, a monastery would contain a disproportionately large number of doddering old men, or sick and helpless individuals. "*Stagnarii*" or "*stationarii*" they are significantly called. Besides, a monk was supposed to be bled for his health four or five times a year. While recovering from this operation he could stay in the infirmary.

The Church usually rejected candidates for regular priesthood who labored under serious physical disabilities. The monasteries had to be less arbitrary. Thus they probably obtained more than their share of blind, semi-invalids, purblind, halt, deaf, etc. In 1161, at an abbey near Boulogne, there are said to have been so many lame, one-eyed, or one-armed monks that the abbot refused to admit any more defectives for thirty years. This was probably an extreme case.

For similar reasons many women, unmarriageable through physical defects, seem to have been placed in nunneries.

behaving wayfarer; but the guest master, a canny old religious, naturally provides better quarters and supper for those likely to put a denier in the alms box than for those who may have just fled the provost.

This is a bare summary of the important buildings of the establishment. If St. Aliquis had been a Cistercian convent, following the rule of St. Bernard of Clairvaux, its structures would have been extremely plain—no mosaics, stained glass, silken hangings, or floral carvings in the church; nor anything else calculated to distract the monks from thinking upon the heavenly mysteries. Said he, austerely: "Works of art are idols which lead away from God, and are good at best to edify feeble souls and the worldly." Bernard was a mighty saint, but all do not follow this hard doctrine. The monks of St. Aliquis, for their own part, are sure that the Heavenly Ones are rejoiced every time they add a new stone leaf to the unfading foliage about the cloister arches, or carve the story of David and Jonathan upon the great walnut back to the prior's seat in the chapter house.

A BENEDICTINE MONK (THIRTEENTH CENTURY)

From a manuscript in the Bibliothèque nationale. He is clad in a frock, a robe supplied with ample sleeves and a cowl.

The monks of St. Aliquis, being Benedictines, are "black monks." If they had been Cistercians they would have been "white monks"—that is, with white frocks and cowls. The cowl is a cumbersome garment enveloping the whole body, but it is worn only at ceremonies. Ordinarily the monks wear black scapularies, covering head and body less completely. They also have

short mantle-style capes. New outer garments are issued
to them every year, new day shoes every eighteen
months, new boots once in five years, and a new pair
of woolen shirts once in four years. They are also
granted both a thin and a thick tunic, a fur-lined coat
for cold weather, also undershirt and drawers—in short,
no silly luxuries, but no absurd austerities.

The control of the whole community rests with the
abbot. Under the monastic rule and vows the monks
owe him implicit obedience. If he is a practical, efficient
man, the whole establishment is happy and prosperous;
if the reverse, it is soon in debt, the property is wasted,
the monks live evilly or desert; and the whole place often
is ruined. Abbeys resemble seigneuries—they are either
growing or dwindling. Many church canons forbid abbots to abuse their office, to live luxuriously, to waste
the abbey property, or to take important steps without
consulting the older monks, but such decrees are hard
to enforce. Fortunately, the head of St. Aliquis—
Abbot Victor, is a moderate, kindly, yet withal a worldly
wise man. He was the younger son of a petty noble
and was thrust into the monastery somewhat because
his worldly heritage would have been very small. The
monastic life, however, agreed with him. He became
popular with the brethren of peasant stock, yet never
let them forget that his parents had been gentle. As
prior he knew how to deal with Conon and other seigneurs.
When the old leader died, there had been one cry from
all the monks assembled in the chapter house. "Let
Victor be our abbot!" Since then, despite inevitable
grumblings, he has ruled acceptably, avoiding alike
Cistercian severity and that lax rule which has made
certain monasteries the hatching nests of scandal.

Victor wears on ceremonial occasions a miter with

gold fringe, although it cannot be adorned with pearls like a bishop's. He has also handsome gloves (especial emblems of his office), a crozer (a pastoral staff), and a ring. His administration is aided by a whole corps of officers. First of all is the prior, named by the abbot and the abbot's chief lieutenant, who is his superior's deputy and general man of affairs.[1] Next the subprior, the third in command; then the third and fourth priors, known as *circatores* because they have to make frequent circuits of inspection; while below them come the *precentor,* in charge of the singing and chanting; the *sacristan,* responsible for the bells, lights, and ornaments of the church; and all the heads of the kitchen, storehouses, infirmary, and monastery finances. There is also the garnerer—a sagacious monk who collects the grain due from the abbey lands and either sells it profitably or turns it over to the storekeeper (*celerer*).

The activities of the monks are multifarious, but everything is really subordinate to the duty of chanting the holy offices in the church. The brethren go to bed, even in wintertime, at sunset. Then by the light of cressets, bowls of oil with floating wicks, they rise at midnight, put on their clothes, sit down on stone seats at either end of the dormitory, and next file in silent procession to the great, dark church. There they chant a long service, with the organ rumbling under the gloomy vaulting—a service made still longer by the prayers for the dead. As solemnly as before they file back to the dormitory and sleep until daybreak in winter, until actual sunrise in summer; whereupon they all rise again,

[1] In monasteries affiliated with the great abbey of Cluny the highest officer was the prior; the only abbot for the entire group of establishments was at Cluny. Various other small dependent monasteries had merely a prior, supposedly dependent on the abbot at a superior monastery.

go to the church, and chant Prime. Tierce follows about 9 A.M.; Sext at noon; Nones at 3 P.M.; and Vespers at about sundown. This continues every day through a long life. No wonder the monks all know by heart their offices for the day and night as given in the breviary.

After Prime a meeting is held in the chapter house. A section is read from the Rule, the abbot or priors call off the work for each monk, individual complaints can be uttered, and corrections and public reproofs are given by the officers. At the Tierce service mass is said; then the morning work goes on until the Sext, after which the first regular meal is eaten, although some bread soaked with wine is allowed earlier to the weaker brethren. Talking during the meal is discouraged, but there is nevertheless much whispering while the reader (allowed to eat earlier) tries to center attention upon the pulpit. The brethren then rise and sing grace, ending up with the "Miserere," which is chanted in procession marching through the cloister. Everybody thereupon retires to the dormitory and enjoys a siesta until it is time for Nones. Work is next resumed until Vespers just before supper. After supper there is another meeting in the chapter house, with more reading from a pious book. Then once more to the church to chant Complines; after that (since St. Aliquis is a well-ordered monastery) all the monks are compelled to go straight to bed and do not sit up for carnal chatter. All the doors of the establishment are securely locked. The officers make the rounds to see that every monk is safe on his cot—and so the whole brotherhood settles for the night.

Life in the monastery thus has a strict routine which soon becomes a perfect habit with most of the inmates. Of course, monks working in the fields are not required to come in for all the daytime offices—they can drop their tools when the great bell rings and pray in silence reverently standing. In nunneries about the same divisions of time are applied, although chaplains have to come in to say mass. The one thing impressing every visitor to a well-ruled monastery is the intense sense of order as compared with the tumult and coarse informality characteristic of even the better castle. To a certain type of mind this regularity is indescribably fascinating apart from any question of its advantages in religion.

To ask how the different brethren of St. Aliquis come to enter its portals is to ask as many individual questions. The abbot is typical of many companions, who were placed there because worldly prospects were small and because they were decently urged by their relatives. Sometimes the pressure was not mild. There are a few brethren who seem discontented men without vocation, chafing against irrevocable vows taken practically under compulsion, and yearning to be back in the world. There is also one coarse, scar-visaged old man who was a robber knight. "Tonsure or the scaffold?" so the duke had put the question. To such a person the monastery is nothing but an honorable prison. There are, however, two or three other elderly ex-cavaliers here for a better reason—they have been overwhelmed with a consciousness of their crimes and are genuinely anxious to redeem their souls. A considerable proportion of the monks are gentle, although the majority are non-nobles. If of the latter class, however, they have been subjected to searching scrutiny before entrance, to make sure they will be useful members of the community. If they are mere clownish peasants, they are often taken only as *conversi* (lay brethren), who learn a few prayers, but spend most of their time on the abbey farms and who do not sleep in the dormitory.

The greater number of the monks have apparently joined voluntarily in early manhood—because they are repelled by the confusion and grubbing hardships of the world, because they have a hankering for an intellectual life, and because they are genuinely anxious to deliver their souls. After a round of fêtes, tournaments, and forays, many a young knight has suddenly turned from them all, announced to his companions: "What profit? Where will I spend eternity?" said farewell to his beloved destrer, and knocked at the convent door. Sometimes he has sickened too late of his choice. More often in this new world of chants, solemn offices, books, honest toil, gently spoken words, and quietness he has discovered a satisfaction not possessed by his brother who is still messire the seigneur.

In the monastery there are, however, certain very young boys, who it is to be hoped will prove contented with their profession. Their parents or guardians have taken them to the abbot, and in their ward's behalf have uttered vows that bind the helpless children forever. "I offer this my son [reads the formula] to the Omnipotent God and to the Virgin Mary for the salvation of my soul and the souls of my parents. . . . And so shall he remain in this holy life all his days until his final breath." Earnestly do the wiser brethren pray that these practically orphaned boys do not become a source of sorrow to themselves and of discord to the community in future years.[1]

[1] While such children would be sometimes presented out of motives of genuine piety, to save their own souls or to redeem those of their relatives, often they were thrust into the convent merely to dispose of unwelcome heirs or to avoid the cost of rearing them. Wise abbots would, of course, sift out such cases carefully.

St. Aliquis is a well-ordered monastery. Its monks, however, point with some pharisaical satisfaction at certain neighboring establishments. It is well said that "ten are the abuses in the cloister—costly living, choice food, noise in the cloister, strife in the chapter, disorder in the choir, a neglectful discipline, disobedient youths, lazy old men, headstrong monks, and worldly officers." It is alleged that all these evils and worse ones have existed in the monastery of St. Ausonne, five leagues away. This community had an excellent name for sanctity until twenty years ago. Then a foolish abbot admitted too many "younger sons" who were being forced in by their relatives. The duke, likewise, imprudently pardoned a whole gang of highwaymen on condition that "they should turn religious." Also, several self-seeking cavaliers deliberately entered the order, in sinful expectation that family influence could procure their election as abbots or bishops—posts of great worldly consequence. Thus it was that our old enemy, Satan, entered into St. Ausonne. All accounts are that he still refuses to be ejected.

The evil tidings of this convent presently spread to Rome; and the Holy Father, deeply grieved, ordered the Bishop of Pontdebois to visit the establishment and restore discipline.[1] It was well that he took a troop of armed sergeants with him, or he would have been stoned by the furious inmates. The monks of St. Aliquis lift their hands in horror at the least of the stories told about his discoveries. Part of the bishop's report reads like this: "Brother Regnaud is accused of great

---

[1] Bishops theoretically had themselves the right of inspection unless a monastery had a direct papal charter; but in any case the monks would probably resist episcopal interference vigorously unless the Pope gave the bishop specific orders to intervene.

uncleanness of life. Bartholomée, a cantor's assistant, often gets drunk and then does not get up for the matins service. Roger, the third prior, frequents taverns. Jean, the fourth prior, is an habitual tippler. Morell, another cantor's assistant, is given to striking and evil speaking. Firmin, in charge of the abbey lands, does the like, etc."

These charges, however, are mere details. The real sorrow is that from the abbot down the whole organization of St. Ausonne has fallen utterly away from the monastic ideal of a "school for the Lord's service" (to quote St. Benedict). The abbot has been not merely very worldly, but very miserly. Recently a jongleur sought hospitality at St. Ausonne. The monks offered him merely black bread and water, although their own supper was far more sumptuous than the "two cooked dishes and half a pint of wine" allowed by the Benedictine rule. On leaving the abbey, the minstrel met the abbot returning from pushing his political fortunes at Paris. He profusely thanked the prelate for his monks' noble hospitality, because they had given him choice wine, rich dishes, and finally presented him with good shoes and a belt. The abbot returned home in a rage and caused his guest master to be flogged for squandering the monastery property. The minstrel, of course, spread the tale of his revenge, and so indirectly prompted the visitation of the establishment.

In fine, the bishop reported that from St. Ausonne many monks ranged the country "with wandering feet"—as mere religious vagabonds, levying alms upon the peasantry, and sometimes bearing letters from their abbot allowing them to quit the cloister at pleasure. The abbot himself, defying the canons, would have elaborate hunting parties with hawks and hounds. The Church law merely permitted monks to kill rabbits and crows dangerous to the crops; but the bishop actually found a kennel of great dogs and a sheaf of boar spears within the holy compound. The dietary at St. Ausonne was fit for a castle. Venison was served on Friday, and the amount of wine consumed was astounding. Women are never supposed to set foot within the inner precincts of a monastery, but, to spare the Church further scandal, one conceals what the bishop discovered to be the practice at this establishment.

The St. Ausonne monks, too, have cast reproaches upon their more honest brethren elsewhere. One of them, after visiting the St. Aliquis convent, is discovered to have complained: "One cannot talk in the refectory; and all night they 'bray' the offices in the church. The meals are very poor; they give us beans and un-shelled eggs. The wine is too thin and too mixed with cows' drink [water]. No—never will I get drunk on *that* wine. At St. Aliquis it is better to die than to live!"[1] Another brother seems to have drifted round the duchy, visiting the more disorderly seigneurs, becoming their boon companion, cozening their women, and boasting that his ideal of life was "a big salmon at dinner time and sitting by a fountain with a friendly dame."

With such monks sheer sacrilege in performing the sacred offices was possible. The story goes that at the morning office they were all very drowsy. Soon their heads would fall on the service books at the close of every line. The choir boys were expected to keep up the chant; but the latter, impious young mortals, soon learned how to begin quiet games the moment the last monk had fallen asleep. Then when the proper time has expired the boys would all call out loudly "Let us

---

[1] These complaints are identical with those actually made by a worldly monk who visited the venerable abbey of Cluny.

bless the Lord!" "Thanks be to God!" the monks would respond, awakening with a start; and then everybody would go comfortably away.

The report of the bishop will probably produce one of two orders from Rome—either the Holy Father will appoint a new abbot strictly enjoined to rule the convent with a rod of iron and to restore discipline, or the whole establishment will be broken up as hopeless and its inmates distributed around among other and stricter monasteries. Cases as bad as St. Ausonne's are rare, but they breed infinite scandal and provide outrageous tales for the jongleurs. So long as monasticism exists there will be institutions afflicted with idleness and luxury—"the lust of the flesh and the lust of the eyes and the pride of life." Doubtless no monastery is exempt from evil thoughts and evil deeds, yet it is pitiful that the saints allow such institutions as St. Ausonne to exist to bring into contempt the tens of thousands of monks who are trying to serve God with sincerity.

Chapter XX: The Monastery of St. Aliquis: The Activities of Its Inmates. Monastic Learning.

FTER a monk has taken the great vow "renouncing my parents, my brothers, my friends, my possessions, and the vain and empty glory of this world. . . . and renouncing also my own will for the will of God, and accepting all the hardships of the monastic life," how is he to be employed? For, as St. Benedict with great sagacity has written, "*Idleness is the enemy of the soul.*" The ancient hermits devoted their entire time to contemplation, hoping for visions of angels; but it is recorded too often that they had only visions of the devil. "Therefore," continues the holy Rule, "at fixed times the brothers ought to be employed with manual labor, and again at fixed times in sacred reading." Thus, in general, the monks of St. Aliquis are busied with two great things, *work* in the fields and *study*, with the copying or actual writing of profitable books.

The monastery being passing rich, its administration constitutes a great worldly care. Ever since the institution came into existence, about the time that Heribert rendered the region fairly safe by erecting his fortress, the monks have been adding to their property. Church foundations never die. Mortmain prevents them from crumbling. Income is obtainable from many sources, but probably the best lands have come to the abbey through the reception of new members. Few novices are received unless they make a grant of their entire possessions to the institution, and, while most younger sons and peasants have little enough to give, every now and then the abbey receives a person of considerable wealth. Besides such acquisitions, there is no better way for laymen to cancel arrears with the recording angel than by gifts of land or money to an abbey. Some of these gifts come during lifetime, sometimes on one's deathbed. Noblemen complain that the monks thus defraud them of their possessions. "When a man lies down to die," bewails the epic poem "Hervis de Metz," "he thinks not of his sons. He summons the black monks of St. Benedict and gives them his lands, his revenues, his ovens, and his mills. The men of this age are impoverished and the clerics daily grow richer." Often, too, a person when on his deathbed will actually "take the habit" and be enrolled as a monk, thus, of course, conveying to the abbey all his possessions. This, we are told, is "the sweetest way for a human conscience to settle its case with God."

Property thus comes to an abbey from every direction. No gifts are refused as "tainted money." Giving to Heaven is invariably a pious deed, and ordinarily justifies whatever oblique means were used to get the donation. So the monks of St. Aliquis have been accumulating tillage lands, meadows, vineyards, and often the rentals for lands held by others. These rentals are payable in wheat, barley, oats, cattle and also in pasture rights. Some donations are given unconditionally, some strictly on condition that the income be used in providing alms for the poor, lodgings and comforts for the sick, or saying special masses for the repose of the soul of the benefactor. Abbot Victor has therefore to supervise many farms, forests, mills, etc., scattered for many miles about. He also receives the tithe (church tax) for five or six parish churches in the region, on condition that he appoint their priests and support them out of part of this income.

For these lands the abbot owes feudal service, and over them he exercises feudal suzerainty, possessing, therefore, an overlord and also vassals, just as did the nobles who held these same fiefs before they passed to the abbey. He is, accordingly, a regular seigneur, receiving and doing homage, bound to do justice to his vassals, and able to call them to arms whenever the secular need arises. By church law he cannot, of course, lead them in person to battle, but has to accept Conon as his advocate; and it is as advocate (or, as called elsewhere, *vidame*) of the abbey of St. Aliquis, able to lead its numerous retainers into the field and act in military matters as the abbot's very self-sufficient lieutenant and champion, that the baron owes much of his own importance.[1] For example, he gets one third of all the fees payable to the abbey for enforcing justice among its dependents, and when he is himself in a feud he will sometimes attempt to call out the abbot's vassals to follow his personal banner, even if the quarrel is of not the least concern to the monks.

Nevertheless, such an overpowerful champion is usually necessary to a monastery. Despite the fear of excommunication, unscrupulous lords frequently seize upon abbey lands or even pillage the sacred buildings, trusting to smooth over matters later by a gift or a pilgrimage. The temptation presented by a rich, helpless monastery is sometimes almost irresistible.

---

[1] Abbots and their advocates were continually having friction over their respective prerogatives. If Victor and Conon got along in fair harmony, they were somewhat exceptional both as prelate and as seigneur.

In nonmilitary matters, however, the monks control everything. They direct the agriculture of hundreds of peasants. They maintain real industries, manufacturing far more in the way of church ornaments, vestments, elegant woolen tapestries, elaborate book covers, musical instruments, enameled reliquaries, as well as carvings in wood, bronze, and silver, than they can possibly use for their own church. All this surplus is sold, and the third prior has just returned from Pontdebois to report his success in disposing of a fine bishop's throne, which Brother Octavian, who has great skill with his chisel, has spent three whole years in making. The monks also maintain a school primarily for lads who expect to become clerics, but which is open also to the sons of nobles, and, indeed, of such peasants as can see any use in letting hulking boys who do not expect to enter the Church learn Latin and struggle with pothooks and hangers.

The monks, too, have another great care and expense— the distribution of alms, even more lavishly than at the castle. The porter is bound always to keep small loaves of bread in his lodge, ready to give to the itinerant poor. Every night swarms of travelers, high and low, have to be lodged and fed by the guest master, with none turned away unless he demands quarters a second night—when questions will be asked.[1] In bad years the monasteries are somehow expected to feed the wretched by thousands. All this means a great drain upon the income, even if the monks themselves live sparely.

There is often another heavy demand made on the abbot's revenues. Having so many and such varied parcels of land, he is almost always involved in costly lawsuits—with rival church establishments claiming the

[1] See also p. 319.

property, with the heirs of donors who refuse to give up
their expected heritages, with creditors or debtors in the
abbey's commercial transactions and with self-seeking
neighboring seigneurs. "He who has land has trouble"
is an old proverb to which Victor cheerfully subscribes.
He is not so litigious as many abbots; but his time
seems consumed with carnal matters which profit not
the soul.

The activities in a large, well-ordered monastery are
ample enough to give scope to the individual genius of
about all the brethren, although every abbey is likely to
have its own special interests. Some South French
monasteries make and export rare cordials and healing
drugs. Others boast of their horticulture, the breeding
of cattle, or the manufacture of various kinds of elegant
articles, as already noted. However, the mere cultivation of the fields, where the brethren toil side by side
with the lay helpers, although also acting as overseers,
consumes the energies of much of the convent. The
remainder of the time of most monks is devoted to forms
of learning. The great establishment of Cluny sets the
proper example. There every brother, at least while he
is young, must practice humility by digging, pulling
weeds, shelling beans, and making bread. But this work
is largely for discipline.[1] If he has the least inclination
he will soon be encouraged to devote himself to copying
manuscripts, studying books, perfecting himself in
Latin, and finally, in actually writing original Latin
works himself.

All day long, save at the times for chanting the offices,
the older brethren and many of the younger are in the

---

[1] A great abbey like Cluny would have so many lay servitors that
it could dispense with manual labor by the monks, save where
personal aptitude was lacking for anything else.

little alcoves round the cloister, conning or copying huge volumes of parchment or vellum, or whispering together over some learned problem. All the formal literature is in Latin. It was, until recently, something of a disgrace to prove oneself unclerkly by using the vulgar tongue, "Romance" being accounted fit only for worldly noblemen and jongleurs.[1]

At St. Aliquis, as in every convent, monks still are wont to argue among themselves, "How far is it safe to study pagan rather than Christian writers?" Undoubtedly Horace, Ovid, and Livy are a delight to any student who can read Latin. What wealth of new ideas! What marvelous vigor of language! What vistas of a strange, wonderful world are opened to the imagination! Unfortunately, however, all these authors died worshiping demons; their souls are in hell, or at least in limbo, its uppermost and least painful compartment. Did not Pope Gregory I write to a bishop who was fond of classical studies, "It behooves not that a mouth consecrated to the praise of God should open for those of Jupiter"? Did not Odilon, abbot of Cluny, renounce his beloved Virgil (the

A PIECE OF FURNITURE SERVING AS A SEAT AND A READING DESK

Restored by Viollet-Le-Duc from a thirteenth-century manuscript. At the left of the writing table is placed an inkstand; near the seat is a circular lectern which holds the chandelier and can be turned at the will of the reader.

---

[1] The result was that French was able to develop as a very forceful, expressive language, unspoiled by pedantry, before many serious books were written in the vernacular. The same was somewhat true also of English, German, and other modern tongues.

most favored of all heathen writers) after a warning
dream, beholding therein a wondrous antique vase,
which as he reached to grasp it, proved full of writhing
serpents? Nevertheless, the pagan authors are so seduc-
tive that the monks persist in studying them, although
always with a guilty feeling that "stolen waters are
sweet, and bread eaten in secret is pleasant."

In the monastery school advanced instruction is given
to the younger monks, as well as to the very few laymen
who have been through the primary instruction in the
trivium—grammar, rhetoric, and dialectics (the art of
reasoning) all taught, of course, in Latin. Apt pupils are
then encouraged to continue under one or two monks of
superior learning in the *quadrivium*—astronomy,
arithmetic, geometry, and music. Systematic instruction is hardly ever given in anything else, although odds
and ends of certain other sciences can be absorbed around
St. Aliquis.

The fundamental textbooks are Donatus's grammar
for instruction in Latin, and then for almost everything
savoring of real learning, Latin translations of Master
Aristotle. For a long time the monks have had to content
themselves with the logical Works of the famous Grecian,
explaining the processes of argumentation, but by 1200
they can enjoy the enormous advantage of using Latin
versions of the Physics, the Metaphysics, and the Ethics—
the great works of The Master of Those Who Know
(to quote Dante, writing eighty years later). Some of
these books have come directly from the Greek, but others
have been distorted by passing through an Arabic version
that in turn has been made over into Latin. There are
also various Arabic commentaries of considerable value.
Curious it doubtless is that Heaven, who has denied
salvation alike to Greek and to Moslem, should suffer

unbelievers to possess a worldly wisdom surpassing
that of good Christians, but the Bible truly says,
"The children of this world are in their generation
wiser than the children of light." On all secular
matters, indeed, Aristotle is a final authority. "Thus
says Aristotle" is the best way to silence every hostile
argument. Only very rarely can a man hope by his
own cogitations to overthrow the dicta of this wonderful sage of Athens.

A great deal of the monkish student's time is taken up
with abstract problems of philology and logic. Nevertheless, the abbey contains many parchments widening
to one's knowledge of the world. For example, you can
read in Vincent de Beauvais's *Mirror of Nature* a
minute account of the universe and all things within it.
You can learn the astonishing fact that the world is a
kind of globe suspended at the center of the cosmos.
Many other wonderful things are described—as, for
example, lead can be transmuted into gold, and all kinds
of wonders which defy ordinary experience, but which
are not to be doubted, since God can, of course, do anything. Or one can turn to Hugues de St. Victor's treatise
On Beasts and Other Things and learn all about
the habits of animals—concerning how stags can live
nine hundred years and how the dove "with her right
eye contemplates herself, and with her left eye God."
There are books also on medicine, parts of which contain
sober wisdom, worthy of attention by the murderous
physicians, but elsewhere giving such directions as that
since autumn is "the melancholy season," people should
then eat more heartily than in summer and should refrain
from love affairs.

As for the more abstract sciences, in music the monks
know the four principal and the four secondary sounds—

337

the *do, re, mi,* of the scales, the seven modulations and the five strings of the viol. In geometry they can, with the aid of a stick, "lying on the ground find the height of walls and towers." In arithmetic they can multiply and divide with great facility and keep accounts like a king's treasurer. In astronomy they understand the motion of the planets and their qualities—Saturn, which is "proud, wise, and ambitious," and Mars, "malevolent and bad, provoking strife and battles," and how the sun is hung in the midst of the planets, three above and three below, and much more similar wisdom; although one must proceed carefully in astronomy, for its connection with astrology is close, and from astrology to the black art is not a long journey.

The good monks have perhaps made their best progress in botany and geology. Some of the brethren have gathered collections of curious minerals, of herbs, and also of dried bird and animal skins; although the interest seems to be in the healing qualities of various substances rather than in the nature of the things themselves. Thus it is certain that figs are good for wounds and broken bones; aloes stops hair from falling; the root of mandrake will make women love you; and plenty of sage in a garden somehow protects the owner from premature death. As for geology, that consists of the collecting and arranging of curious stones. It is of course settled in Genesis that the world was made in a very few days. The infidel Avincenna has indeed advanced the theory that mountains are caused by the upheaval of the earth's crust and by action of water. One must hesitate, however, about believing this. It seems hardly compatible with Holy Writ.

On the other hand, the books on animals unhesitatingly tell about remarkable creatures which are mentioned in

Aristotle or in Pliny or by the Arabs. Unicorns, phœnixes, and dragons are well understood, likewise sea monsters, as, for example, great krakens, which drag down ships with their tentacles, sirens or mermaids, and finally "sea bishops" (probably a kind of seal) which piously "bless" their human victims before devouring them.

Besides the study of these older books, the monks are writing certain books themselves. The most important is the great chronicle, begun some years ago by the learned Brother Emeri. It commences with the creation of the world and Adam and Eve, tells about the Greeks and Romans and Charlemagne and his heirs, and then in much greater detail gives the recent history of the Duchy of Quelqueparte, the happenings at the abbey, and also much about the barons of St. Aliquis. Emeri is now dead, but the chronicle is continued from year to year. It is really a compendium of varied learning. From it, for example, you learn all about the wars of Julius Cæsar, the Crusades, the great lawsuit of ten years ago over some of the abbey lands, the feud between Conon and Foretvert, and how in 1216 a two-headed calf was born on a neighboring barony, and in 1217 a meteor struck near Pontdebois.

The Latin in this chronicle is, on the whole, very good, sometimes almost equal to Livy's, and the story is embellished by constant citations not merely of Virgil and Horace, but of Homer and Plato. One would suppose from this that the authors were familiar with Greek. Such, however, is by no means the case. All the quotations from Greek authors and many of their Latin ones are taken from commonplace books. Nevertheless, the narrative seems the more elegant for this borrowed learning. The monks are proud of their chronicle and

339

never fail to boast how much more complete, accurate, and erudite it is than similar works compiled at the rival institutions.

When the monks are not actually studying, they are often copying. St. Aliquis has more than two hundred volumes in its library. Parchment is very expensive, but very durable. When the abbot sees his way to procure material for another volume, he is likely to send to some friendly convent to borrow a book which his monks do not yet possess. Then some of the most skillful brethren are put to work making a copy, if possible more beautiful than the original. In from six months to a year the work will probably be finished, although, if a duplicate is to be made of a work already on hand, there will be less haste and the process may extend over years.[1]

Copying is an excellent means of propitiating Heaven. St. Bernard said emphatically, "Every word which you write is a blow which smites the devil," and Cassiodorus, much earlier, asserted: "By the exercise of the mind upon the Holy Scriptures you convey to those who read a kind of moral instruction. You preach with the hand, converting the hand into an organ of speech—thus, as it were, fighting the arch-fiend with pen and ink."

Parchment, we have said, is a costly article. To provide a single book scores of sheep must die. A new style of writing material, however, is just coming into vogue. Paper, a substance made of linen cloth, now is being produced in small quantities in France, although, as

[1] This would be especially true of copies of the Bible, of which every abbey would have at least one example; and additional specimens would be prepared very deliberately with the intention of making the new work just as beautiful and permanent as possible.

usual, it seems to have been an invention of the Arab Infidels. Some day, perhaps, paper will become so plentiful and cheap that books can be multiplied in vast numbers, but as yet practically everything has to be on parchment, which is certainly far less destructible than paper, whatever the cost.[1]

In the cloister alcoves a dozen copyists are pursuing their task with infinite patience. Their question is not "how fast?" but "how well?"—for they are performing "a work unto God." As a rule, they write their sheets in two columns, making their characters either in round-ish minuscule or in squarer Gothic. The initials are in bright colors—some with a background of gold. Here and there may be painted in a brilliant miniature illustration. The work of the best copyists is beautifully legible. The scribes put their heart and soul into their productions. They expect the volumes will be memorials to their faithfulness and piety scores of years after they are departed.

When the sheets are completed, the book is bound in leather much the same as in other ages, although sometimes the sides are of wood. In any case, there are likely to be metal clasps and bosses of brass upon the covers. A few of the most precious volumes are adorned with plates of silver or carved ivory. So year by year the library grows. It need not be remarked that every copy is *read* and *reread* with devoted thoroughness. What the learning of the Feudal Age, therefore, lacks in breadth is somewhat compensated for by intensity. The older and more studious monks know almost by heart *all* the facts in their entire collection. The younger brethren revere them as carrying in their own heads

[1] The introduction of paper was, of course, absolutely necessary, if the invention of printing were to have any real value.

practically everything significant in the way of worldly wisdom.[1]

Thus we catch some glimpse of the superficial and material side of a typical monastic establishment. Into its spiritual and intellectual atmosphere we cannot find time to penetrate. Our present duty is to "return to the world" and to examine the oft-mentioned but as yet unvisited Good Town of Pontdebois.

[1] It is perhaps proper to say that Dante (1265–1321), a person, of course, of remarkable intellect, was able to master the *entire fund* of learned information and science available in his time. This was not true of the next great mediæval scholar, Petrarch (1304–71). By his period the supply of human knowledge had become too vast for any one brain. Petrarch had to become a specialist.

Chapter XXI: The Good Town of Pontdebois: Aspect and Organization.

S the summer advances, Conon, his baroness, and his familiars make their annual visit to the great fair always held at this time at Pontdebois. Practically nothing except wheat, cattle, and a few like staples are ordinarily bought and sold in or around St. Aliquis. Of course, a messenger can be sent to the town for articles that are urgently needed, but, as a rule, the baron's family saves up all its important purchases until the fair, when many desirable things not ordinarily to be had in the city are put on sale. This present season the fair seems the more important because on account of the expensive fêtes Conon cannot afford to visit Paris and must make his purchases nearer home.

It is only a few leagues to Pontdebois, but messire travels with a considerable retinue—at least twenty men at arms well equipped, besides body servants for himself and his wife, and a long string of sumpter beasts to bring back the desired commodities, for the castle must really stock itself for the year. The baron hardly fears an attack by robbers so near to his own castle and to a friendly town, but he takes no chances. The best of seigneurs disclaim any responsibility for the fate of travelers who proceed by night, and one sire who controls some miles of the way has possibly a quiet understanding with certain outlaws that they may lurk in his forests and watch the roads without too much questioning, provided they refrain from outrages upon important people and make him liberal presents at Christmas and Easter.[1] In any case, a number of merchants, packmen, and other humble travelers who had gone safely as far as St. Aliquis, are glad to complete the journey in the baron's formidable company. Conon in turn gladly protects them; it adds to his prestige to approach Pontdebois with a great following.

The roads are no worse than elsewhere, yet they are abominable; trails and muddy ruts they seem most of the year, ordinarily passable only for horses and mules, although in the summer rude two-wheeled carts can bump along them. To cross the streams you must, in some places, depend on fords very dangerous in the springtime. One unfordable river, entering the Claire, is indeed crossed by a rude wooden bridge. The building of bridges is fostered by the Church. A great indulgence was proclaimed by the bishop some years ago when this bridge was constructed as a pious work, especially useful for pilgrims. Unfortunately, no one is responsible for its upkeep. It is falling into disrepair, and already is so tottering that as men pass over it they repeat those formulas, "commending their souls to God," which the Church provides for use whenever one is attempting unstable bridges.

On the journey you meet many humble travelers obliged to trudge weary miles. There is a poor peasant seeking a farm now on a distant seigneury. He has a donkey to carry some of his household gear and one of the children. His wife is painfully carrying the youngest infant. The poor man himself staggers under a great

---

[1] Another abuse would be to levy a heavy toll on all travelers passing a castle, irrespective of whether there was any legal license to demand the same.

sack. Travelers of more consequence ride horseback,
with a large mail or leathern portmanteau tied on their
beast's crupper. Their burdens are heavy because one
often has to spend the night in abominable quarters,
and consequently must, if possible, carry flint, steel, and
tinder for making a fire, some kind of bedding, and very
often a tent. Along the road, too, are any quantity of
beggars, real or pretended cripples and other deformed
persons, wandering about and living on charity; or blind
men with staffs and dogs. The beggars' disguise is a
favorite one for robbers. The wretches, too, who whine
their, "Alms, Messire! Alms!" and hold up a wrist minus
the hand, or point to where an eye has been gouged out,
probably have suffered just punishments for crimes,
although some of them may have mutilated themselves
merely in order to work on the sympathies of the gullible.

As the party approaches Pontdebois the houses become
better and closer together, and just outside the gate is
a group of taverns, available for those who prefer to
carouse or lodge without rather than within the city
walls. Conon is on terms of hospitality with a rich
burgher who has found the baron's favor profitable, and
he leads his company promptly inside the gates, but
many of the humbler travelers turn off to these taverns.
Adela gives an aristocratic sniff of disdain as they ride
past such places. They are assuredly very dirty, and
from them proceeds the smell of stale wine and poor
cooking. The owners, smooth, smirking men, stand by
the road as travelers come in sight and begin to praise
their hostelries. "Within," one of them is calling out,
"are all manner of comforts, painted chambers, and soft
beds packed high with white straw under soft feather
mattresses. Here is your hostel for love affairs. When
you retire you will fall asleep on pillows of violets, after

you have washed out your mouth and rinsed your hands with rose water!"

His victims, however, will find themselves in a dirty public dining room, where men and women alike are drinking and dicing around the bare oaken tables. At night the guests will sleep in the few chambers, bed wedged by bed, or perhaps two in a bed, upon feathers anything but vermin-proof. In the rear of most inns, too, there is a garden where guests are urged to carouse with the unsavory females who haunt the establishments. The visitors will be lucky if they can get safely away without being made stupidly drunken and then robbed, or having the innkeeper seize their baggage or even their clothes on the pretense that they have not paid their reckoning.

Leaving these taverns at one side, the St. Aliquis company rides straight onward. Before it the spires and walls of Pontdebois are rising. The circuit of gray curtain walls and turrets reaches down to the Claire, on which barges are swinging, and across which stretches the solid wooden bridge which gives the Good Town its name. Above the walls you can see the gabled roofs of the more pretentious houses, the great round donjon, the civic watchtower, and, above all else, the soaring fabric and stately mass of the cathedral with the scaffolding still around its unfinished towers. Several smaller parish churches are also visible. The baron's company is obliged to halt at the gate, such is the influx and efflux of rickety carts, sumpter beasts, and persons thrusting across the drawbridge. "Way, good people," Conon's squires cry. "Way for Messire of St. Aliquis!" and at last, not without a cracking of whips to make these mechanic crowds know their betters, the party forces a path down the narrow streets.

A visit to Pontdebois is no real novelty to the castle

folk, yet they always experience a sense of bustle and vastness upon entering. Here are eight thousand, indeed, some assert ten thousand, people, all living together in a single community.[1] How confused even the saints must be when they peer from heaven and try to number this swarm of young and old, rich and poor, masters and apprentices, packed in behind one set of walls! To tell the truth, the circuit of Pontdebois is not very great; to render the walls as defensible as possible and to save expense, the fortifications have been made to inclose the smallest circumference that will answer. As a result, the land inside is precious. Houses are wedged closely together. Streets are extraordinarily narrow. People can hardly stir without colliding with others, and about the only real breathing spaces are the market place and some open ground around the cathedral. Behind the bishop's palace, also, there is a small walled-in garden. Otherwise, it appears almost as if not one green thing could grow in Pontdebois. The contrast with the open country whence the travelers have just come is therefore startling.

Even the best of the streets are dark, tortuous, and filthy. There is almost no paving.[2] The waste water of the houses is flung from the windows. Horrid offal is

---

[1] If Pontdebois really had as many as eight thousand permanent inhabitants, it was no mean community in feudal times. Many a city would have only two or three thousand, or even less. A place of ten thousand or more would rank as the most important center for a wide region. There were few of such size in France.

[2] Even in Paris at this time the only paving was on the streets leading directly to the city gates. The remainder continued to be a mere slough, a choice breeding place for those contagious diseases against which precautions were assumed to be useless and to which men were bound to submit as to "the will of God." Supplications to some healing saint, like St. Firman or St. Antoine, usually seemed more efficacious than any real sanitary precautions.

thus cast out, as well as the blood and refuse from the numerous slaughterhouses. Pigs are privileged as scavengers, even in the market place. The streets are the darker because the second stories of the houses project considerably over the first, the third over the second, and also the fourth and fifth (which often exist) over those lower. Consequently, there is almost a roof formed over the lanes, cutting off rain, light and air. In the upper stories, neighbors not merely can gossip, but can actually shake hands with their friends across the street. All the thoroughfares, too, are amazingly crooked, as if everybody had once built his house where it pleased him, and afterward some kind of a bypath around it had been created! At night these twisting avenues are dark as pitch. No one can get about without a lantern, and even with one it were better, if possible, to stay at home. To prevent the easy flight of thieves, it is common to stretch many heavy chains across the streets at night. Notwithstanding, footpads often lurk in the covert of black corners.

Pontdebois has few quiet residence sections. It is a community of almost nothing but little shops and little industries—the two being often combined under one roof. The shops generally open directly into the streets, with their stalls intruding on the public way like Oriental bazaars. The streets, in fact, seem to be almost the property of the merchants. Foot passengers can barely find a passage. Carts cannot traverse the town during business hours, and Conon's company on horseback might have found itself absolutely blocked had it not chanced to arrive almost precisely at noon, when the hum and bustle very suddenly cease and the worthy folk of Pontdebois forsake their counters and benches to enjoy hearty dinners.

As it is, they reach the market place just as the city hangman has finished a necessary ceremony. One Lambert, a master woolen weaver, had been caught selling adulterated and dishonestly woven cloth, contrary to the statutes of his guild. The hangman has solemnly burned the offending bolts of cloth before a jeering crowd of apprentices, while Lambert's offense has been cried out with loud voice. The man is disgraced and ruined. He will have to become again a mere wage earner, or quit the city outright. His misfortune is the choice news of the hour. The smell of the burning cloth is still in the air when Conon's party rides by the pillory and halts at the house of the rich Othon Bouchaut, who is ready to receive them.

Maître Othon is one of the principal burghers. He has grown rich by importing wares from Venice, Constantinople, and the lands of the Infidels. It is scandalous (say some nobles) how he, villein born, with hands only accustomed to hold a purse or a pen, is able to talk to a great seigneur without groveling as every good peasant ought. He and his wife even wear gold lace, pearls, and costly stuffs on fête days, as if they were nobles; and they are said actually to have broken the law forbidding non-nobles to wear furs. Very deplorable, but what can be done? Othon is so rich that he can stir up trouble even for the duke. Nothing remains but to speak him fair and accept his hospitality.

This powerful merchant's house is in the market-place. It rises five stories high, and is built of beams filled in with laths, mortar, and stucco. On the ground floor are storerooms for costly Oriental goods, and desks where the master's clerks seem forever busy with complicated accounts. On the next are the rooms for the family, and, although without the spacious magnificence of the great hall at St. Aliquis, Adela remarks a little enviously that her host's wife enjoys many comforts and luxuries hardly known in the castle. The upper stories are full of small chambers for Othon's family, his clerks, and the younger apprentices who are learning his business. Before the front door swings the ensign of the house—a gilded mortar (in token of the powdered spices which the owner sells). The houses of Pontdebois have no numbers. The ensigns serve to identify them. One of Othon's neighbors lives at the "Crouching Cat," another at the "Tin Pot," another at the "Silver Fish," and so on all through the town.

The house of Othon also appears to be quite new, as do many others. This, however, is a doubtful sign of good fortune. Only a few years ago much of Pontdebois was burned down. The narrow streets, the thatched roofs, the absence of any means of checking a blaze save a line of buckets hastily organized, make great fires a standing menace to every city.[1] Othon complains that at any moment he may be reduced almost to beggary by the carelessness of some wretched scullery maid or tavern apprentice. He will also say that somehow in the pent-up city there is greater danger of the plague than in the country castles or even in the villages with their dungheaps. A dozen years ago Pontdebois lost a quarter of its population by an outbreak which spared neither rich nor poor, before which physicians and religious processions seemed alike helpless, and which demoralized the community before the saints mercifully halted the devastation.

[1] Rouen had six severe fires between 1200 and 1225, and yet was not exceptionally unfortunate. If a city were close to a river, it was liable also to very serious freshets. Of course, every place was in fairly constant danger of being stormed, sacked, and burned down in war.

The Communal Donjon

There are only a few stone houses in Pontdebois. Even the best houses of the citizens are usually of wood and mortar. Not yet have risen those magnificent stone city halls which later will be the glory of North France and Flanders. But on one side of the market place rises the communal donjon. The Good Town is like a seigneur (indeed, somewhat it *is* a seigneur placed in commission): it has its walls and therefore its strong citadel. The donjon forms a high, solid, square tower dominating the public square. At its summit there is always a watchman ready, at first danger of fire or attack, to boom the alarm bell. The tower itself is large enough to have good-sized rooms in its base. Nearest the ground is the council chamber where the worshipful echevins can deliberate. Above that is the archive room, where the elaborate town records are kept. Directly under the council chamber, however, is the prison, where general offenders are mewed up no more comfortably than in the abysses of St. Aliquis.

The soul of the communal donjon, however, hovers around its bells. There in the dark tower hang shrill Jacqueline, loud Carolus, and, deepest and mightiest of all, Holy Trinity, and several others. A peal of powerful bells pertains to every free town. Of course, they ring lustily and merrily on holidays; indeed, strangers to the city think they are rung too often for repose.[1] But if they all begin leaping and thundering together, that is probably a sign for a mass meeting of the citizens in the open plaza before the donjon. The magistrates may wish to harangue the populace from the balcony, just above the council room, descanting upon some public danger

[1] Modern travelers are to this day impressed by the amount of bellringing which goes on in such unspoiled mediæval-built Flemish towns as Bruges.

or deliver a peaceful explanation of some new municipal ordinance. In any case, a commune without its donjon and bells is like a ship without its rudder, and if ever Pontdebois succumbs to superior power, the first step of the conqueror will probably be to "take away the bells"— that will be the same thing as annulling the city liberties.

Pontdebois has been a Good Town with a charter of privileges for about a hundred years. As early as Charlemagne's day a village existed upon the site. The location proved good for trade, but the inhabitants, despite success in commerce and industry and increasing numbers, were for a long time mere villeins dependent upon the lord bishop of the town and region, and with no more rights than the peasants of the fields had. However, in dealing with men who were steadily becoming richer, and who were picking up strange ideas by foreign intercourse, it proved much harder to keep them content with their station than it did the run of villeins. Besides, the dukes of Quelqueparte, although very loath to grant privileges to their own villeins, were not averse to having privileges given to the subjects of such independent and unreliable vassals as the bishops of Pontdebois. Consequently, when the townspeople about A.D. 1100 began raising the cry, "Commune! Commune!" in the episcopal presence, the bishop could not look to his suzerain for much support. Indeed, it was being realized by intelligent seigneurs that granting a charter to a town often meant a great increase of wealth, so that if the lord's fiscal rights were carefully safeguarded, he was actually the gainer by an apparent cession of part of his authority. The upshot was that about A.D. 1110, when a certain bishop needed a large purse to cover his travel to the Holy Land, for a round sum the townsfolk bought from him a charter—a

precious document which practically raised them out
of the status of villeins and protected them against those
executions and tyrannies which the run of peasants had
to accept resignedly, as they did bad winters.

This charter read in part much as follows: "I, Henri,
by the grace of God Bishop of Pontdebois, make known
to all present and to come, that I have established the
undermentioned rules for the inhabitants of my town of
Pontdebois. Every male inhabitant of said town shall
pay me every year twelve deniers and a bushel of oats
as the price of his dwelling; and if he desires to hold land
outside the walls four deniers per year for each acre.
The houses, vines, and fields may be sold and alienated
at the pleasure of the holder. The dwellers in this town
shall go neither to the *ost* [feudal levy] nor on any other
expedition unless I lead the same in person. They are
allowed six echevins to administer the ordinary business
of the town and to assist my provost in his duties. I
especially decree that no seigneur shall withdraw from
this town any inhabitants for any reason, unless they
are actually 'his men' or owe him arrears in taxes, etc."[1]

After securing this charter, the men of Pontdebois
began to hold up their heads in a manner grievous to the
neighboring nobles, and even more grievous to the
wealthy clergy, for prince-bishops were often the original
suzerains of the towns, and their authority was the most
seriously curtailed.[2] The books are full of the wrath of

---

[1] Of course, no two communal charters were ever alike, although
many were run in a common mold. Many towns received not a full
charter, but "rights of burgessy"—*e.g.,* guaranties against various
common forms of oppression, although the laws were still actually
administered by officers named by the seigneur.

[2] Bishops often had their cathedral and episcopal seat at the largest
place in their dioceses—the very places most likely to demand
charters.

the ecclesiastics over the changed situation. "'Commune!' a name new and detestable!" pungently wrote Abbot Guibert of Nogent, even when the movement was young; while Bishop Ives of Chartres assured everybody that "compacts [with city folk] are binding on no one: they are contrary to the canon law and the decision of the holy fathers." Even as recently as 1213 a synod at Paris has denounced communes as the creations of "usurers and exactors" who have set up "diabolical usages, tending to overthrow the jurisdiction of the Church."

However righteous the anger of these holy men, it has proved vain. The communes ever wax stronger, and annually some new seigneur is compelled to sell a charter or even to grant one for nothing. The kings watch complacently a movement which weakens their unruly feudatories. Sometimes the townsfolk have grown insolent and tried to defend their privileges by sheer violence. Once there was a very tyrannous bishop of Laon. He foolishly tried to cancel a charter granted the city, and boasted: "What can you expect these people to do by their commotions? If my negro boy John were to seize the most terrible of them by the nose, the fellow would not even growl. What they yesterday called a 'commune' I have forced them to give up—at least as long as I live!" The next day the yell, "Commune! Commune!" rang in the streets. A mob sacked the episcopal palace and found the bishop hiding in a cask at the bottom of the cellar. The howling populace dragged him into the street and killed him with a hatchet. Then, to add to this sacrilege upon an anointed bishop, they plundered most of the nobles who chanced to be in the town. After such deeds it is no wonder that the king went to Laon and re-established order with a strong hand. Nevertheless, some years later, a new charter was granted the town, and the succeeding bishops have had to walk warily, despite inward groanings.

Fortunately, Pontdebois has been spared these convulsions. As a rule the local prelates have been reasonable and conciliatory. The bishop is still called "suzerain." He receives the fixed tax provided in the original agreement. He has jurisdiction over the citizens in spiritual matters, which include heresy, blasphemy, insults, and assaults upon priests and outrages to churches. Likewise much of what might be called "probate litigation"—touching the validity of marriages and children, and consequently the wills and property rights affected thereby. However, in most secular particulars the citizens have pretty complete control. They levy numerous imposts, direct taxes, tolls, and market dues; they enroll a militia to defend the walls and to take the field under their own officers and banner when the general levy of the region is called out; they pass many local ordinances; and they name their own magistrates who administer "high justice." They can even wage local wars if they have a grievance against neighboring barons, being themselves a kind of collective seigneur. The one thing they *cannot* do is to coin money; that is a privilege carefully reserved to the king and to the superior nobility.

Practically all these powers are exercised by the six echevins, with a higher dignitary, the mayor (*maire*), at their head.[1] There is little real democracy, however, in Pontdebois. The richer merchants, like Othon, and the more prosperous masters form practically an oli-

---

[1] The echevins were often known instead as "jurés" and their numbers were frequently much greater than six. The mayors might be called "provosts" or "rewards."

garchy, excluding the poor artisans and apprentices from any share in municipal affairs save that of paying taxes and listening to edicts by the magistrates. The same officers are re-elected year after year. They use the town money much as they see fit, refusing public reckoning and blandly announcing that "they render their accounts to one another." There are, therefore, certain discontented fellows who even murmur, "We 'free burghers' are worse taxed and oppressed than are Baron Conon's villeins at St. Aliquis."

Nevertheless, there is often a great desire to become even a passive citizen of Pontdebois. If you can live there unmolested for "a year and a day," you escape the jurisdiction of the lord on whose estate you have been a villein. You are protected against those outrages which are possible on even the best seigneuries. Most of all, you gain a chance to become something more than a clodhopping plowman. Perhaps your grandchildren at least will become wealthy and powerful enough to receive a baron as their guest, even as does the rich Othon.

So one may wander about the twisting streets of Pontdebois until nightfall, when the loud horns blow curfew—"cover fires." After that, the streets are deserted save for the occasional watchman rattling his iron-shod staff and calling through the darkness, "Pray for the dead!"

Chapter XXII: Industry and Trade in Pontdebois. The Great Fair.

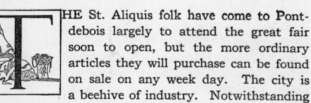

HE St. Aliquis folk have come to Pontdebois largely to attend the great fair soon to open, but the more ordinary articles they will purchase can be found on sale on any week day. The city is a beehive of industry. Notwithstanding much talk about commerce in the Feudal Ages, the means of communication and transport are so bad that it is only the luxuries—not the essentials—that can be exported very far. It takes thirty days in good weather to travel from Paris to Marseilles. It takes sometimes a week to go from Pontdebois to Paris; and there is no larger industrial city much nearer than Paris. The result is that almost everything ordinarily needed in a château, village, or even in a monastery, which cannot be made upon the spot, is manufactured and sold in this Good Town.

Industrial life, however, seems to exist on a very small scale. There are no real factories. An establishment employing more than four or five persons, including the proprietor, is rare. Much commoner are petty workshops conducted by the owner alone or aided by only one youthful apprentice. This multiplicity of extremely small plants gives Pontdebois a show of bustle and activity which its actual population does not warrant.

When you do business in a town, simply name your

desires and you can be directed to a little winding street
containing all the shops of a given industry. There is the
Glass Workers' Street, the Tanners' Row, the Butchers'
Lane, the Parchment Makers' Street (frequented by
monkish commissioners from the abbeys), the Gold-
smiths' Lane, etc.

As a rule the goods are made up in the rear of the

CLOTH MERCHANTS
From a bas-relief in the cathedral of Rheims (thirteenth century).

shop and are sold over a small counter directly upon the
street, where the customer stands while he drives his
bargain. Written signs and price cards are practically
unknown. The moment a possible purchaser comes in
sight, all the attendants near the front of the shops
begin a terrific uproar, each trying to bawl down his
neighbor, praising his own wares and almost dragging

in the visitor to inspect them. Trade etiquette permits shopkeepers to shout out the most derogatory things about their rivals. Father Grégoire, wishing to buy some shoes, is almost demoralized by the clamor, although this is by no means his first visit to Pontdebois. As he enters the Shoemakers' Lane it seems as if all the ill-favored apprentices are crowding around him. One plucks his cape. "Here, good Father! Exactly what you want!" "Hearken not to the thief," shouts another; "try on our shoes and name your own price!" A third tries to push him into yet another stall. "Good sirs," cries Grégoire, in dismay, "for God's sake treat me gently or I'll buy no shoes at all!" Only reluctantly do they let him make his choice, then conclude a bargain unmolested by outsiders. In the fish, bread, and wine markets the scenes can be even more riotous, while the phrases used by the hucksters in crying their wares are peculiar and picturesque.

As always in trade, it is well that "the buyer should beware"; fixed prices are really unknown and inferior goods are inordinately praised. Nevertheless, the city and guild authorities try hard to protect purchasers from misrepresentation. The officers are always making unannounced rounds of inspection to see how the guild ordinances are being obeyed.[1] The fate of the rascally woolen maker has been noted. Heavy fines have also been imposed lately upon a rope maker who put linen in a hemp cord, and a cutler who put silver ornaments in a

[1] These regulations for a long period were of marked value for insuring a high grade of workmanship according to traditional methods, but later they became a most serious impediment to any improvements in industrial processes. Originality, new designs, and labor-saving devices were practically prohibited, and some industries were destined to remain almost stagnant down to the French Revolution.

bone knife handle. This, however, was not to protect purchasers, but because they had gone outside the line of work permitted to members of their guild and trenched upon another set of craftsmen. Indeed, a very short residence in Pontdebois makes one aware that within the chartered commune the question is not, as in strictly feudal dominions, "Whose 'man' is he?" but "To what guild does he belong?" Everything apparently revolves around the trade and craft guilds.

Some of these guilds, like that of the butchers, are alleged to be much older than the granting of the charter; but it is undeniable that the organizations have multiplied and grown in power since that precious document was obtained.[1] Each special industry goes to the seigneur (in this city to the bishop) for a special grant of privileges and for a fee he will usually satisfy the petitioners, especially as they desire the privileges mainly to protect them against their fellow craftsmen, not against himself. In Paris there are more than three hundred and fifty separate professions; in Pontdebois they are much fewer, yet the number seems high. Many guilds have only a few members apiece, but even the smallest is mortally jealous of its prerogatives. One "mystery" makes men's shoes, another women's, another children's. Some time ago the last mentioned sold some alleged "children's shoes" which seemed very large! Result— a bitter law suit brought by the women's shoemakers. Christian charity among the guildsmen has not been restored yet. In Paris they say that the tailors are

[1] Among the oldest traceable guilds in Paris were the Master Chandlers and Oilmen, who received royal privileges in 1061. The butchers, tanners, shoemakers, drapers, furriers, and purse makers, were other old Parisian guilds.

pushing a case against the old-clothes dealers because the latter "repair their garments so completely as to make them practically new." There will soon be handsome fees for the kings' judges, if for nobody else.[1]

Such friction arises, of course, because each guild is granted a strict monopoly of trade within certain prescribed limits. A saddle maker from a strange city who started a shop without being admitted to the proper guild would soon find his shop closed, his products burned, and his own feet in the stocks by the town donjon. The guilds are supposed to be under strict regulations, however, in return for these privileges. Their conditions of labor are laid down, as are the hours and days of working. The precise quality of their products is fixed, and sometimes even the size of the articles and the selling price. Night work, as a rule, is forbidden, because one cannot then see to produce perfect goods, although carpenters are allowed to make coffins after sunset. On days before festivals everyone must close by 3 P.M., and on feast days only pastry shops (selling cakes and sweetmeats) are allowed to be open. Violaters are subject to a fine, which goes partly to the guild corporation, partly to the town treasury; and these fines form a good part of the municipal revenue.

The guilds are not labor unions. The controlling members are all masters—the employers of labor, although usually doing business on a very small scale. A guild is also a religious and benevolent institution. Every corporation has its patron saint, with a special chapel in some church where a priest is engaged to say masses for

---

[1] The fullers were always suing the weavers. Could the latter, if they wished, dye the cloth which they themselves had woven? Bakers were always at law with keepers of small cookshops who baked their own bread, etc.

the souls of deceased members.[1] If a member falls into misfortune his guild is expected to succor him and especially, if he dies, to look after his widow and assist his orphans to learn their father's craft. Each organization also has its own banner, very splendid, hung ordinarily

beside the guild's altar, but in the civic processions proudly carried by one of the syndics, the craft's officers. To be a syndic in an influential guild is the ordinary ambition of about every young industrialist. It means the acme of power and dignity attainable, short of being elected echevin.

The road to full guild membership is a fairly difficult one, yet it can be traversed by lads of good morals and legitimate birth if they have application and intelligence. A master can have from one to three apprentices and also his own son, if he has one who desires to learn the trade. The apprentices serve from three to twelve years.

The more difficult the craft the longer the service; thus it takes a ten-year apprenticeship to become a qualified jeweler. The lads thus "bound out" cannot ordinarily quit their master under any circumstances before the proper time. If they run away they can be haled back and roundly punished. They are usually knocked about plentifully, are none too well clothed, sleep in cold garrets, are fed on the leavings from the

---

[1] Certain saints would naturally be the patrons of certain particular crafts—*e.g.*, St. Joseph of the carpenters, St. Peter of the fishmongers, etc.

master's table, and can seldom call a moment their own except on holidays. Their master may give them a little pocket money, but no regular wages. On the other hand, he is bound to teach them his trade and to protect them against evil influences. Often enough, of course, matters end by the favorite apprentice marrying his master's daughter and practically taking over the establishment.

At the end of the apprenticeship the young industrialist becomes a hired worker, perhaps in his old master's shop, perhaps somewhere else.[1] He is engaged and paid by the week, and often changes employers many times while in this stage of his career. The guild protects him against gross exploitation, but his hours are long— from 5 A.M. to 7 P.M. during the summer months. Finally, if he has led a moral life, proved a good workman, and accumulated a small capital, he may apply to the syndics for admission as a full master himself. A kind of examination takes place. If, for example, he has been a weaver he must produce an extremely good bolt of cloth and show skill in actually making and adjusting the parts of his loom. This ordeal passed, he pays a fee (divisible between the city and the guild) and undergoes an initiation, full of horseplay and absurd allegory. Thus a candidate for the position of baker must solemnly present a "new pot full of walnuts and wafers" to the chief syndic; and upon the latter's accepting the contents, the candidate deliberately "breaks the pot against the wall"—a proclamation that he is now a full member of the guild. The last act is of course a grand feast—

---

[1] A master could not employ more than one or two paid workers, lest he build up too big a business and ruin his competitors. The guild system seems deliberately contrived to perpetuate the existence of a great number of *very small* industries.

the whole fraternity guzzling down tankard after tankard at the expense of the new "brother."

There is one quarter of the town which the St. Aliquis visitors hardly dare to enter. Thrust away in miserable hovels wedged against one angle of the walls live the "accursed race"—the Jews. Here are dark-haired, dark-eyed people with Oriental physiognomies. They are exceedingly obsequious to Christians, but the latter do not trust them. These bearded men with earrings, these women with bright kerchiefs of Eastern stuffs, all seem to be conducting little shops where can be bought the cheapest furniture, household utensils, and particularly old clothes in Pontdebois. In this quarter, too, is a small stone building which Conon and his followers wonder that the echevins suffer to exist—a very ancient synagogue, for the Jewish colony is as old as the town. The few Christians who have periled their souls by venturing inside say the windows are very small and that the dark, grimy interior is lighted by dim lamps. Here also are strange ancient books written in a character which no Gentile can interpret, but by whispered report containing fearful blasphemies against the Catholic faith. Why are such folk permitted in Pontdebois? Maître Othon has to explain that if God has consigned these Jews to eternal damnation he has permitted many of them while in this world to possess inordinate riches. Some of the most abject-looking of these persons, who are compelled by law to wear a saffron circle on their breasts, can actually find moneys sufficient to pay the costs of a duke's campaign. Every great seigneur has "his Jew," and the king has "the royal Jew" who will loan him money when no Christian will do so in order to wage his wars or to push more peaceful undertakings.

The Jews are indeed hard to do without because the Church strictly forbids the loaning of money on usury, yet somehow it seems very difficult to borrow large sums simply upon the prospect of the bare repayment of the same. The Jews, with no fear for their souls, do not hesitate to lend on interest, sometimes graspingly demanding forty, fifty and even sixty per cent.[1] This is outrageous, but ofttimes money must be had, and what if no Christian will lend? There are certain worthy men, especially Lombards of North Italy, who say that it were well if the Church allowed

MONEY-CHANGERS (CHARTRES)

lending at reasonable interest, and they are beginning to make loans accordingly. This suggestion, however, savors of heresy. In the meantime the Jews continue despised, maltreated, and mobbed every Good Friday, but nevertheless almost indispensable.

The great object which brings so many visitors to Pontdebois is the annual fair held every August in the field by the river, just south of the town. Then can be

---

[1] The extreme difficulty of collecting loans made to powerful seigneurs went far to explain these astonishing rates of interest. The chances of an unfriended Jew being unable to collect any part of his loan were extremely great. As a rule his hopes lay in becoming the indispensable man of business and financier of a king or other great lord who would support him in recovering principal and interest from lesser debtors, in return for great favors to himself. Thus Richard I of England is alleged to have made the Jews settled in his realm furnish nearly *one third* of his entire revenues, as recompense for allowing them to use his courts to collect from their private debtors.

purchased many articles so unusual that they are not regularly on sale in the city shops, or even at the more general market which is held in the square before the donjon upon each Thursday. The Pontdebois fair cannot, indeed, compete in extensiveness with the Rouen or Dijon fairs, the famous Lendit fair (near St. Denis and Paris), nor, above all, with the great Champagne fairs at Troyes and elsewhere, for these are the best places for buying and selling in all France. Nevertheless one must not despise a fair which attracts nearly all the good folk of Quelqueparte who are intent on gains or purchases.

In some respects the fair has many features like the tourney at St. Aliquis. Long files of travelers on beasts or on foot are approaching, innumerable tents are flaunting bright pennons, and the same jongleurs who swarmed to make music or to exhibit tricks at Conon's festival are coming hither also. But the travelers are not, as a rule, knights in bright armor, but soberly clad merchants. Their attendants lead, not high-stepping destrers, but heavily laden sumpter mules; the tents are not given over to gallant feasting and gentle intrigues, but to vigorous chaffering for that thing which all knights affect to despise—good money. Therefore, although the bustle seems the same, the results are very different.

There is a special complication at these fairs. In what kind of money shall we pay? The royal coinage is supposed to circulate everywhere and to represent the standard, but the king's power cannot suppress a whole swarm of local coinages. There are deniers of Anjou, Maine, Rouen, Touraine, Toulouse, Poitou, Bordeaux, and many other districts besides the good royal coins from Paris; also a plentiful circulation of Constantinople bezants, Venetian zechins, German groats, and English silver shillings, in addition to many outlandish

A FAIR IN CHAMPAGNE IN THE THIRTEENTH CENTURY

In the center of the picture, a commoner and his wife going to make more purchases; at the right, in front of a shop, cloth merchants and their customers; a shop boy on his knees unpacks the cloth, another carries the bales; at the left, a beggar; another establishment of a draper; a group of people having their money weighed by the money changer; farther back, a lord and his servants going through the crowd; at the left a parade of mountebanks; at the right, other shops; and in the background the walls, houses, church, etc.

infidel coins of very debatable value. To add to the trouble, there are varying standards for weights and measures. You have to make sure as to which one is used in every purchase.[1]

The "royal foot" is a pretty general measure, but sometimes it is split into ten, sometimes into twelve, inches. Still worse is the pound weight. A Paris pound divides into sixteen ounces, but that of Lyons into fourteen, that of Marseilles into only thirteen. Clearly one needs time, patience, and a level head to trade happily at this fair!

When you consider the number of tolls levied everywhere upon commerce—a fee on about every load that crosses a bridge, traverses a stretch of river or highway, passes a castle, etc.—the wonder grows that it seems worth while to transport goods at all. The fees are small, but how they multiply even on a short journey! Along the Loire between Roanne and Nantes are about seventy-four places where something must be paid. Things are as bad by land. Clergy and knights are usually exempt, but merchants have to travel almost with one hand in their pockets to satisfy the collectors of the local seigneurs. The result is that almost nothing is brought from a distance which is not fairly portable and for

[1] Mediæval coinages varied to such an extreme extent that it is almost impossible to make correct general statements about their modern values. In the time of Philip Augustus, probably the North French money table was something like this:

1 pound (livre)—2 marks—20 (earlier 24) sous—240 deniers—4760 obols.

A sou, merely a money of account, was equal to about 20 modern francs ($3.86 gold), and the denier, a regular coin, to about one franc (19.3 cents, gold). The copper obols were thus worth about one cent. But money in the Feudal Age had a purchasing power equal to at least ten times what it is to-day, and attempts at close estimating are decidedly futile.

which there is a demand not readily met by the local workshops.

Nevertheless, a good fair is a profitable asset to an intelligent seigneur. The present fair was instituted seventy years ago by an unusually enterprising lord bishop. He induced the barons of the region to agree to treat visitors to the fair reasonably and to give them protection against robbers. He also established strict regulations to secure for every trader fair play when disposing of his wares, commissioned sergeants to patrol the grounds, and set up a competent provost's court right among the tents, so that persons falling into a dispute could get a quick decision without expensive litigation.[1] In return he laid a small tax on every article sold. The arrangement worked well. Succeeding bishops have been wise enough to realize that contented merchants are more profitable than those that have been plundered. "Hare! Hare!" cry the prelate's sergeants on the first day—announcing the opening—and then for about two weeks the trafficking, bargain driving, amusements, and thimble rigging will continue.

The time of a fair is carefully calculated. Many merchants spend all the warmer months journeying with their wares from one fair to another. Many of the traders at Pontdebois have spent half of June at Lendit, where "everything is for sale, from carts and horses to fine tapestries and silver cups." The wares at this present fair are almost equally extensive, although the selection may be a little less choice. Besides all kinds of French products, there are booths displaying wonderful silks

[1] The courts of Champagne took particular pains to assure merchants of honest treatment and protection, and their fairs were unusually successful. Champagne, of course, by its central location between the Seine and the Rhine, the Midi and Flemish lands, was exceedingly well placed to attract merchants.

from Syria, or possibly only from Venice; there are blazing Saracen carpets woven in Persia or even remoter lands, while local dyers and fullers can stock up with Eastern dyestuffs—lovely red from Damascus, indigo from Jerusalem, and many other colors. You can get beautiful glass vessels made in Syria or imitated from Oriental models in Venice. The monks will buy a quantity of the new paper while they purchase their year's supply of parchment; and Adela will authorize the St. Aliquis cook to obtain many deniers' worth of precious spices—pepper, cinnamon, clove, and the rest essential for seasoning all kinds of dishes, even if their cost is very dear. The spices are sold by a swarthy, hawk-visaged Oriental who speaks French in quaint gutturals, is uncouthly dressed, yet is hardly a Jew. It is whispered he is a downright miscreant—*i.e.,* an outrageous Infidel, possibly not even a Mohammedan. Perhaps he is native to those lands close to the rising place of the sun whence come the spices. Ought one to deal with such people? Nevertheless, the spices are desirable and he sells them cheaper than anybody else. There are many other unfamiliar characters at the fair, including a negro mountebank, quite a few Germans from the Rhenish trading cities, and a scattering of so-called Italians, mostly money changers and venders of luxuries, who, however, seem to be really Jews that are concealing their unpopular religion for the sake of gain.

After the fair commences, many articles are on sale daily; but others are exhibited only for a short time. Thus, following the custom at Troyes, for the first day or two cloths are displayed in special variety; after that leather goods and furs; then various bulk commodities, such as salt, medicinal drugs, herbs, raw wool, flax, etc.; next comes the excitement of a horse and cattle market, when Conon will be induced to buy for his oldest son a palfrey and for his farms a blooded bull;[1] and after that various general articles will hold the right of way.

The Pontdebois masters are required to close their shops and do all their business at the fair grounds in order that there may be no unjust competition with the visiting traders. Indeed, all business outside the fair grounds is strictly forbidden in order to prevent fraudulent transactions which the bishop's officers cannot suppress. Thus, besides the costly imported wares, you can get anything you ordinarily want from the curriers, shoemakers, coppersmiths, hardware, linen, and garment venders, and the dealers in fish, grain, and even bread.

THE SALE OF PELTRIES (BOURGES)

All this means a chaffering, chattering, and ofttimes a quarreling, which makes one ask, "Have the days of the Tower of Babel returned?" The sergeants are always flying about on foot or horseback among the winding avenues of tents and booths, and frequently drag off some vagabond for the pillory. They even seize a cut-purse red-handed and soon give the idlers the brutal pleasure of watching a hanging. There are a couple of tents where notaries are ready with wax and parch-

[1] Frequently, however, the cattle markets might be held at special seasons entirely apart from the general fairs.

ments to draw up and seal contracts and bargains. Flemish merchants are negotiating with their Bordeaux compeers to send the latter next year a consignment of solid linseys; while a Mayence wine dealer is trying to prove to a seigneur how much his cellars would be improved by a few tuns of Rheingold, shipped in to mellow after the next vintage.

Along with all this honest traffic proceed the amusements worthy and unworthy. There are several exhibitors of trick dogs and performing bears. In a cage there is a creature called a "lion," though it is certainly a sick, spiritless, and mangy one; there are also male and female rope dancers and acrobats, professional story tellers, professors of white magic, and, of course, jongleurs of varying quality sawing their viols, or reciting romances and merry *fabliaux*—clever tales, though often indescribably coarse. There are, in addition (let the sinful truth be told) perfect swarms of brazen women of an evil kind; and there is enough heady wine being consumed to fill a brook into the Claire. The sergeants continually have to separate drunkards who get to fighting, and to roll their "full brothers"—more completely overcome—into safe places where they can sleep off their liquor unkicked by horses and uncrushed by constantly passing carts.

This bustle continues two weeks. By that time everybody who has come primarily to buy has spent all his money. If he has come to sell, presumably he is satisfied. The drunkards are at last sad and sober. "Hare! Hare!" cry the sergeants on the evening of the last day. The fair is over. The next morning the foreign merchants pack their wares, strike their tents, and wander off to another market fifty miles distant, while the Pointdebois traders and industrialists resume their normal activity. They have stocked up with necessary raw materials for the year, they have absorbed many new ideas as to how they can make better wares or trade to more advantage; yet probably most of them are grumbling against "those Germans and Flemings and Jews whom the bishop turns loose on us. Blessed saints! how much money they have taken out of the neighborhood!" But the bishop, when his provost reports the tax receipts, is extraordinarily well satisfied.

Chapter XXIII: The Lord Bishop. The Canons. The Parish Clergy.

AFTER Conon and his baroness have soiled their gentle blood by discreet trafficking at the Pontdebois fair, the seigneur must needs pay a ceremonious call upon the lord bishop. He might indeed have accepted lodgings at the episcopal palace, but it is well not to be put under too many obligations even to so conciliatory a prelate as Bishop Nivelon. Between the lay and ecclesiastical lords there are compliments, but little affection. Both unite in despising the villein and distrusting the monks, but there the harmony often ends.

The lord bishop occupies almost the apex of the ecclesiastical power, barring only the Pope and his cardinals; and all the lay world ought to honor the clergy. A familiar story illustrates the recognition due even to the humbler churchmen. Once St. Martin was asked to sup with the emperor. He was offered the cup before it was passed to the sovereign. This was a great honor. He was supposed merely to touch the vessel to his lips, then hand it on to his Majesty. Instead, to the surprise yet admiration of all, he gave it to a poor priest standing behind him, thereby teaching the plain lesson that a servant of God, even of the lowest rank, deserves honor above the highest secular potentate.

The clergy is divided into two great sections—the religious (the monks) and the secular clergy who are "in the world" and have the "cure of souls." The parish priests belong, of course, to this second class. They celebrate mass and administer the sacraments and consolations of religion. They are possibly reckoned by the laity a little less holy than the monks, but their power is incalculable. At their head in each diocese (ecclesiastical province) is the bishop. Since the wealth of the Church embraces at least one fifth of all the real estate of France[1] and the control of this vast property is largely vested in the bishops, it is easy to see what holding such an office implies. There is no seigneur in Quelque-parte so rich as Bishop Nivelon, barring only the duke himself—and the duke would justly hesitate, quite apart from feelings of piety, to force a quarrel with so great a spiritual lord.

EPISCOPAL THRONE OF THE
THIRTEENTH CENTURY
Restored by Viollet-Le-Duc, from an ivory
in the Louvre.

[1] *One third* of the real estate of Germany was alleged to have belonged to the church. Of course, much of this belonged to monasteries, to the endowments of canons (cathedral clergy), or of the parish priests, etc., but the bishops assuredly enjoyed or at least controlled the lion's share.

It will be hard for other ages to realize the part that is played by the Church in the feudal centuries. The clergy are far more than spiritual guides. They are directors of education and maintain about all there is of intellectual life, science, and learning. They help the weak secular authorities to preserve law and order. They supply practically all the teachers, lawyers, and professional nonfeudal judges in Christendom, and very many of the physicians. As already stated, that multitude of legal cases known as "probate," involving the disposal of wide estates, often go directly to the Church Courts.

If an ordinary man appears interested in literary matters, he is frequently set down as a "clerk," even if he does not openly claim to have received holy orders. It is indeed very desirable legally for a common person (not a privileged noble) to be barely literate. If he can do this and is arrested on any charge, he can often "plead his clergy." The test is not to produce a certificate showing that he is a priest or monk, but to be able to read a few lines from the Bible or other sacred book. If he can read these fateful "neck verses," he may sometimes escape a speedy interview with the hangman. He is then ordinarily handed over to the bishop or the bishop's official (judicial officer) and tried according to the merciful and scientific canon law, which, whatever the offense, will seldom or never order the death penalty, save for heresy.[1] The worst to be feared is a long imprisonment in the uncomfortable dungeon under the bishop's palace.

[1] In the case of heretics, the Church did not execute the offenders by its own officers. It merely "relaxed" them to secular officials, who at once put the old civil laws against misbelievers in force. Of course, the Church could not secure the immunity of traitors and great criminals, yet even those were usually treated more tenderly if they could claim ecclesiastical jurisdiction.

With conditions like this, what wonder if very worldly elements keep intruding into the secular clergy. Many a baron's son balances in his mind—which is better, the seigneur's "cap of presence" or the bishop's miter? The bishop, indeed, cannot marry; but the Church is not always very stern in dealing with other forms of social enjoyment. Sometimes a powerful reforming Pope will make the prelates affect a monkish austerity—but the next Pope may prove too busy to be insistent concerning "sins of the flesh." A great fraction of all the bishops are the sons of noble houses. Merely becoming tonsured has not made them into saints. They are the children of fighting sires, and they bring into the Church much of the turbulence of their fathers and brothers in the castles.

A BISHOP OF THE TWELFTH CENTURY

From an enameled plaque representing Ulger, bishop of Angers (1125–1149). He wears the albe, the dalmatica, the chasuble, the amice, and the miter. He blesses with the right hand, an attitude in which bishops are often represented.

Certainly, men of humble birth can become prelates. It is one of the glories of the Church that, thanks to her, the children of poor villeins can receive the homage of the great in this world. Pope Sylvester II was the son of a mere shepherd of Aurillac. Suger, the mighty abbot of St. Denis and vice gerent for Louis VI, was the son of an actual serf. Pope Hadrian IV, the only Englishman who has ever mounted the throne of St. Peter, seems to have had an origin hardly more exalted. All this shows what

fortune can sometimes await bright and lucky boys who
enter betimes the convent schools instead of following the
plow.[1] But Heaven seldom reverses the natural order.
As a rule, when a noble enters the church, family influence and the social prestige of his caste will get behind
him. He is far more likely to be elected bishop and to
enjoy the seats of glory than are his fellow clerics,
learned and devout, who have no such backing.

Nivelon of Pontdebois is an example of the average
bishop of the superior kind. He was the second son of a
sire of moderate means. Family influence secured him,
while fairly young, the appointment as canon at the
cathedral. The old bishop conveniently happened to
die at a time when both the duke and his suzerain, the
king, thought well of the young canon and were anxious
to conciliate his relatives. Nivelon, too, had displayed
sufficient grasp on business affairs, along with real piety,
to make men say that he would prove a worthy "prince
spiritual." The canons (with whom the choice nominally
lay) made haste to elect him after a broad hint from both
the duke and the king. Confirmation was obtained from
Rome after negotiations and possibly some money
transfers.[2] Since then Nivelon has ruled his diocese well.
He has been neither a great theologian nor a man of
letters, as are certain contemporaneous bishops, nor a
self-seeking politician and a mitered warrior like others.
There have been no scandalous luxuries at his palace,

[1] One could go on multiplying such cases. For example, Maurice
of Sully, who was bishop of Paris under Philip Augustus, was the
son of a poor peasant. He managed his diocese admirably and
bequeathed not merely considerable wealth to his relatives, but
large properties to two abbeys and also funds for poor relief.

[2] The question of the technical relations at this time of both
Papacy and royalty to the appointment and investiture of French
bishops is one that must be left for more detailed and learned
volumes.

and he has never neglected his duties—which none can deny are numerous.

There is plenty of excuse for Nivelon if he allows religious tasks to be swamped by secular ones. He apparently differs largely from a seigneur n that his interests and obligations are more complex. On his direct domains are parish churches, abbeys, farms, peasant villages, and forests which he must rule by his officials and provosts just as Conon rules St. Aliquis. He has many noble fiefs which owe him homage and regular feudal duties in peace and war. His knightly vassals wait on him, as do regular lieges, and are bound on state occasions to carry him through his cathedral city seated on his episcopal throne. He does not himself do ordinary homage to the king, but he must take to him a solemn oath of fealty, and assist with armed levies on proper summons. There are many clergy around his palace, but also a regular baronial household—seneschal, steward, chamberlain, marshal, and equerry, though not, as with the laxer prelates, a master of the hawks.

So much for Monseigneur Nivelon's temporal side; but, since he is a self-respecting prelate, his ecclesiastical office is no sinecure. He has to ordain and control all the parish priests (curés), and spends much of his time inspecting the rural churches and listening to complaints against offending priests, suspending and punishing the guilty. Indeed, his days are consumed by a curious mixture of duties. Just before Conon ceremoniously calls upon him he has been listening first to a complaint from a castellan about the need of new trench-buts for the defense of a small castle pertaining to the bishopric, and then to the report of his "official" concerning a disorderly priest accused of blaspheming the Trinity while in his cups in a tavern.

Once a year Nivelon has to hold a synod in the choir of his cathedral. All the nonmonastic clergy of the diocese are supposed to be present, and he has to preach before them, stating home truths about Christian conduct and administering public reprimands and discipline. Often his routine is interrupted by the commands of the king that he, as a well-versed man of the world, shall come to Paris to give counsel, or even go to England or Flanders as the royal ambassador. If the king does not demand his time, the Pope is likely to be using him to investigate some disorderly abbey,[1] or as arbiter between two wrangling fellow ecclesiastics. It would be lucky if a summons did not presently come, ordering the bishop to take the very tedious and expensive journey to Rome to assist at some council (such as the Lateran Council of 1215) or be party to some long-drawn litigation.

A BISHOP OF THE
THIRTEENTH
CENTURY

From the tomb of Evrard de Frouilloy, bishop of Amiens, died in 1229 and was buried in the cathedral of that city. He wears beneath the albe, the chasuble.

A conscientious bishop can, indeed, be no idler. If he has any spare time he can always spend it sitting as judge in cases which if he is compelled to be absent he deputes to his official. The canon law is far more scientific than local customs. Nivelon, or his deputy, has also a clear understanding of issues which will leave even so well-meaning a seigneur as Conon hopelessly be-

[1] Some abbeys would be directly under the bishop and liable to visitation and discipline by him at any time. Others would be supposed to be directly under the authority of the Pope (see p. 326) but the Vatican would often send orders to a competent bishop to investigate and act on charges against them.

fuddled. The Church courts refuse to settle cases by duels. As a rule, too, they discourage ordeals, despite the alleged intervention of God therein. Trials in the bishop's court betake of inquests based on firm evidence taken before experienced judges. The result is that many honest suitors try to get their cases before the Church tribunals—and, as stated, the jurisdiction of the Church is very wide. A bishop, therefore, if he wishes, can put in almost his whole time playing the Solomon; or, if he prefer, he can almost always find the estates of the diocese enmeshed in financial problems which it will tax his best energies to disentangle.

All these things Nivelon is supposed to do or must get done. What wonder (considering mortal frailty) that many men who seek the episcopate for temporal advantage often bring their great office into contempt? It is true that sometimes very worldly young clerics, when once elected, are sobered by their responsibilities and become admirable prelates. There is a story of a college of canons which decided to elect to the vacant bishopric a fellow member "who was excellent in mother wit," but who, when they sought him to tell of his honor, was actually dicing in a tavern. Forth they dragged him, "weeping and struggling," to the cathedral, and thrust him into the episcopal chair. Once enthroned, however, he proved sober and capable, thus proving how, despite his original sins, "the free gift of virtue which had come upon him (by consecration) shaped the possibilities of an excellent nature."

This is all very well, but the sacred honor does not always work such reformation. The monks never conceal the faults of the rival branch of the clergy. A monkish preacher has lately declaimed: "The bishops surpass as wolves and foxes. They bribe and flatter in order to extort. Instead of being protectors of the Church, they are its ravishers." Or again, "Jesus wore hair cloth; they silken vestments. They care not for souls, but for falcons; not for the poor, but for hunting dogs. The churches from being holy places have become market places and haunts for brigands." Most of this is mere rhetoric, and such sweeping generalizations are unjust. If the majority of bishops are not ascetics, neither are they rapacious libertines. Nevertheless, even as one ill-ruled abbey brings contempt on many austere establishments, so a few faithless bishops bring scandal on the whole episcopate. Some years ago Pope Innocent III had to denounce a South French bishop as "serving no other God but money, and having a purse in place of a heart." This wretch was charged with selling Church offices, or leaving them vacant in order to seize their incomes, while the monks and canons under him (says the Pope) "were laying aside the habit, taking wives, living by usury, and becoming lawyers, jongleurs, or doctors."[1]

Acts like these have forced the Council of Paris in 1212 to forbid bishops to wear laymen's garments or luxurious furs; to use decorated saddles or golden horse bits, to play games of chance, to go hunting, to swear or let their servants swear, to hear matins while still in bed, or excommunicate innocent people out of mere petulance. Bishops, too, are not supposed to bear arms, but we have seen how they sometimes compromise on "bloodless" heavy maces. Nivelon occasionally lets a

[1] Manasses (a great cleric, chancellor of the chapter of Amiens) caused himself to be represented on his seal not holding a pious book, as was usual, but in hunting costume on horseback, a bird on his wrist and a dog following. He was evidently a worldly noble "who had the tastes of his class and led a noble's life."

secular advocate or vidame lead his feudal levy, but at times he will ride in person. A bishop, of course, was King Philip's chief of staff at Bouvines,[1] although in excuse it should be said he had been the member of a military monastic order; but Bishop Odo of Bayeux fought at Hastings (1066) before any such authorized champions of the Church existed. One need not multiply examples. That bishops shall genuinely refrain from warfare is really a "pious wish" not easily in this sinful world to be granted.

A bishop can, however, justify this assertion of the Church militant. He must fight to maintain the rights of the bishopric against the encroaching nobility. Around the royal domain conditions are reasonably secure, but here in Quelqueparte, as elsewhere in the average feudal principalities, it is useless to ask the suzerain to do very much to defend his local bishop, the two are so likely to be very unfriendly themselves. Anathemas cannot check the more reckless seigneurs. In 1208 the Bishop of Verdun was killed in a riot by a lance thrust, and in this very year 1220 the Bishop of Puy (in the south of France) has been slain by noblemen whom he had excommunicated. The murderers have doubtless lost their souls, but this fact does not recall the dead! Jongleurs (who echo baronial prejudices) are always making fun of bishops, in their epics alleging that they lead scandalous lives and are extraordinarily avaricious, even when summoned to contribute for a war against the Infidels. The truth is, the bishops, being often recruited from the nobility, frequently keep all their old fighting spirit. The bishop opposes a neighboring viscount, just as the viscount will oppose his other neighbor, a baron. Frequently enough the

[1] See p. 244.

382

war between a bishop and a lay seigneur differs in no respect from a normal feud between two seigneurs who have never been touched by tonsure and chrism.

There are other frictions less bloody, but even more distressing to the Church. If there is an exempt abbey in the diocese—independent of the bishop and taking orders from only the Pope—the abbot and the bishop are often anything but "brethren." Each is continually complaining about the other to the Vatican. However, even if the local abbey is not directly under the Pope, its head is likely to defy the bishop as much as possible. Abbots are always trying to put themselves on equality with bishops and intriguing at Rome for the right to wear episcopal sandals, a miter, etc. So the strength of the Church is wasted, to the great joy of the devil. It is counted a sign that the Bishop of Pontdebois and the Abbot of St. Aliquis are both superior prelates, that their relations are reasonably harmonious.

However, it is with the nobles that Nivelon has his main troubles. One of the reasons why Conon wishes to see the bishop is to complain of how certain St. Aliquis peasants are being induced to settle on the Church lands. Villeins somehow feel that they are better treated by a bishop or abbot than by the most benevolent of seigneurs. "There is good living under the cross," runs the proverb. Also, the baron wishes to urge the bishop not to excommunicate a fellow noble who is at issue with the prelate over some hunting rights. It is all very well for the bishop to devote to the evil one and the eternal fire a really sacrilegious criminal. The fact remains that many nobles allege that they are excommunicated, and unless reinstated lose their very hopes of heaven, merely because they have differed from great churchmen as to extremely secular property ques-

383

tions. The fearful ceremony of excommunication is liable to fall into contempt except when used in the most undoubted cases. A resolute baron, sure of his cause, can defy the anathema and, if his followers stand by him, may hold out until he forces a compromise.

If the struggle is bitter, however, the bishop has another weapon. He can put the offending seigneur's lands and castles under the Interdict. Doubtless it is a harsh thing to deny all religious services and sacraments, save the last unction to the dying, to thousands of innocent persons merely because their lord persists in some worldly policy. Yet this is done frequently, and is, of course, of great efficacy in getting pious people, and especially the womenfolk, to put pressure upon their seigneur to come to terms with the Church. Sometimes an "intermittent" interdict is established. Thus, for a long time the Count and the Bishop of Auxerre were at enmity. The count, a hardened scoffer, was no wise troubled by excommunication. Then the bishop ordained that as soon as the count entered the city of Auxerre all the offices of religion, except baptism and last unction, should be suspended. The moment he and his men departed the church bells rang and religious life resumed. The instant he returned there was more bell ringing—whereat the churches were closed. The count did not dare to stay very long in the city, because of popular murmurs; yet he and the bishop kept up this unedifying war for fifteen years until the Pope induced the king to induce the count to submit to the Church by a humiliating penace.

Excommunication and interdict are thus weapons which a lord spiritual can use against a lord temporal, to supplement crossbows and lances. Unfortunately they have fewer terrors against foes which all bishops,

including Nivelon, have within their own household—
the chapters of canons at the cathedrals.

To be a canon is almost equal to enjoying the perquisites of some less valuable bishopric without the
grievous cares of the episcopal office. The chapter of
canons constitutes the privileged body of ecclesiastics
who maintain the worship at the cathedral.

As you go through Pontdebois you see the great gray
mass of the new episcopal church rising ahead of you.
Presently a solid wall is reached, protected by a gate and
towers. This is the cathedral "close," a separate compound next to the majestic church and communicating
with it by a special entrance. Within this close one
passes under strictly ecclesiastical jurisdiction. Here
is a pretentious residence, the bishop's palace, and a
pleasant garden, and here is also a group of smaller
houses—the habitations of the canons. These last form
the chapter of canons who enjoy as a corporate body a
quantity of lands, seigneurial rights, officers, and goodly
income quite separate from the bishops. Supposedly
they are controlled by a Rule, but it is a rule far less
severe than that of most monks.

The chapter here, as elsewhere, is largely recruited
from the local noble houses. Church law nominally
forbids it, but the fact remains that many, if not most,
canons are practically nominated, whenever there is a
vacancy in the chapter, by this or that powerful seigneur.
To get a relative a prebend (income from endowment)
as canon is often equivalent to providing for life for a
kinsman to whom you might otherwise have to cede a
castle. It is well understood that since years ago a baron
of St. Aliquis endowed with large gifts a certain prebend,
his successors have the naming of its occupants, as often

as it falls vacant. After Conon has visited the bishop, he will pay a friendly call on "his canon," not without a certain desire to verify the reports that this elderly cleric is in poor health and not long for the present world. If such rumors are correct, the baron must consider whether a certain remote cousin feels summoned to endure the hardships of a religious life, and what substantial favors this ambitious cousin and his father could give Conon for the privilege.

A canon who performs *all* his duties is hardly idle. He is supposed to take part in the incessant and often extraordinarily elaborate services at every cathedral. He should possess a good physical presence, and intone the offices with elegance and precision. Every week day he has to chant through five services, and on Sunday through nine. On certain great feasts and holidays there are still more. Anthems, responses, psalms, prayers, hymns, also public processions should keep him turning leaves of the ponderous ordinaries and manuals until he knows every chant therein by heart.

It is possible, however, to find substitutes in all the less important services. There are plenty of humbly born poor priests hovering around every cathedral, glad of a pittance to act as the lordly canon's deputies. A worldly minded canon therefore does not feel this duty of chanting to be very arduous. Of course, if he is absent too often, or from very important ceremonies, there is comment, scandal, and a reprimand from the bishop; but a wise bishop does not interfere with his canons except on grave provocation. They form an independent corporation with well-intrenched privileges. Their head, the dean, is entirely conscious that he is the second cleric in the diocese and that he need not look to the bishop for dignity and glory. The bishop himself has been to a certain extent chosen by these very canons. It will depend considerably upon their attitude toward him whether his dying moments are not embittered by the knowledge that his dearest enemy is not to be elected his successor. Finally, a chapter of canons can make a bishop's life a Gehenna by filing complaints against him with the archbishop (always glad to interfere), or directly at Rome. When men say that Nivelon has got along tolerably with his chapter as well as with his neighboring abbot and seigneurs, they prove again that he is an unusually tactful prelate.

It is a fine thing, therefore, to be one of the dozen-odd canons, young or old, who inhabit the sacred close at Pontdebois. They can be identified by their special costume, the loose surplice of linen with wide sleeves covering the cassock, and by the "amice," a headdress of thick black stuff with a flat top and terminating on each corner in a kind of horn.

Baron Conon points out to his sons these well-fed men of florid complexion, contented and portly, moving with slow dignity about the cathedral close. "How would you enjoy being a canon?" he asks of small Anseau, his youngest boy. "There are no better dinners than those in the chapter refectory; and remember that your brother will have to get the castle."

Anseau shakes his head and scowls: "I might be a monk, yes," he rejoined; "monks save their souls and go to heaven—but a canon—ugh! They must weary God by their idleness. François may have St. Aliquis; but let him give me a good destrer and good armor. I will seek my fortune and win new lands."

"The saints bless your words," cries his father, "there spoke a true St. Aliquis! And remember this: When cavalier or jongleur rails hardest against worthless churchmen, it is not bishop, priest, or monk whom half the time they have in their pates, but slothful canons. Yet I must see the Revered Father Flavien, and learn if his cough *is* really as bad as they say!"

Nivelon secures peace by letting his canons largely alone—to their great content. Fortunately, the good

laymen of Quelqueparte do not depend entirely upon their spiritual administrations. The "cure of souls" rests with the parish priests. These are scattered all through the diocese. Their management takes up a large part of the bishop's crowded time.

Every church requires at least one priest in residence to say mass and afford religious comfort to the laity. If competent bishops could always have appointed this clergy, much sorrow would have been eliminated. Unfortunately, the bishop can only name a fraction. Practically every noncathedral church has its patron, the heir or beneficiary of the wealthy personage who once endowed the local establishment. This patron may be the bishop himself, but often the honor may be enjoyed by an abbey, or a chapter of canons, or, in a majority of cases, by some very secular seigneur. Conon will say. "I hold the

A DEACON
(THIRTEENTH
CENTURY)

He wears an albe, the dalmatica, the amice, the stole, and the maniple. From a statue in the cathedral of Chartres.

patronage of eight churches," just as he will say, "I hold St. Aliquis castle." The patron is entitled to a share of the tithe (tax for religious purposes) and other income of the parish, before turning the remainder over to the officiating priest. He can, in addition, "present to the living"—that is, name the new curé for the parish upon every vacancy. The bishop is supposed, indeed, to confirm the candidate, and should not do so without investigation as to the other's fitness, but he will hesitate to offend the patron by refusal to proceed with the ceremony unless the impediment is gross and patent. The candidate is asked to decline a Latin noun, to conjugate a simple verb, to chant a few familiar psalms with fair voice—that is probably about all the test for learning. To make matters worse, if the candidate fears his own bishop, he can go to another diocese and probably get a licence from a less exacting prelate. A bishop is obliged to honor the certificate issued by his equal. He can seldom then refuse after that to invest the priest with the parish.

The last stage of scandal comes when the patron actually takes money for presenting a candidate. This is, of course, a terrible crime against the Church: it is simony—after the fashion of the accursed Simon Magnus, who was guilty of trying to purchase "the gift of God with money." Nivelon has just had to induct into a parish an ill-taught, worldly fellow, the son of a rich peasant, who somehow persuaded the Viscount of Foretvert that he was fit to have the spiritual conduct of five hundred Christians. The bishop has heard ugly rumors about "two hundred deniers," yet for lack of real proof is helpless. It is feared these scandals are frequent, but many times, if candidate and seigneur are willing to imperil their souls, what can be done?

As a rule, however, conscientious patrons name well-reputed lads from their barony, the sons of thrifty peasants or of petty nobles, who have been to the school attached to a convent or cathedral, and who have de-

veloped an aptitude for saying masses rather than for
plowing or fighting. The favor is bestowed rather as a
reward for faithful service by the youth's family or to
insure the same in the future, than for any direct money
consideration. To be a parish priest is not a very high
honor. After the patron has taken his share of the tithe,
and the bishop another share, the curé is likely to be
left with barely enough income to put him among the
better class of peasants.

Yet, after all, he is now caught up into the great body
politic of the Church. The latter will not let him starve.
It will give him a decent old age. It will protect him
against those gross cruelties which seigneurs may inflict
on any peasant. It will make him the most important
individual in the average village—often the only person
therein understanding the mysteries of parchments.
If he is a worthy man, his influence as counselor, friend,
and arbiter will be almost boundless. He will receive
a personal respect almost equal to that due to a cavalier.
Finally, there is always the chance that he may win
some magnate's favor, and by good luck or merit rise
to greater things. Father Grégoire, Conon's chaplain,
although nominally only a poor priest, is probably more
influential in St. Aliquis than Sire Eustace, the seneschal—Conon sometimes complains good naturedly that
he is more powerful than Conon himself. So then, apart
from any desire for strictly religious leadership, it is no
bad thing for a lad of humble origin to be appointed
parish priest.

If, however, to receive a parish means not a holy
trust, but a sordid opportunity, what a chance for making the fiends rejoice! Every jongleur, when he runs
out of more legitimate stories, chatters about godless
priests. Charges against the parish clergy are the small

coin of filthy gossip—how they violate their vows of celibacy in a shameless manner; how they frequent taverns, take part in low brawls, drink "up to their throats," and lie torpid in the fields; how they fight with their parishioners; how they sell strong drink like tapsters; how they play dice, gamble and often cheat their opponents, etc.

Another set of charges is that if their means admit, they wear armor like nobles, or dress like foppish laymen, and ride out with hawks or dogs. More familiar still are the accusations of extreme covetousness; of the outrageous exaction of fees for administering the sacraments, even to the dying; of performing shameless marriages for money; of refusing burial services until they have been bribed; and, in short, of converting themselves into financial harpies.

All this is undeniable. Yet it must be remembered that the number of parish clergy is very great, and the proportion of evildoers is (considering their manner of appointment) no more than might be expected. Many of the parish priests are true ministers of God who counsel the simple, persuade the erring, comfort the sorrowing, and leave the world better than they found it. A few, too, spend their leisure in genuine pursuit of learning, like that Father Lambert of Ardes (in Flanders) who is deeply read in old Latin authors and Christian fathers and who has composed an excellent local chronicle—worthy to rank with the best produced in the monasteries.

Taken, therefore, at large, despite much dross, the men of the Church do not cast away their great opportunity. If alms and charity relieve the wretched, if letters and science have a genuine power, if the world retains other ideals than those of the tourney, the feud, and the foray, if villeins are taught that they, too, are men with immortal souls no less than are the barons, the glory belongs surely not to the castle, but to the monastery and to the parish. And when a good churchman dies, especially, of course, if he has been an effective and benignant bishop, all the region knows its loss. When the late Bishop of Auxerre departed, it was written, "It would be impossible to tell how great was the mourning throughout the entire city, and with what groaning and lamentations sorrow was shown by all who followed his funeral." While of the great and good Bishop Maurice of Paris, builder of Notre Dame, it was recorded, when he passed in 1196, that "he was a vessel of affluence, a fertile olive tree in the house of the Lord. He shone by his knowledge, his preaching, his many alms, and his good deeds."

Like every other institution, the Church of the Feudal Age is entitled to be judged by its best and not by its worst.

Chapter XXIV: The Cathedral and Its Builders.

ARON CONON and Adela had still another duty ere they returned to St. Aliquis. They were fain to go with their sons, and each burn a tall candle before the altar of Our Lady in the cathedral. All dwellers near Pontdebois are intensely proud of their great church. It has been building now these forty years. At last it is fairly complete, although the left tower has still to be carried up to the belfry, and very many niches lack the sculptured saints presently to occupy them. A worthy cathedral, like a worthy character, is growing continually. Probably the Feudal Age will end before Notre Dame de Pontdebois is completed as its pious designers have intended.[1]

The cathedral is the center for a large group of buildings whereof most are in the noble pointed (Gothic) style of architecture. As just explained, in the sacred close there is the bishop's palace and the houses of the canons; there are also a cloister for promenading, a school (much like that at the monastery), a room for a library, and a synodal hall for meetings of the canons and where the bishop can conduct litigation. There is, in addition, a hospital for sick clerics. The whole forms a little world sequestered from the uproar and

---

[1] Few or no cathedrals were *really* completed at any time, in the sense that all the details of their design were brought to perfection.

sordid bustle of the marts and workshops of Pontdebois. As you enter the cathedral compound, exterior cares are suddenly left behind you—a great sense of peace is realized. One hears the wind softly whistling through the soaring tracery of the massive right tower. There is a whirring flutter of doves from their homes under the flying buttresses. Through a section opened in the floral tracery of a great window comes the rumbling of an organ and the deep Gregorian chant of some hymn from the psalter. Utter contrast it all is either to the hammering and chaffering of the city, or the equally worldly clatter of the castle court! The vast tower pointing upward speaks even to the thoughtless, "Fortress and city, trade and tourney endure only for the instant—the things of the Spirit abide forever."

The cathedral, by its vast and soaring bulk, completely dwarfs the comparatively small and mean houses of the town. They are of thatch and wood. It is of stone. They lack even a tawdry magnificence. The cathedral could gaze with contempt on royal palaces. This fact teaches even more clearly than words the enormous place occupied by the Church in the Fuedal Age. It is not by its literature and learning (though these are not to be despised), but *by its sacred architecture and sculpture* that the spirit of this era displays its power and originality. In contemplating so magnificent a fabric, it is best to remember that it is the work of men of ardent faith, profoundly convinced that in the church building there dwells continually upon the high altar God himself, invisible but ever present. Squalid dwellings may suffice for man, but not for the Creator. And since God actually takes his abode in such an edifice, every art must contribute to its splendor. Architects, sculptors, painters, jewelers, all perform their

NOTRE-DAME AND THE BISHOP'S PALACE AT THE BEGINNING OF THE THIRTEENTH CENTURY

From the restoration of M. Hoffbauer. At the left the Petit-Pont and the buildings of the archbishop's palace, destroyed in 1831; the cathedral, of which the choir and the south transept were finished only at this date; behind the cathedral, on the ground occupied to-day by a public garden, was the church of Saint-Denis du Pas, built previous to the cathedral and destroyed in 1813.

best, each rendering his homage to the Eternal. The cathedral, therefore, sums up all that is noblest in the art of the time when it is erected.

Since the nave of such a church often can be used for secular mass meetings without fear of impiety, and since a whole countryside will claim the right to throng the edifice on great festival days, a cathedral has to be far larger than an ancient pagan temple.[1] It must possess an interior meet for elaborate processions, stopping often at each of twenty-odd altars lining its walls. To erect a building like this is an undertaking in which a whole countryside can be asked to join. About forty years ago the old cathedral, built in the ancient Romanesque (round-arched) style with a wooden roof, was falling into disrepair, and the new pointed, stone-vaulted architecture was developing through all France. People from regions round made remarks about the "impiety" of the clergy and folk near Pontdebois in "dishonoring heaven." Various prelates taunted the ruling Bishop Thibaut with his mean cathedral. This Thibaut, however, had been an energetic as well as a devout man. By prudent administration of the diocese he had saved considerable money. He next persuaded his canons to curtail their luxuries and to contribute generously. Means, too, were taken to lure money from the faithful. The holy relics were exhibited. Indulgence from purgatory was promised to donors. Conscience-stricken barons were urged to atone for their crimes by liberal gifts to the new enterprise. Civic

[1] For example, Notre Dame de Paris covered four times the floor area of the Parthenon at Athens (a decidedly large Greek temple) with its nave thrice as high as the older building. Of course, a Greek temple was primarily for housing a holy image; the great sacrifices and the throng of worshipers would be outside the edifice in the open, unlike a Christian church.

pride and excited piety won the deniers from the Pontdebois trade and industrial masters. A rich countess left
a notable legacy on condition that the canons should
always pray for her soul on the anniversary of her death.
So between coaxing and religious feeling a goodly fund
was collected—and, as was wisely said, "the new cathedral has saved many souls"—meaning that many sinful people were happily moved to redeeming acts of
generosity. There were even gifts, it is said, from
brigands and evil women, likewise a good many less
debatable presents in kind, as when a baron gave both
the necessary oak and the pay of the carvers for making
the magnificent choir stalls, besides presenting the
great stained-glass rose window. Whatever the source,
no donation was denied, the bishop counting it fortunate if even the booty of thieves could be turned to the
glory of God.

Bishop Thibaut found a skillful architect, a Norman,
half cleric, half layman, who had assisted on one of the
great churches at Rouen. The plans this man drew up
were very elaborate, but he did not live to see them
more than half executed. Even if workmen and money
failed not, it was dangerous to rush the erection of the
great piers, buttresses, and vaulted ceilings. At Auxerre,
where they tried to hasten the work, much of the choir
suddenly collapsed "like a crash of thunder," though
Heaven mercifully prevented the loss of life. At Noyon
they began to build in 1152. Their cathedral was nearly
finished by 1200. Notre Dame de Paris was begun in
1163, and the choir was fairly completed by 1177; but
the great towers and façade certainly cannot be finished
before 1225. Rheims was begun in 1211, but undoubtedly
even the work on the choir cannot be ended under thirty
years from that date. If Pontdebois is reasonably com-

plete after forty years of effort it is therefore being built more expeditiously than the average cathedral. Indeed, many wiseacres shake their heads. "Too much haste," they mutter; "when one builds for God and in order to last till His Judgment Day, it is very sinful to hurry."

First the choir was finished with all energy possible, for here the canons must constantly chant their offices. The nave, which was more for popular gatherings, waited till later. There was great rejoicing when at last the main portal was so far completed that a very fine and tenderly carved statue of Christ could be set above the same. *"Our beautiful God!"* the people lovingly call the image; and from that time, year by year, the work went forward, every member or ornament that was added seeming to suggest something additional, as if the achieving of perfection were to be a work for eternity.

To erect the main structure of his cathedral, Thibaut had called in a traveling fraternity of workmen, the Lodging-House Keepers of the Good God, who obeyed the Master of the Work—*i.e.,* an architect. They would stay for years in one place, recruiting new members as old ones died, then moving elsewhere when no longer needed. This fraternity erected the main structure of the building; then Thibaut passed away, money failed, and enthusiasm somewhat lapsed. However, twenty years later, a new fraternity were put to work on the façade and towers. This was more delicate work, involving a great deal of skillful carving. They were obliged to stop again before completion had been attained. Probably a score of years hence, still another such fraternity will raise the second tower. Meantime, every year, a few skillful craftsmen, sustained by donations, add a statue here and a gargoyle yonder, put richly painted glass into another window, or complete the intricate carving around the railing to the pulpit stairs. Now and then there is a special exhibition of relics to attract worshipers and their alms.[1] One of the results is that the style of the different parts of the cathedral differs subtly according to the respective periods of their construction. There is not a contradiction, but only a pleasing variety. One feels that *the cathedral is something living.* It has come into being, not by arbitrary creation, but by a natural growth; like a mighty, comfort-spreading tree.

As we wander about this glorious fabric, with its hundreds of statues,[2] its blazing windows, its vaulted roof which hangs its massive weight of stone so safely above our heads all attempts at detailed description become futile. Let them be left for other books and other moods. Later generations doubtless will record at great length that about the middle of the twelfth century a great activity in church building, as a surpassing work of Christian piety, began to manifest itself especially in northern France. This activity was not to spend itself for more than a hundred years.[3] It absorbed much of the best thought and energy of the time. In addition, it developed a genuinely new type of architecture, a real

[1] One device was to take an extra-precious relic and intrust it to monks, who would place it in a cart and drive through a wide region haranguing the faithful and holding out a purse for them to fill. At Rouen one of the cathedral towers was known as the "Butter Tower," because it was largely built with money given for permission to eat butter in Lent.

[2] At Rheims, prior to the German bombardment of 1914, there were more than two thousand statues.

[3] During this period there were built in France some eighty cathedrals and more than five hundred large and superior churches in this Gothic style.

THIRTEENTH-CENTURY WINDOW
IN THE CATHEDRAL OF CHAR-
TRES, REPRESENTING SAINT
CHRISTOPHER CARRYING
CHRIST

innovation upon those models traceable back to the pagan Greek. We come to the reign of the pointed arch which adapts itself to endless curves and varieties. We have, too, the grouped columns which uphold the groins of the lofty vaulting, their members radiating outward like the boughs of a stately forest. These columns and piers can be made amazingly light, thanks to the daring use of flying buttresses, an invention not merely of great utility, but of great beauty. Thanks also to these grouped pillars, groins, and buttresses, the walls between the bays (intervals between the columns) are in no wise needed to uphold the roof of stone; and as a result these bays can be filled up with thin curtain walls crowned above with enormous windows which are filled with a delicate tracery and a stained glass that throws down upon the pavement of the church all the rainbow tints of heaven. Each bay is likely to contain a separate chapel or at least an altar to some particular saint. Over the portal, where the main entrance gives access to the long nave, radiates the mighty rose window, the final triumph of the glass and tracery. And so through all the vast structure— huge in proportions, yet, as it were, a harmonious mass of fair carving and jewel work, until (even as says Holy Writ) "the whole body fitly joined together, and compacted by that which every joint supplyeth, according to the effectual working in every part, maketh increase of the body unto the edifying of itself in love."

So the apostle of the making of a Christian man, so, too, of the making of the august church. And after saying this, what profit to add that this cathedral has a length of about four hundred feet, that the ceiling of the nave rises at least one hundred feet above the pavement, that the rose window is nearly forty feet in diameter, that the higher tower is much more than two hundred?[1] Numbers are for sordid traffic, they are not for a work wrought out of a passionate love of man toward God.

We cannot stay to linger over the symbolism which they tell us is in every part of the church; how the "Communion of Saints" is proclaimed by the chapels clustering around the choir and nave; how the delicate spire which rises at the center of the transepts teaches that "vanquishing earthly desire we should also ascend in heart and mind"; how the triple breadth of the nave and two aisles, likewise the triple stretch of the choir, transepts and nave, proclaim the Holy Trinity; and how the serried armies of piers and columns announce the Prophets and Apostles who uphold the fabric of the

[1] Such figures would indicate that Pontdebois Cathedral was somewhat smaller than Notre Dame de Paris. It could rank up well among the great churches of France, yet not at all in the first class.

Church; while font, altar, crucifix, and crosses innumerable attest the earthly pilgrimage and redeeming passion of Jesus Christ.

But the cathedral is more than a great collection of allegories. Everywhere in stained glass, and still more in the multitudinous images, is told the Bible story. The characters are not clothed in Hebraic fashion. "Baron Abraham" and "Sire David" appear in ring mail like doughty cavaliers. The history of the good warrior Judas Maccabæus perhaps is told in greater detail than that of prophets like Isaiah and Jeremiah. But very few important stories are omitted, and, above all, the great pageant of the life of Jesus is worked out in loving detail. The child, who is brought time and again to visit the cathedral, knows almost every essential Bible narrative, albeit he may never learn to read even French, much less to con the Latin of the Vulgate. Likewise, in the cathedral rest the tombs of brave seigneurs and worthy bishops, each covered either with an effigy showing his armor and his beloved hunting dogs couched at his feet, or in his pontificals; and the tombs also of noble women, sculptured as richly clad, who have made life beautiful by their worthy living, and who now rest securely until God's great Judgment. So the cathedral is both a temple for the hopes of the present, and an inspiration from the remote and nearer past.[1]

[1] St. John of Damascus, writing in the Orient in the eighth century, gave what amounted to the standard justification of holy images and pictures in churches and for the veneration of the same:

"I am too poor to possess books, I have no leisure for reading. I enter the church choked with the cares of the world; the glowing colors attract my sight like a flowery meadow; and the glory of God steals imperceptibly into my soul. I gaze on the fortitude of the martyr and the crown with which he is rewarded, and the fire of holy emulation is kindled within me. I fall down and worship God *through* the martyr; and I receive salvation."

After he had prayed beside his father and mother, little Anseau stole away from the altar and wandered timidly about the church. In a corner of a transept he found a stone craftsman completing a small image of St. Elizabeth to adorn some niche. The sculptor was polishing the back of the statue no less carefully than the front. "Why such trouble?" asked the boy curiously. "No one can see the back." "Ah, my fair damoiseau," replied the other, smiling, "no man, of course; *but God can see.* This is for the Cathedral; and is God 'no one'?"

The next day, having spent all their money and become wearied of the mechanic bustle of Pontdebois, Baron Conon and his company rode back to St. Aliquis. After they had traveled for miles, the great mass of the cathedral was still visible behind them.

The Feudal Age has produced very much that is evil—it has also produced the Gothic church and its builders. By which ought the epoch be judged?

Seven hundred years afterward the donjon of St. Aliquis is an ivy-covered ruin. Vanished is the monastery; vanished, too, the peasants' huts. In the smoky industrial city on the site of Pontdebois not one ancient stone seems left upon another. But, hold! Soaring high above ugly roof and factory chimney, with its airy pinnacles denouncing a life of materialism and doubt, visited by admiring pilgrims from beyond the Sea of Darkness, the great fabric of the gray cathedral remains.

Index

Index

406